CAPITOL REVOLUTION

THE RISE OF THE MCMAHON WRESTLING EMPIRE

TIM HORNBAKER

ECW PRESS

FOR THEIR EVERLASTING
LOVE AND SUPPORT,
THIS BOOK IS DEDICATED TO
ABRAHAM "AVRASH"
AND SHEILA
TABITHA

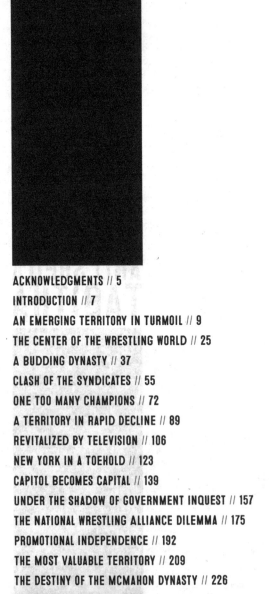

ACKNOWLEDGMENTS

The creation of *Capitol Revolution* was undeniably an outgrowth of my book on the NWA (*National Wrestling Alliance: The Untold Story of the Monopoly that Strangled Pro Wrestling*), and a logical next step for me as a writer. During a lengthy research period, I accessed a variety of historical collections and reviewed thousands of articles, government documents, and personal correspondence, particularly material written by many of the promoters mentioned in the book. These letters were of the utmost importance—establishing the tone of relationships behind the scenes and clearing up many long-standing questions about specific events and controversies in wrestling history.

Of course, I am grateful to a number of people for their patience, understanding, and assistance. First and foremost, I thank my wife, Jodi, for her unwavering encouragement and support through a number of eventful years. Also, Timothy and Barbara Hornbaker, Melissa Hornbaker, Virginia Hall, Sheila

Babaganov, Debbie and Paul Kelley, Chad Porreca, Frances Miller, and John and Christine Hopkins.

Additionally, I'd like to thank Michael Holmes and everyone at ECW Press for their insightful comments and creative ideas, which helped make this book a reality.

Amy Miller and the entire Interlibrary Loan Department of the Broward County Main Library in Fort Lauderdale, Florida, were, once again, instrumental in providing primary resources for my work. The employees of the Magazine and Newspaper Section were also helpful in responding to any of my questions during my many hours of microfilm research.

Last, but not least, I would like to especially thank a number of friends, contributors, and fellow researchers: John Pantozzi, Daniel Chernau, Kit Bauman, Jim Bowman, J. Michael Kenyon, Scott Teal, Steve Yohe, Don Luce, Fred Hornby, Mark Hewitt, Libnan Ayoub, Steve Johnson, Greg Oliver, Koji Miyamoto, Bob Bryla, Dave Meltzer, Graham Cawthon, Jim Zordani, Hisaharu Tanabe, George Rugg, and too many others to name. These knowledgeable individuals were always available to correspond and offered a great deal of assistance in the creation of this project. More information about the history of professional wrestling can be found at www.legacyofwrestling.com.

INTRODUCTION

When Vincent James McMahon and Capitol ruled the Northeast, professional wrestling was shrouded in secrecy. Wrestlers lived their gimmicks in and out of the ring, and promoters warned against stepping out of character in public. Most behind-the-scenes dramas stayed behind the scenes, and a majority of fans knew very little about the business of the sport. Instead, spectators focused on the product, suspended their disbelief, and enjoyed the grappling mayhem at their local arena. There was no question that the industry was surrounded by an incredible aura, and wrestling developed into a multi-million-dollar brand of entertainment.

Promoters tended to shy away from acknowledging wrestling's grand heritage, and it was obvious there was very little appreciation for the sport's past. The reason was simple: they felt there was no money in it. Insiders were concerned about their next box office attraction and considered historical information worthless. In terms of conservation of history, promoters routinely discarded documents and other records without a second thought. Never did anyone think how important such source material would be to researchers in the future. Altogether, the surreptitious nature of the industry remained intact, and any real appreciation of wrestling's traditions were repressed.

From the perspective of World Wrestling Entertainment (WWE), the evolution of McMahon's original World Wide Wrestling Federation (WWWF), the old stigmas attached to "wrestling history" prevail under the watchful eye of Vincent Kennedy McMahon. Only recently has the WWE decide to embrace aspects of its elusive past. Honoring the heroes of yesteryear in a centralized hall of fame has become an annual event, and a plethora of DVDs have been released with footage of old-time stars. Additionally, a long-awaited tribute was paid to Bruno Sammartino, and his status as a "Living Legend" emphasized across the WWE universe. Without his commitment to the promotion in the 1960s and '70s, the organization would not be where it is today.

Other products, such as the *50 Years of Sports Entertainment* DVD and the territorial footage featured on the subscription-based WWE Network, demonstrates a new willingness to appreciate wrestling's history. But for all the information that is suddenly being distributed to the public as part of a coordinated marketing strategy, just as much remains undisclosed. The true development of the Northeastern territory and the Capitol Wrestling Corporation is a story begging to be told. And the detailed legacy of the McMahon family—arguably the most influential family in wrestling history—deserves to be broken down and disseminated without prejudice. Finally, the truth about the origins of the WWE can be told.

(1)
AN EMERGING TERRITORY IN TURMOIL

During World War I, professional wrestling was in a state of flux as syndicate leaders struggled to maintain their relevance. A lack of new and exciting superstars was hurting the industry, and while top-tier wrestlers Ed "Strangler" Lewis, Joe Stecher, and Wladek Zbyszko were capable box office attractions, wrestling needed a boost. The fact that Earl Caddock, the generally accepted world heavyweight champion, was overseas in combat also hurt big-time grappling—especially after various title claimants appeared in his absence. The confusion damaged wrestling's reputation and left many wondering who was in charge of the sport.

In the East, Jack Curley was considered the most powerful sponsor of pro wrestling. Nearing 41, he was originally from San Francisco but had traveled throughout the Americas and Europe in his quest to become one of the sport's top promoters. Based out of New York City, he masterminded the first-rate spectacles at Madison Square Garden, wrestling's premier venue, and his shows were highly successful. He was cordial with promoters and managers across the country and, because of that, was able to import many recognizable wrestlers for his programs. His shows offered a diversity of talent, from quicker light heavyweights to the bulky mastodons who relied on their strength to defeat foes.

Curley expertly managed the politics of professional sports, and he was a diplomat in many respects: He synchronized efforts with city officials, laying the groundwork for his public events while cleverly handling the erratic personalities of various boxing and wrestling personnel. There was rarely a dull moment among the upper tier of wrestling leaders, and he ably balanced the fragile environment made up of Billy Sandow and Tony Stecher, managers of Lewis and Joe Stecher, respectively. Between 1917 and 1921, harmony prevailed for the most part, and a number of high-profile matches were staged, which advanced the principal storylines.

From 1916, when he first put down roots in the New York metropolitan area, Curley was the primary wrestling impresario, and his local monopoly went unchallenged. That changed in 1921, when a perceived insult motivated well-known boxing promoter George Lewis "Tex" Rickard to enter the sport. The supposed offense related to the American tour of Georges Carpentier and the way Curley overshadowed Rickard because of his personal friendship with the French fighter. Rickard was unwilling to forgive and essentially declared war on Curley, pledging to take over all preeminent grappling in New York. Rickard used his political pull to banish his foe from the Garden—if any future wrestling shows were staged, he'd run them himself.

The spiteful retaliation didn't end there. Rickard's beliefs were impressed upon the members of the newly instituted New York State Athletic Commission, and Chairman William Muldoon, the "Iron Duke," agreed that the theatrical wrestling presented by Curley was substandard at best. A champion wrestler 40 years before, Muldoon considered himself to be the best judge of virtuous and honest wrestling in the state, and he spearheaded the commission's drive to oust Curley by refusing to issue him a license.

Although gaining steam, Rickard was hurt by the fact that most of the prime wrestlers and managers were already aligned with

Curley, making up what was known as the "Trust." Rickard nevertheless pushed forward and put his faith behind "Trustbuster" Marin Plestina, a big 34-year-old Yugoslavian managed by vociferous J.C. "Joe" Marsh. Plestina brought credibility to wrestling, not shenanigans, Rickard believed, and if he was as good as Marsh said, he'd quickly take out the pretenders and assume the heavyweight championship mantle.

Plestina's first obstacle was a Nebraskan named John Pesek, a wrestler who lived up to his nickname of "Tigerman" by displaying cat-like reflexes and astonishing ferociousness. He was a rare breed of grappler, mixing strength and aptitude with otherworldly instincts. To this day, few pro wrestlers rate alongside Pesek in terms of legitimate shooting and hooking skills, and Plestina, regardless of his size and ability, was outmatched from the initial bell.

But Pesek, an operative working on behalf of Curley, wasn't in New York to win. He was in town to send a message to Rickard and set out to single-handedly ruin his program. He did it with a deliberately unprofessional display, completely unbefitting center stage at the Garden. He threw out the rulebook when he entered the ring on November 14, 1921, and lunged at Plestina with the intent to maim. He frequently butted and gouged at his opponent's eyes, and an uninformed observer would've thought the illegal maneuvers were part of the catch-as-catch-can repertoire. Pesek was disqualified three separate times for fouling and what little wrestling took place was an utter disappointment. While Pesek was criticized, his syndicate allies knew he had delivered a flawless execution. His mission to tarnish Rickard's promotional endeavors was accomplished.

Rickard was annoyed. He disliked the atmosphere of wrestling and saw little hope of making any money. Boxing was his priority, and he wanted it to remain that way. In January 1922, he worked out an arrangement to turn over the matchmaking duties for grappling at the Garden to sportsman William Wellman. About 10 years earlier, at the age of 21, Wellman had managed all aspects of the stadium and was considered a prodigy. With a concise plan and financial backers, he was taking on the negative odds and all the naysayers in an attempt to resurrect the sport. He admittedly knew next to nothing about wrestling, but he did understand promotions, and his experience, he felt, was going to be instrumental in churning out a moneymaker.

Whereas Rickard didn't have the support of the Trust, Wellman did, and his friendly relations with Curley gave him an advantage. Years earlier, he had been responsible for getting Curley his first position at the Garden, and Curley was ever loyal to his longtime associate. He gave his approval to Trust workers to appear on Wellman's shows, and in the wrestling business, that was akin to getting the Pope's blessing.

Nevertheless, the success of the new combine completely rested in the hands of the public. For a show featuring the Zbyszko Brothers, Caddock, Ed "Strangler" Lewis, and ex-Olympian Nat Pendleton on February 6, 1922, an estimated 12,000 people turned out. A couple of weeks later, half that attendance showed up for a Garden program headlined by Lewis and Cliff Binckley. Wellman was unable to sustain the high overhead and reassessed his commitment to promoting wrestling. In the meantime, New York's wrestling scene fizzled into nothingness, and Curley went overseas to Europe, where he concentrated on boxing.

The focal point of professional wrestling was still the world heavyweight championship. On March 3, 1922, in promoter Tom Law's Midwestern haven of Wichita, Kansas, the crown passed from Stanislaus Zbyszko back to Strangler Lewis. The title switch wasn't unexpected, as Lewis and his manager Billy Sandow had proven to be two of the shrewdest men in the sport. They were continuously plotting and planning to increase their monetary intake, much like Frank Gotch and Farmer Burns in the old days, and their scheming not only accounted for today's business but tomorrow's and the day after's as well.

Under the rule of Lewis and Sandow, wrestling was becoming more sophisticated. Their booking practices shifted from an ordinary, straight-laced strategy to one that embraced Lewis as a purposefully devious heel. The change in image was shocking to fans in cities that had seen Lewis perform previously, and when his sportsmanship was called into question, audiences turned on him in a split second. Normally the champion was regarded as honorable, but Lewis and his crippling headlock were sinister, and many times, the rancor of crowds nearly bubbled into riots. In these instances, Lewis needed police protection to escape the ring.

Lewis's metamorphosis motivated people to support his underdog challengers, such as Joe "Toots" Mondt, Mike Romano, Dick Daviscourt, and Stanley Stasiak. In competitive championship matches, fans were often subjected to a third fall gimmick that led to Lewis retaining. For example, in Chicago on April 29, 1924, the champion was engaged in a grueling bout against Romano. After winning the second fall with a headlock, Romano had won over the crowd and was going strong into the third. Lewis, on the other hand, was exhausted, holding onto the ropes to remain upright. Both Romano and the audience sensed victory, and the wrestler attempted to pull the heavier champion off the ropes to the middle of the ring. But Romano lost his grip and stumbled, giving Lewis time to pounce. He quickly applied a double wristlock and took the win.

The stunned audience was angry. They had seen their Italian idol hoodwinked by Lewis's unwillingness to resemble a true champion in the third fall. The Strangler then took advantage of Romano's mistake and triumphed. In response to the unjust scenario, fans littered the ring area with bottles.

Lewis appeared to become more and more beatable, much to the delight of spectators, but he always eked out a win. In Boston at the Arena on May 8, 1924, a large audience rooted for Stasiak to finally strip the Strangler of his title. He was on his way, winning the first fall, but the constant choke holds applied by Lewis were making him blindingly mad. Finally he cracked and fouled the champion, and the match was stopped. Stasiak was disqualified and Lewis retained. Once again, people voiced their complaints and nearly ran amok. Police were on hand and stifled the animosity before it got out of control.

Sandow was the brains behind the syndicate. Born Wilhelm

Baumann in Rochester, New York, the 40-year-old manager and promoter was a proficient manipulator and well connected throughout the nation. He smartly fostered the creation of a stable of wrestlers, formed a circuit of towns for Lewis to travel, and used the exceptional skills of Pesek as a "policeman." In wrestling parlance, that means Pesek was used as a barrier between rogue grapplers and the champion. If a certain jurisdiction ordered Lewis to wrestle outlaws like Plestina or Jack Sherry, the potential challenger would have to defeat Pesek first. Such a result was doubtful; thus, Lewis was safe from having to wrestle a legitimate contest against an unknown commodity.

In Tulsa, Wichita, and Chicago, three of Sandow's most important cities, he staged a system of elimination matches to build up challengers and make title contests against Lewis seem more consequential. It also added fan encouragement to the challengers' momentous undertaking, as if the wrestler and audience were united in the climb toward the championship. Attendance would typically skyrocket for the culminating bout against Lewis and then play out in dramatic fashion.

The value of the heavyweight championship was measureless to Sandow and Lewis. Their ownership of the title meant financial success and the kind of press attention competitors envied. When Sandow proposed ideas, sportswriters listened, and the noteworthy concept of a wrestler-versus-boxer mixed matchup between champions Lewis and Jack Dempsey was seriously bandied about. To Sandow, it was an opportunity to attract a record attendance and make a copious amount of money.

Finding a way to arrange the affair so that it didn't hurt either athlete's box office appeal was tougher than imagined. There were several options. At the forefront was the legitimate, freewheeling shoot. Opposite was the worked shoot, which portrayed the bout to be genuine but was anything but. Then there was the draw or inconclusive/disqualification finish. The latter, if done the right way, would preserve the integrity of both men, although the always-unpopular DQ ending could inspire a backlash. But it was clear that a loss for either Lewis or Dempsey would likely cause irreparable damage.

In New York, William Muldoon was not thrilled about the idea and refused to issue a license for any prospective bout locally. There were still hopes of staging the contest elsewhere, but, despite the enormous interest, plans faded and were forgotten.

Another significant virtue of controlling the heavyweight championship was that promoters from all over North America were vying for appearances from the titleholder in their town. Sandow was able to be highly selective. He set the financial terms beforehand and dictated whom Lewis was going to face. Budding promoters Tom Packs of St. Louis and Lou Daro in Los Angeles were eager to feature Lewis on a regular basis.

After spending most of 1922 in France, Jack Curley affiliated himself with a new venture in New York City, the Cycle Sports Corporation. The outfit was run by 42-year-old Matthew "Matty" Zimmerman, the manager of the Leblang's famous Broadway bargain ticket agency. He also worked as a matchmaker for the Lexington Avenue Athletic Club. Zimmerman had obtained authorization from the athletic commission to operate sports at the 71st Regiment Armory, and Curley was hired as an assistant. Once again, Curley's connections to talent were instrumental, and Wladek Zbyszko, George Calza, and Ernest Siegfried were spotlighted.

Curley lured champion Lewis to town for a March 26, 1923, match against Cliff Binckley, but the show received so much commission interference that it had to be canceled at the last minute. First, Muldoon announced the main event could not be billed as a championship contest because Binckley wasn't an authentic contender. Going a step further, the commission decided to pull the plug on sanctioning the bout, pressuring Curley and Zimmerman to replace Binckley with either Siegfried or Zbyszko. They were unable to make the last-minute substitution, and the show was called off.

Lacking high-quality performers and matches that could

garner widespread interest, Cycle Sports struggled but planned another push for attention beginning in October 1923. Curley booked two impressive German newcomers, Hans Steinke and Dick Shikat, plus collegians Frank Judson and Nick Lutze. In the headliner, Zbyszko was matched against Plestina in what would end up being a two-hour, 30-minute draw. Another show was staged in early December, but the kind of returns they anticipated failed to materialize.

Surprisingly, in spite of the poor conditions in the area, Rickard was again motivated to try his hand at wrestling promotions. He envisioned a grand tournament for Madison Square Garden to begin on January 3, 1924, and invited the biggest names to participate. Sportswriter W.C. Vreeland of the *Brooklyn Daily Eagle* wondered if the top wrestlers had "deserted" the syndicate of Curley for Rickard because the latter had control of the valuable Garden. Whether any of the star grapplers would really appear remained to be seen.

In what was turning out to be a season of bombshells, the New York State Athletic Commission rendered a decision in December 1923 that shockingly favored Curley and hurt Rickard. Muldoon and his commission mates concluded that, owing to the diminished popularity of wrestling, only one license was needed in New York City—and that it belonged to Curley and Zimmerman. Even though Rickard had publicly announced his upcoming tournament and made preparations, it was forcibly abandoned.

On January 16, 1924, the wrestling license of the Cycle Sports Club expired. Curley, not wasting any time, immediately obtained commission approval for a new organization, the Mayflower Athletic Corporation. After being shunned by Muldoon for nearly three years, Curley was back in his rightful spot, running pro wrestling shows under his own marquee. No longer did he have to mask his leadership position by claiming to be a press agent or some kind of mid-level guy. He'd finally returned to the top of the New York pyramid, and the only thing that he still needed was the heavyweight title. Commandeering the championship would be accomplished by hook or by crook.

Lewis and Sandow were comfortable with the power they had achieved. However, they were aware that long-reigning champions often became stale at the box office. If that was indeed happening, they were realistic enough to make a change but stubbornly refused to relinquish the title without some kind of guarantee. As had been the case for seven or so years, the championship was passed to temporary titleholders, yet it always returned to Lewis. Other than Joe Stecher, who was competing on an abbreviated schedule, there were no other legitimate options for a new champion anywhere in the United States. There were a number of up-and-comers with potential, but no one was ready to fill the role.

Stanislaus Zbyszko, nearing 45 years of age, was considered a dinosaur. Wladek was in the prime of his career, but he was missing the overwhelming elegance of a one-of-a-kind, industry-changing champion. Former titleholder Earl Caddock was retired, and John Pesek, at 175 pounds, was thought to be too small to successfully reign as the heavyweight kingpin. Others, like Renato Gardini, Joe "Toots" Mondt, and Jim Londos were supporting-cast players in 1924. They were able to main event as challengers, but Sandow and Lewis didn't feel they were title worthy.

After examining the landscape, Sandow and his champion decided to implement an "outside the box" scheme. The concept was to elevate mammoth 6'6", 260-pound former football star Wayne Munn to the title. Pushing Munn would ensure they'd retain control of the championship since he was a member of their syndicate. They'd also benefit financially via booking and appearance fees for the new titleholder, splitting the money several different ways. And when Munn was milked for all he was worth, Lewis getting the title back was a cinch.

Munn's popularity in the central states and Midwest, the central corridor for the Lewis group, was significant. He was expected to draw big numbers in his home state of Nebraska, in Kansas City, where he played football, and from Tulsa to Chicago. The Munn idea was brilliant to a degree. Capitalizing on a newfangled array of maneuvers and brute strength, he was offering a fresh hero for fans to gravitate toward in the midst of a stale wrestling world.

He was an exciting change of pace from the usual grapplers on the circuit, and audiences were intrigued by the possibilities.

The major downside to the plan was that Munn was a rookie on the mat. He could easily rely on his strength, but if taken down by a skilled shooter, he was completely unprotected from being twisted into submission. He didn't have the kind of experience necessary to wiggle out of dangerous predicaments and was slightly naive about the harsher side of pro wrestling. The scarcity of forethought by Sandow and Lewis to acknowledge Munn's vulnerabilities left them in a perilous situation, and calculating enemies were going to be working overtime to take any advantage they could.

Ironically, Munn made his pro wrestling debut at the 71st Regiment Armory for Curley on February 12, 1924. He was a striking figure physically, and his impressive ring presence eclipsed his qualifications. A few years earlier, he'd spent time in the boxing ring, and while he was initially lauded for his size and might, his body couldn't deliver. His mass was too much against nimbler foes. Defeated in three successive bouts, he retired from the fight business and turned to grappling under the tutelage of Lewis. The New York newspaper *The Sun and the Globe* remarked that because of Munn's brawny appearance, he represented a "new type of wrestler."

In the same article, the writer said wrestling was experiencing the dawn of a "new era" by spotlighting an array of homegrown talent. Seven of the eight performers on the February 12 program were born in the United States, including Munn, Strangler Lewis, and Pat McGill. The only exception was Mike Romano of Italy. Conversely, promoters in the past had gone to great lengths to feature foreign athletes, hoping to attract and entertain recent arrivals from various points in Europe and Asia. Although it was a notable change, the majority push of American-born performers was short-lived, and Curley was especially receptive to booking a card full of international grapplers.

In 1937, writer Marcus Griffin penned the revealing book *Fall Guys: The Barnums of Bounce* and introduced the public to the phrase "The Gold Dust Trio," his description of the controlling syndicate behind the ascension of Munn in 1924–25. Sandow and Lewis were two members of the combination, and Toots Mondt was the third wheel, a bright and skilled grappler from northern Colorado. Mondt's "discovery" by Sandow and Lewis a few years earlier had changed the life of the Rocky Mountain mainstay. Formerly known as a light heavyweight, he graduated from regional combat to national matches with standing among the leading challengers to Lewis's title.

Mondt's growth as a performer was two-sided. On one hand, he developed a legitimate wrestling science and toughness competing in straight contests and in carnival athletic shows. His mat talents came from both natural instincts and development, and at his peak, Mondt had few peers—ranking with the cream of the crop, Lewis and Pesek. The other side of his education was strictly about making money. A product of vaudeville, he was wise to entertaining audiences and thrilling people so he'd not only gain their money the first time around, but in repeat performances later on. It all came down to the athletic drama and having the keen sensibility to work the audience in such a way that they were entertained regardless who won.

Scripting personal feuds between performers, gimmicks, and other planned scenarios were driven into the wrestling lexicon with Mondt's guidance. He was also behind the subtle and not-so-subtle heel turn by the Strangler, which led to loud and passionate responses from audiences throughout their promotional territory. Mondt was instrumental in playing to the sentiments of fans from the Midwest to the West Coast, and he not only gained the respect of Sandow and Lewis but became one of the most important people in pro wrestling.

The cunning decisions of the Sandow-Lewis-Mondt combination resulted in a stream of "hundreds of thousands of dollars" into their "coffers," according to Griffin. Based on their track record, there was no reason to believe Munn was going to be anything but successful. In fact, the payoff was expected to be huge.

Curley's February 12, 1924, promotion at the 71st Regiment Armory with Lewis, McGill, and Munn in featured roles drew an estimated 3,000 people. As it happened, he watched the heavy-weight champion arrive and quickly depart without much satisfaction. The high-level meetings that had occurred in years past were absent, and Curley clearly found himself on the outside of the dominant faction. His opinion on the future of the championship was meaningless to the powers that be, and because of the dismal attendance in New York, he'd be lucky to receive any future bookings by the titleholder, whoever it was at the time.

Mindful of his standing in the industry and the expected heavy decline of his business, Curley was disheartened. He'd been riding a high since he regained a prevailing position in New York and wanted to recover all of his lost influence. But Sandow and Lewis were blocking any positive growth, and the title was the main ingredient to any power shift. Sandow had successfully moved the center of the wrestling world from the Northeast to the central states and created a tightly guarded fortress for his syndicate that ostracized anyone they disliked, feared, or deemed insignificant.

With the proper promotional machine in place and a variety of expectations, the Munn plan went ahead as scheduled on January 8, 1925, in Kansas City. Fan excitement for the affair was expressed by 15,000 people jamming the Convention Hall, the largest local wrestling crowd in history. Munn carried the support of the audience in his trek to upset Lewis, and during the important first fall he proved he was the real deal. He used his strength to escape the stranglehold and, after 21 minutes, applied a body and crotch hold to defeat the champion. The animated contest continued in the second but ended unexpectedly when Munn tossed Lewis over the top rope. The champ landed on the platform holding up the ring and then collapsed onto the hard floor below.

Evidently injured, Lewis lay prone on the floor as doctors ran to his aid. Munn, who was caught up in the excitement, tried to exit the ring to continue the fight but was stopped by the referee, Walter Bates. Sandow cried foul, shouting at the top of his lungs, and demanded the official award the match to Lewis. Bates agreed to disqualify Munn, but not for the entire match, only for the second fall. He proceeded to give Lewis 15 minutes to return to the ring to continue the bout. If he was unable to revive, Munn was going to be declared champion. Gallantly, Lewis returned. His body was bandaged and a serious back injury was suspected. He was no match for the unstoppable Munn in the third fall. After less than a minute, Lewis was pinned.

Wrestling had a new champion, and the Sandow-Lewis-Mondt scheme was delivered to the public with perfection. Although he was the heavyweight kingpin, Munn's limited repertoire was clearly acknowledged by mainstream sources. The Associated Press remarked that he had the grappling knowledge of a "novice," and outside of his pure strength, his body and crotch hold was his only real "weapon." A weekly newspaper out of Chicago, *Collyer's Eye*, broke the facade and declared the title change and "injury" to Lewis as scripted events. The paper claimed Munn was susceptible to defeat by "at least fifty" competitors in legitimate matches, all due to the new champ's inexperience.

Curley followed up with his own ridicule of Munn. He openly identified the rival Trust as being made up of Sandow, his two brothers, Max and Julius Baumann, and a gaggle of wrestlers from Lewis to Pesek to Mondt. In criticizing Munn, Curley said he wasn't even a good third-rate wrestler and that he was "not good enough to win from a fair middleweight." He named 10 grapplers willing to put up $10,000 to battle Munn for the title—all of whom were outsiders to the Sandow syndicate.

Yet inside the seemingly impenetrable Sandow complex, there was one wrestler who, perhaps greater than anyone else in the combination, had loyalty to Curley. He was Stanislaus Zbyszko. Back in the early part of the 1910s, Zbyszko and his manager Jack Herman worked closely with Curley, and Stanislaus's brother Wladek was managed by the New York impresario for many years. If Curley was going to resort to an old, underhanded trick to win back the championship, he needed an insider with access to Munn.

The ethics of pro wrestling has always been questionable. There was no honor among thieving promoters, and regardless of how honest a man might have been away from the ring, his will was repeatedly tested in an environment made up of conniving swindlers. Lacking a central authoritative body to regulate the sport, wrestling was essentially run by promoters and managers, and their affiliations and partiality tended to swing toward the biggest moneymakers on the horizon—not athletes with genuine ability. And, not to be ignored, the core fundamentals of pro wrestling were built on fakery, lies, and deceit. The public was sold on grappling matches that were said to be honest but were predetermined. It was a scam from beginning to end.

Curley appealed to Zbyszko because he had access to Munn and Sandow didn't think he had any reason to worry. Time and again, Zbyszko had demonstrated his value as a member of the troupe. He was perceived to be trustworthy and did what he was told. But that wasn't going to be the case on April 15, 1925, in Philadelphia. Curley asked him to do the unthinkable and pull off an in-ring double-cross of Munn. It was an extraordinary request and for financial considerations, plus the prestige of regaining the heavyweight championship, Zbyszko agreed.

The betrayal of Munn by Zbyszko was a remarkable scene. Often wearing a smile, the Polish heavyweight jostled Munn to the mat and applied stylish techniques to twist and turn the much bigger champion onto his back. The first fall came after eight minutes and 11 seconds and the second in just four minutes and 53 seconds. Munn, standing as much as eight inches taller than Zbyszko, was said to be "helpless" and appeared surprised when toppled. In an instant, the power balance of wrestling shifted from Lewis and Sandow to Curley, and the latter was all too ready to assert himself as the central ruler. In a somewhat comedic side note, newspapers added years to the already aged Zbyszko, making him anywhere from 55 to 58. His real age was believed to be somewhere in the region of 44 to 47.

Zbyszko wasn't seen as a long-term champion. To Curley, the most sensible replacement titleholder was Joe Stecher of Nebraska. For the last three years, Stecher had bounced in and out of active competition, freely venturing into idleness to concentrate on semipro baseball and other hobbies only to stage a comeback months later. In November 1924, he rejoined the circuit and worked on his conditioning to make another run at the heavyweight title. Having won the crown several times before, he was exceedingly familiar with the demands of being champion. He was highly skilled, tall, and possessed great strength in his legs, explaining why his finisher was the leg scissors hold.

On the canvas, Stecher was instinctual and intelligent. His fast-paced aggressiveness could be matched by an impressive defensive ability, and he rated among the top-three catch-as-catch-can heavyweight grapplers in the world. Outside the ring, he relied heavily on his brother Tony to handle political issues and contracts. The importance of his sibling was never more evident than in December 1916, when Joe, traveling east without Tony by his side, suddenly walked out of a grueling match against former Olympian Johan Olin of Finland. The unexpected action caused his forfeit and gave Olin a claim to the world title. Pundits believed that had Tony been at Joe's side, the champion would have finished the match.

Wrestling the championship away from the Sandow syndicate meant big money, and the Stechers were eager to resume their alliance with Curley. On May 30, 1925, before 15,000 people in St. Louis, "Scissors" Joe toppled Zbyszko in two straight and won his claim to the title. That same day in Michigan City, Indiana, not far from Chicago, Lewis beat Munn in another match billed as being for a "championship." It was said that because Lewis never completely relinquished the title to Munn in the first place, nor did he give up his diamond belt, he still held a tainted version of the crown. Thus, when he beat Munn, he added to his credibility. The story was convoluted to say the least, but now, with two rivaling titleholders, it became a battle of press agents. The fans had to decide which story and lineage they believed more.

In the end, Stecher was regarded as having the stronger claim, and he lived up to his reputation on the circuit from New York to Los Angeles. Curley went into rebuilding mode, trying to impress locals with a mixture of new faces and old favorites at the 71st Regiment Armory. Between 1925 and '27, he regularly promoted Wladek Zbyszko, Nat Pendleton, Hans Steinke, and Renato Gardini and began to push popular "Golden Greek" Jim Londos. Youngsters Ray Steele, Karl Sarpolis, Abe Coleman, and Jim Browning were receiving their first New York jobs and doing well for themselves. They were clearly on the road to stardom.

Pesek jumped sides in the war, aligning with Stecher and wrestling the champion in two heated Los Angeles bouts in 1926. Late that year and going into 1927, a silent peace accord was drafted between Stecher and Lewis, but Curley stood on the sidelines, unwilling to make amends with the Strangler or Sandow. He did gain an important ally in Toots Mondt, who settled in New York City and found employment in Curley's office. Mondt was no longer wrestling with gusto and traveling as part of the Sandow group. He appeared for matches, but his ability to book contests and work with talent was far more valuable.

In New York, 10,000 fans saw Stecher retain his title over Ivan Podubbny on February 1, 1926, indicating that area fans were still supportive if awoken by the right kind of spectacle. Growth was apparent when smaller venues in Queens (Ridgewood Grove) and Manhattan (St. Nicholas Arena) began to offer recurring events. Curley's promotional alliance grew as well, and he formed a strong bond with Philadelphian Ray Fabiani. His ties to Tom Packs in St. Louis and Ed White in Chicago continued to produce fruitful results.

The wrestling scene was far from stable, and personal animosities, vengeful maneuvering, and greed were keynotes to the sport's future. On a never-ending rollercoaster ride, Curley was determined to stabilize things in New York once and for all. His feud with Sandow, and an even greater conflict with Boston promoter Paul Bowser, were setting the stage for a tumultuous couple of years. But in the midst of strife, the New York wrestling market would become the most valuable in the world.

(2)
THE CENTER OF THE WRESTLING WORLD

By the end of 1927, "Scissors" Joe Stecher was exhausted. His body and mind were tired from the extensive traveling over the past two and a half years as world champion. Feeling financially comfortable, he could envision walking away from the bright lights to live the quiet farm life of Nebraska. His many contributions to wrestling were well known, and during his reign, he assisted in building up the important St. Louis and Los Angeles territories. The idea of passing the title to Ed "Strangler" Lewis had once been preposterous, but now it made sense. He was the rightful heir.

In the Ridgewood community of Queens, New York, there were thousands of people who believed differently. The city was enjoying its first full year of activities at the newly built Ridgewood Grove Arena, and spectators enjoyed everything from musical events and dances to boxing and wrestling. The venue was owned by the Palmetto Amusement Corporation and operated by its president, Isaac T. Flatto, and general manager, Wesley Hamer. Wrestling was under the rule of Paul Rudolph "Rudy" Miller, a

38-year-old from Dresden, Germany, and he successfully brought top-flight talent to the arena.

Miller had gained a measure of importance in wrestling a few years earlier, when two German grapplers brimming with talent had appeared on the American scene, and, because of his ability to communicate with them, Miller had taken over as their manager. They were Hans Steinke and Dick Shikat.

Steinke settled in Hicksville on Long Island and became the pride of New York City. Of the various outlets, none rooted for him like the fans at Ridgewood Grove. It got to the point that an estimated 2,000 people, mostly Germans, formed the "Hans Steinke Social Club" and petitioned officials for a title match for their hero against Stecher. In 1928, he was voted the most popular wrestler over Henri Deglane, Jim Londos, Renato Gardini, and others. For his win, he received a specially designed diamond-studded gold belt.

Undefeated in several years, Steinke was a legitimate contender, and many felt he should "go over" Stecher when the time was appropriate. He stood 6'3" and weighed anywhere from 235 to about 250 pounds. In the boroughs of New York, he was favored by fans and particularly by promoter Jack Curley, who was dead against Strangler Lewis getting the championship back. The last thing he wanted to do was relive the monopolistic days of Sandow and Lewis. But Joe and Tony Stecher were doing business for themselves and worked out an arrangement with Sandow and promoter Tom Packs of St. Louis, where the title switch would occur.

Before the match took place, widespread grumbling caused the New York State Athletic Commission to issue a decree stating that Stecher's title was invalidated in the state until he wrestled and beat Steinke. The commission's edict was pointless on the eve of Stecher's defense against Lewis on February 20, 1928. The Strangler won the first and third falls and captured the world heavyweight championship before more than 7,500 people at the Coliseum. The bout's design and execution were flawless, and, much to the dismay of the New York crowd, Ed Lewis was again the titleholder.

The New York State Athletic Commission didn't wait long before it again issued a statement. Instead of Stecher, this time it was Lewis, and the Strangler would not be recognized in the state until he defeated Steinke. Over the next couple of months, various newspapers boldly billed the 35-year-old Steinke as a claimant to the heavyweight championship, and Curley's press department worked overtime to convince sportswriters and fans that the "German Oak" was the rightful kingpin. Mostly he was acknowledged as the "uncrowned champion," and whatever title billing he received seemed to fade in the summer of 1928.

Of the two German wrestlers signed by Rudy Miller, it was Shikat, not Steinke, who was destined for genuine world title recognition. Four years younger than his countryman, Shikat was deemed more marketable, and his speed and athleticism were eye-catching attributes. He was taken under the tutelage of Joe "Toots" Mondt and schooled in the finer points of catch wrestling. His abilities matured, and Philadelphia instead of New York was his central proving grounds. It didn't take long for the large German population to get behind Shikat, and promoter Ray Fabiani, working closely with Mondt and Curley, brokered a path to maximize his potential at the box office.

On par with the development of wrestling in the New York area was the expansion and growth of the sport in Boston, where Paul Bowser was in charge. Bowser and Curley were solid enemies and had been for a number of years. The exact origin of their feud isn't known, but they both sought power and had the extraordinary capacity to see wrestling on a national scale, while most promoters only concentrated on a single city. In 1923, they clashed under unique circumstances in the ring when Bowser pit John Pesek against Curley's undefeated Olympian Nat Pendleton in a shoot match in Boston. The unscripted bout carried the honor of both promoters, but Bowser had the last laugh when Pesek took the contest in two straight falls.

The defeat humiliated Curley. All the time and money poured into making Pendleton an untarnished future champion was lost, and he detested Bowser even more. Curley was also annoyed for another reason. While he was without a world titleholder because of his troubles with Sandow, Bowser thrived. The Boston promoter did stellar business with Sandow and Strangler Lewis, and their friendly association remained strong for years.

Of all the hostilities in professional wrestling, none was more encompassing than the Curley-Bowser war. They were almost complete opposites. Each hated the thought of his rival getting the better of him, and Curley wanted retribution. Within a short time, they were working to running opposing promotions in each other's towns, all in effort to land a crushing blow. Of course, the ultimate victory would be putting their foe out of business.

One of Curley's past opponents, Tex Rickard, made peace, and they entered into a business agreement in 1928 that was bound to benefit both. The deal was to debut pro wrestling at the "new" Madison Square Garden on March 19 and vault the sport back to the "big-time circuit," as sportswriter Ed Hughes of the *Brooklyn Daily Eagle* remarked. In the main event, Steinke retained his top billing with a defeat of Gardini in a match that went over an hour, and Londos wrestled Ray Steele in an entertaining 30-minute draw in the semifinal. *New York Evening Post* reporter William Morris commented that the show, also featuring Pesek, Shikat, and Abe Coleman, was a "highly successful debut," and attendance was around 3,500.

Around this time, Bowser was supervising the wrestling education of an unlikely prodigy. His new asset was Gus Sonennberg, a gritty warrior from the National Football League. Originally from the Upper Peninsula of Michigan, Sonnenberg, 30, was a lifelong athlete, having excelled in many sports in high school and college, and had received berths on three NFL teams. His more recent exploits were as a member of the Providence Steam Rollers, and in 1928 the squad went 8-1-2 and won the league championship. Sonnenberg's hard-nosed style of play and affable attitude earned him the respect of his peers and a herd of supporters.

Wrestling was not a natural vocation for Sonnenberg. He likely wouldn't have crossed over if his teammate John Spellman hadn't done so and revealed the exemplary earnings of off-season grappling. Sonnenberg became a convert, much to Bowser's glee, and the latter quickly realized that he had a superstar in the making.

Winning his first 39 matches, the 5'7½" Sonnenberg showed class and innovation in the ring. His basic strategy was to combine the methods of wrestling and football, but rather than only rely on strength like Wayne Munn, he was going to display agility and nimbleness. The flashy exhibition of speed made him a surefire standout on a bill of sluggish heavyweights. His versatile arsenal included a variety of genuine holds but also featured flying head-butts and shoulder tackles. His ace in the hole, the flying tackle, was a game-changing finisher. Relying on speed, timing, and a large serving of theatrics, Sonnenberg lined up his opponents and catapulted himself into their midsections, creating a sensation.

The flying tackle was soon seen everywhere professional grappling was featured, from Madison Square Garden to small-town America. It brought excitement and tension, perfect for the dramatic wrestling stage, as the flying tackle wasn't a guaranteed success. Sonnenberg, and others who used the maneuver, occasionally missed their rival completely and sailed from the ring onto the concrete floor. In those instances, the purveyor of the tackle was seriously injured and often unable to continue the match.

On the other hand, when successfully landed into the guts of an opponent, it usually meant a swift and easy victory. And no one was better at it than Sonnenberg, the move's originator. He beat foe after foe all the way up the Sandow syndicate's ladder to champion Ed Lewis. Then, Bowser brokered the deal that would pass the title from the Strangler to the hottest commodity in the business. On January 4, 1929, around 20,000 people cheered Sonnenberg's two-straight-fall win over Lewis at the Boston Garden, and he was subsequently crowned wrestling's world champion.

Sonnenberg's major drawback was the same as Munn's—his inexperience. He didn't have the wherewithal to combat or defend against a wrestler of pure abilities and needed to be protected from conspiring outsiders. If a trusted ally turned on him during a match, a specially provided referee who toured with the champion would decide the bout in way to shield Sonnenberg and his precious championship. The official was the last line of defense against an in-ring betrayal.

Curley's up-and-coming champion, Dick Shikat, was better suited to ward off a legitimate attacker. He had excelled in amateur and Greco-Roman grappling in his native Germany and had many years of competition under his belt. There was no doubting Sonnenberg was a much more colorful performer, but Shikat found his niche and began commanding larger and larger audiences. He beat his longtime friend, the previously unbeatable Steinke, and was greeted by a magnificent cheer from a crowd of 30,000 when he toppled Londos for the vacant world title on August 23, 1929, in Philadelphia.

Before the match, the Pennsylvania and New York State Athletic Commissions withdrew recognition of Sonnenberg as the official titleholder for failing to wrestle worthy opponents. It was a polite way of saying that Sonnenberg was meeting the same members of his syndicate over and over. Curley's press agents ran with the story, telling sportswriters that Sonnenberg was sometimes wrestling the same man multiple times in different cities, the foe using various aliases to conceal his identity.

According to Curley and Fabiani, and their respective contacts within the New York and Pennsylvania commissions, Sonnenberg was not defending against tried-and-true challengers, such as Steinke, Shikat, and Londos. The rush to discredit Sonnenberg was on, and officials in those two states agreed to rescind title recognition. When Shikat went over Londos in August 1929, a new championship lineage was started, and once again, the wrestling landscape reverted back to a war for the hearts and minds of fans. Who were the people going to support: Sonnenberg, the vibrant flying tackle artist, or Shikat, the hard-nosed battler?

The Curley syndicate was on the upslope of prosperity. In terms of talent, they had Shikat, Londos, Pesek, Steinke, Renato Gardini, the Zbyszkos, and Mondt. They imported Fred Grubmier and Rudy Dusek from the famous Iowa-Nebraska corridor, known for producing outstanding grapplers, and also George Zaharias from Colorado. Curley shored up his contingent of foreign athletes by hiring a multilingual 34-year-old named Jack Pfefer to serve as a manager and scout. Pfefer, as part of the Russian Grand Opera, toured the world and reportedly spoke more than a dozen languages. He was instrumental in enlisting many international competitors, including Matros Kirilanko, Ferenc Holuban, and Sandor Szabo.

Mondt's expert coaching of Shikat improved the latter's showmanship, and the champion formed an entertaining routine that had characteristics of both Ed Lewis and Ric Flair. Murray Robinson, sports editor of the *Brooklyn Standard Union*, offered an explanation of Shikat's histrionics after he took in a show at Ridgewood Grove. Robinson was familiar with the overcooked performances of wrestlers in the modern arena and said Shikat delivered a "good show." He specifically mentioned the way Shikat recoiled and backed away from his muscled opponent. The champion would hide in the corner, use the ropes to force a break, and pretend to be fearful—all to raise the ire of the crowd. It worked.

Shikat would ultimately use science and his strength to seize the advantage and defeat his rival to retain the championship. But the way he invoked reactions as a heel agitator was similar to Lewis's practices during his dominance in the 1920s and comparable to the work of Flair, Buddy Rogers, and many other colorful wrestlers throughout the past 80 years. Sometimes even the most subtle tactics were enough to rouse the audience, but when an instigator really worked the angles, snarled, grimaced, and contorted his face in the midst of a lively display, the crowd usually roared with fury. This kind of performance meant big money.

The shenanigans inside the ring were well crafted by the wrestlers, managers, and promoters of each syndicate. Better than 99 percent of the time, matches ended just as they were scripted, and there were very few unexpected occurrences.

The more contentious events were customarily produced by the raging promotional war, which was growing in scope, not only across the United States but also in Canada. With Sonnenberg drawing widespread attention from curious sports fans, Bowser was able to expand his circuit from Boston to Los Angeles and from Toronto to Miami. Promoters were eager to feature the ex-football player and happy to formally affiliate themselves with the Bowser faction. Curley's enterprises did likewise, and his troops marched to box office paydays in a host of new cities. Things took an interesting turn in November 1929, when Curley workers began appearing in Bowser's home grounds in Boston, wrestling under the auspices of Billy Avery at the Mechanics Building. The debut show, headlined by Shikat and George Manich, drew 2,500.

Both syndicates replaced their heavyweight champions in 1930 in an effort to avoid a sense of staleness at the top of their ranks. Shikat was outgunned by wrestling's newest idol, Jim Londos, on June 6, 1930, in Philadelphia before 20,000 spectators. In the many months leading up to the exalted affair, the 36-year-old Londos built up an impressive fan base that was impossible to ignore. He was far more popular than Shikat or any of his contemporaries, and for Curley, there was no smarter business move than to make Londos champion.

Londos, sporting a golden tan, an impressive physique on his 5'8" frame, and a stylish potpourri of wrestling moves, was likable. He looked like a superstar, and his size—given his vast mat knowledge and strength—wasn't a handicap when facing larger foes. Born in Greece, Londos had settled in San Francisco as a young man and spent a number of years competing as an amateur grappler in local clubs. After turning pro, he toiled from region to region, scuffling for meager pay, and worked his way up to semifinals and main events against established stars. Though times were tough, he demonstrated an unsinkable spirit. He appeared destined for greatness and, in 1930, reached the apex of professional wrestling by winning the world heavyweight title.

All across the Curley circuit, arenas were exploding with overflow crowds, and although America was reeling in the aftermath of the 1929 stock market crash and facing the beginning of the Great Depression, people were determined to turn out and support Londos as champion.

Madison Square Garden was still the primary spot for big-time wrestling in New York. Of course, Curley yearned to return to the coveted venue, but in March 1930, Garden officials sidestepped his appointment and hired Stanislaus Zbyszko to be their wrestling matchmaker. Zbyszko followed up with two programs, on April 2 and May 14, but couldn't lure an attendance greater than 4,000 despite booking Ed Lewis, Joe Stecher, and Joe Malcewicz. Tom McArdle, an officer for the Garden, sought better financial returns when wrestling picked up again in the autumn of 1930. The solution for maximum dollar was Curley and his top star, Londos. The deal was made, and Curley booked his first show for November 17, 1930.

It was an exciting time for wrestling in the territory. Casual fans were increasingly attracted to the spectacle of pro grappling, and promotions broadened across the New York metropolitan area and into surrounding states. The extraordinarily favorable conditions almost guaranteed Curley a success on November 17, and the turnout was better than expected. An estimated 20,000 people jammed the Garden to see Londos earn a much-appreciated victory over Gino Garibaldi in 46 minutes. William Morris of the *Evening Post* decided that, based on the success of the show, New York had become the "center" of the wrestling world.

His bold statement was accurate. New York surged to the forefront, driven by the enormous Garden turnout in November and again on December 29, 1930. Curley's second offering drew 20,000 people and a gate of over $48,000 for a booking of Londos against Ferenc Holuban of Hungary. Another 3,000 people were turned away. Giving away 34 pounds, Londos needed but 20 minutes and 45 seconds to beat his opponent and sent the crowd home content. Curley finished the year on a high note.

In late 1930, Paul Bowser was dealing with the overexposure of Sonnenberg and preparing a number of young wrestlers for future glory. His number one project was Edward Nicholas George, better known as Ed Don George and the son of a New York farmer. George was a champion amateur wrestler and had placed fourth in the 1928 Olympics. The opposite of Sonnenberg in terms of size and legitimate skill, George, 25, was flawlessly groomed to capture the world title. On December 10, 1930, in Los

Angeles, he took two of three falls from Sonnenberg and won the championship. A majority of the 10,000 fans in attendance vocalized their support of the title switch.

Ed "Strangler" Lewis disapproved, and he was shocked by the shift from Sonnenberg to George. According to the agreement he had made with Bowser prior to his January 1929 title loss, he was slated to regain the championship when Sonnenberg's reign was due to end. Instead of making arrangements to fulfill his end of the bargain, Bowser eliminated Lewis from the picture completely and gave the title to a highly skilled shooter who, he felt, was virtually impossible to beat in genuine warfare. If Lewis came for revenge, there was no way the overweight and aged Strangler would have the faculties to top George, and Bowser was fully confident in his decision.

Back in Boston, Bowser had to deal with yet another invasion of his sacred territory. This time around, the trespasser was Ray Fabiani, the Philadelphia mastermind and a chieftain in the Curley-Londos tribe. Known as the Fiddler because of his work as a professional violinist, including a stint with the Chicago Opera Company, Fabiani had become a promoter in the mid-1920s. The local sporting public was enthusiastic about his operations at the Metropolitan Opera House, Municipal Stadium, and the Arena in Philadelphia, and wrestlers greatly appreciated his trustworthiness. Londos had made a lifelong friend.

Fabiani's achievements sold Boston Garden officials on the idea of him becoming matchmaker, and on December 19, 1930, he opened up his promotions before 12,000 spectators. In the main event, Rudy Dusek defeated strongman Milo Steinborn, while Jim McMillen, Gino Garibaldi, and Paul Jones entertained fans on the undercard. Dusek was an interesting choice to headline. Born Rudolph Hason, he had grown up in Omaha, Nebraska, and was one of nine children. He wrestled as an amateur and took lessons from the legendary Farmer Burns, developing into an accomplished light heavyweight.

In 1930, Dusek was 29 years old and in the prime of his career on the mat. His status in the Curley organization was a result of his fine workmanship and exceptional wrestling smarts. He was able to carry opponents in the ring to good matches, assist in booking, and mentor younger athletes. He also had three brothers, Emil, Ernie, and Joe, who turned to pro grappling, and they were collectively known as the bruising Riot Squad. Friendly affiliation with Rudy meant bookings for the entire Dusek clan, and that association proved important during the wrestling wars of the 1930s.

The 12,000-person draw at the Boston Garden was a spectacular number for a first-time promotion. Bowser had reason to be concerned. An ideal response was carried out in early 1931, when his troops moved into New York City to chew into Curley's local monopoly. His on-the-ground associate was veteran Jack Herman, a German-born manager and promoter with over 30 years' experience. Herman assumed control of wrestling at the 69th Regiment Armory in Manhattan, and his February 11, 1931, program drew 3,500 fans to see Joe Stecher battle Marin Plestina. In March, champion Ed Don George made his area debut, and 6,000 were present to see him top Jean LaDue.

Columnist Westbrook Pegler addressed the situation in New York in a syndicated piece that appeared in the *New York Evening Post* on March 19, 1931. He cited the overwhelming success of Curley's promotions and reported that $268,000 had been garnered from six programs at Madison Square Garden. Pegler, in contrast, claimed the Bowser-Herman troupe hadn't produced a single gate higher than $2,700.

Pegler predicted they could lure an exceptional attendance with a champion-versus-champion outdoor affair during the summer. Such a match needed the consent of both Curley and Bowser, and the former, firmly in position as the czar of wrestling, didn't need to waste his time on such a proposal.

"I am doing very well as things are," Curley told Pegler. With Londos as his champion, and the excitement created by the Greek sensation, he couldn't fail. There was only continued success ahead, he figured, as long as he pulled the strings without interference.

Bowser was motivated to make a dent in New York and siphon off some of Curley's business. He gained four different venues for wrestling: the 69th Regiment Armory, Broadway Arena, Star Casino, and Jamaica Arena. The Broadway Arena in Brooklyn was exceptionally promising, not for its location or regular patronage but because of the man who was running it. The administrator was Jess McMahon, one of New York's most battle-tested promoters. He obtained a license to operate in February 1931 and staged a number of boxing programs before debuting wrestling on April 9. That day, 1,200 people saw Stanley Stasiak win the headliner over Louis Lowe and Jack Sherry beat Henri Deglane by decision after 30 minutes.

The injection of McMahon into the coarse wrestling environment was notable, and if Bowser sought a man who could build a fundamentally stable promotion from the floor up, Jess was the person to call. Only time would tell if McMahon could swing a winner, but if his past record was any indication, he was certain to deliver the fans of Brooklyn a memorable show, week in and week out.

(3)
A BUDDING
DYNASTY

The entertaining affairs of professional wrestling were news-worthy for the New York press in 1931, but the city had been a much different place 60 years earlier. Absent were the skyscrapers that hovered high above the streets and the smooth pavement for automobiles. The massive centers for shopping and entertain-ment were available in reduced incarnations, and the indomitable corporations that transformed America were barely a gleam in their founders' eyes. In the aftermath of the Civil War and as the country sailed into what was dubbed the Gilded Age, the popu-lation of New York grew sizably, and it became the beacon for opportunity-seeking settlers from all over the world.

On the northwest side of Manhattan Island rested the com-munity of Manhattanville, today also known as West Harlem. It was a charming locale for Europeans of all origins, and the con-glomeration meshed in their pursuits of employment, family, and happiness. On 131st Street and Bloomingdale Road, the Church of the Annunciation was an attractive symbol for Irish Catholics.

Among its vast congregation were Roderick and Elizabeth McMahon, a young Irish couple of 26 and 23, respectively, in 1870.

The McMahons lived on the nearby property of a widow, Ann Fortune, on Lawrence Street between 10th Avenue and Broadway, along with a pair of teachers, Ann's daughter Mary and Angeline Simpson. Another occupant, a 20-year-old named Rick Dowling, was employed as a bartender, and, according to the 1870 U.S. federal census, Roderick's occupation was that of a "liquor dealer." Records do not indicate whether McMahon ran a saloon or worked as some type of distributor, but he remained an active businessman through the remainder of his years.

In 1871, McMahon paid Fortune $5,200 for the property, and he continued to run his enterprise and live out of the same location. As his family swelled to include three children, Mary, Catherine, and Edward, and with another on the way, he decided to separate his professional work from his personal life. He invested $3,500 in a two-story home on 10th Avenue and 130th Street in November 1881, and the McMahons relocated. Five months later, on May 26, 1882, their final child, Roderick James, was born.

Through his involvement in the church and social groups such as the Catholic Mutual Benefit Association, the McMahon patriarch made a lot of friends and was a pillar of the Manhattanville neighborhood. His hard work and dedication earned him admirers for his entrepreneurship, and he was the foundation of his young family. That made his sudden death on October 30, 1888, even harder to understand. The 44-year-old was taken in the prime of his life.

As in other parts of the country, competitive sport was an essential amusement for New Yorkers. Boys from grade school to college gathered on vacant lots a short distance from the Church of the Annunciation to play ball. Organized teams representing various groups engaged in regular baseball competition. The "Eighth Avenues" fielded a squad of younger adolescents, and they were such a skilled unit that other kids watched them practice with dreams of one day joining them on the diamond. In 1893, 13-year-old Eddie McMahon was a hopeful. He was a keen observer of all the players at Pastime Park, where the Manhattan College club played, and shared a love of sports with his brother, Roderick.

The family moved less than a block north, along Amsterdam Avenue, and Roderick, who was also known by the nickname "Jess," attended Public School 43. Soon thereafter, he enrolled at Manhattan College and earned a commercial diploma in 1899. He was a multitalented man, proven by the diversity of his employment in the ensuing years. Always motivated to help support his mother, McMahon toiled as a clerk in a local bank, in the hat business, and in the food industry. However, through all of his varied occupations, the one constant was his involvement in athletics, particularly on the administrative side of things.

As early as March 1900, at 17 years of age, Jess was managing the baseball team of the Olympic Athletic Club, which was based out of his neighborhood and made up of friends. Brother Eddie was more inclined to participate in the on-field happenings, but Jess was content to promote the team. He sought out games by getting space in area newspapers and arranged for suitable training grounds. It was a crucial, sink-or-swim education, but Jess was well organized and immensely smart. He made up for any deficiencies by learning quickly and building on his failures.

Football was a natural next step for the Olympic AC, and members put together a squad of 115-pounders. McMahon went to work looking to challenge comparable semiprofessional teams in 1901 and 125-pounders the following year. On the field, regardless of the age of the players, football lived up to its reputation as a violent sport. With limited pads and protection, if any at all, the athletes went into games like it was combat, and fisticuffs were considered normal. Injuries were rampant, but for New York City clubs, team pride was always on the line. It was motivation to fight through the pain and battle for the honor of their organization, one game at a time.

On the football field, the squad representing the Olympic displayed a striking amount of courage, particularly in 1903, after picking up a handful of former college athletes. Halfback John Thorpe and quarterback Frank Goodman were veterans of Columbia University, and left end Marty Waters had made a name for himself while with the Knickerbocker Athletic Club. The renewed spirit of the team was illustrated in victories over nearly all of their rivals, including impressive shutouts against the West Point Engineers and Fort Columbus. On December 14, 1903, a special indoor football tournament was staged at Madison Square Garden, and the Olympic club entered a four-team bracket for championship honors.

In the first game, McMahon led his squad to a 6–0 victory over the Knickerbocker FC, and a few days later they beat the tough Mohawk AC 12–0 to capture the championship of Greater New York. The New York *Globe and Commercial Advertiser* reported that the Olympic AC "won through superior knowledge of the great fall game and superior physical condition." It was a great achievement and a major feather in the cap of young Jess McMahon.

Once again demonstrating his versatility, McMahon became a public servant and worked as a sewer inspector in 1905–06. In the midst of his tenure, boxing supporters launched a movement to revive the sport in New York City—and the outcome had personal consequences. Prizefighting had been banned by the New York State legislature and Governor Theodore Roosevelt in 1900 after a continuous stream of negativity. Effectively known as Section 458 of the penal code, the prohibition of boxing was staunchly regulated by police, and they wouldn't hesitate to arrest anyone, including the fighters, promoters, and referees, for violating the law.

In November 1905, a major breakthrough for pro-fight advocates occurred when a local magistrate decided that three-round contests held within the confines of a private athletic club were legal. Specifically, such engagements were only for affiliated members, not the public, and no admission fees could be charged at the door. Members paid yearly dues for the right to see the bouts, and this system of bypassing the law was quite normal at the Bleecker, National, and Hudson Athletic clubs. It wasn't until the magistrate pronounced the scheme legal that such boxing gained the necessary accreditation to operate freely.

Almost immediately, Jess and Eddie McMahon went into action to prepare the Olympic Athletic Club for exclusive membership-only boxing exhibitions. Since the club had only operated sanctioned outdoor sports like baseball and football, the McMahons needed to locate a clubhouse that provided enough comfort and accommodations for a crowd. The Marion Hall at 125th Street and Lexington fit the bill. The inaugural show was held on December 16, 1905, and was headlined by Benny Yanger and Rube McCarthy. This marked the first time the McMahon family promoted an indoor ring event.

Innumerable boxing clubs were sprouting up across New York. Despite the condemnation of opponents and police intimidation and interference, the fight business gained momentum and club memberships skyrocketed. Some sportswriters, when remarking about the clientele of the various clubs, would commonly put "membership" or "members" in quotes as a sort of tongue-in-cheek reference to the legitimacy of the organizations. It was believed that a majority of boxing fans at these clubs were not genuine members, but paying customers, and that promoters were covertly breaking the law.

The police watched the situation intently, shutting down any event they believed to be illegal. The Olympic AC wasn't above suspicion. In February 1908 and again in January 1909, officers executed raids on the facility and, in the latter instance, arrested the two fighters engaged in battle and the referee. Nevertheless, the courts continued to affirm the right of clubs to stage restrictive fight exhibitions for the amusement of their associates. The McMahons continued to present quality contests by known and credible athletes. They also featured many up-and-coming locals from Harlem and other parts of New York. Knockout Brown, Joe Wagner, Eddie Walsh, Willie Jones, Abe Attell, Frankie Burns, and Paddy Sullivan were among the highlighted combatants.

Fighters from bantamweight to heavyweight stacked the cards at the Olympic, and the McMahons often brought in foreign competitors, giving the venue an international flavor. The three-round "rule" expanded to 10, and it wasn't uncommon to see an enthusiastic and bloody encounter go the distance. Exhibitions of speed, science, and strength were routine, and the "members" of the Olympic appreciated the McMahons' devotion to their entertainment. The loyalty and gratitude went both ways, and it was clear that the brothers were becoming two of the most influential fight promoters in the city. Not only were they forming a long-term bond with their supporters, they were making allies out of fight managers and the boxers themselves. Their sense of fairness in what was usually corrupt world went a long way.

Audacious promoters, time and again, tested the will of law enforcement and took liberties that threatened boxing as they knew it. Disaster finally struck during the summer of 1909, when the Fairmont Athletic Club went overboard in hyping a contest between Sam Langford and Stanley Ketchel. While it was truly an important fight, officials brazenly touted the occasion with public announcements and arranged a special reservation system for its "members" and their guests. The event provoked high-ranking bureaucrats all the way up to the governor and drew immense criticism. Fairmont directors had little choice but to abandon their plans, and on September 16, 1909, they did just that.

The backlash of politicians paralyzed all of the clubs supporting boxing, and for almost two months the fight game was suppressed by fear. In the interest of letting the tension simmer down, the McMahons went on hiatus at the Olympic, but they were not giving up their lucrative enterprises. Things stood in a state of limbo, pending a formal decree from someone in power. When that statement failed to arrive in a timely manner, the McMahons took the next logical step and proved utterly defiant. On November 8, 1909, the Olympic club reopened to "members," becoming the first to resume boxing in the city. About 200 spectators were on hand.

Police were alerted to the resumption of fisticuffs at the Harlem location and dispatched officers from a West 125th Street station to break up the event. But they were moments too late, and Jess McMahon locked the front door, preventing anyone from entering the building outside of the 200 already admitted. Police turned away hundreds of would-be spectators at the entrance, and while the commotion was being contained outside the venue, Eddie McMahon commenced the boxing program inside. Since they didn't have legal authority to enter the private club without proper cause, the officers stood guard outside—believing that they were successfully interrupting the show. They couldn't have been more wrong, and the patrons escaped unmolested out a back door at the conclusion of the affair.

A week later, the McMahons were at it again, and the police responded the same way. According to the *New York Times*, several of the officers attempted to get inside to see what was happening, but Jess turned them away.

With the Olympic leading the way, other clubs resurrected boxing on a weekly basis and the heavy scrutiny faded. Business continued to prosper for Jess and Eddie going into 1910, and they accepted a proposition to expand their promotional empire to the Manhattan Casino, a classy ballroom further north in Harlem, at 155th Street and Eighth Avenue. The owners of the facility were also a pair of brothers, Edward and Louis Waldron, and the opportunity to make serious money was before the McMahons for the first time in their lives. The casino sat more than 3,000 people, making it much bigger than the Olympic. If they could book the right matches and attract fans from across the city, it was guaranteed profit.

Since prizefighting was still outlawed, the McMahons needed to organize another club to operate boxing at the casino. The new outfit was designated the Empire Athletic Club, and its debut on April 8, 1910, was marked by the 10-round victory of Harlem's own Tommy Murphy over Battling Hurley. Through the rest of the year, the brothers were among the most prolific promoters in the boxing trade, and their standard remained excellent at both the Olympic and Empire Clubs. They were rewarded with capacity houses.

Becoming increasingly affluent, Jess looked to further diversify his interests. Baseball was always a passion, and for a stretch of the 1900s, he held a small share in the Philadelphia Giants, a famous African American ball club. In 1911, McMahon commissioned a former star of the Giants, future Hall of Famer Sol White, to assemble a team to play at his home grounds, Olympic Field, at 136th Street and Fifth Avenue. White was more than successful in his endeavors, gathering a contingent of outstanding athletes and compelling the *Brooklyn Daily Eagle* to say that it was "one of the strongest aggregations of colored ball players ever gotten together."

Known as the Lincoln Giants, the squad featured the likes of John Henry Lloyd, Louis Santop, "Smokey" Joe Williams, Spot Poles, Dick Redding, Dan McClellan, and Pete Booker. Jess McMahon, incidentally, said Lloyd was the "greatest ball player" he'd ever seen when discussing baseball with a reporter from the *New York Age* in 1948. He added that he'd "seen them all," but Lloyd "made an indelible imprint" on his mind. It was impossible not to be awed by the fielding and hitting power of Lloyd, another future member of the National Baseball Hall of Fame. The 5'11" shortstop was an essential part of the Giants, and when White bowed out later in 1911, Lloyd assumed the role of manager.

McMahon ensured his team remained independent and free from third-party booking fees. The Giants, however, were never lacking competition, especially after their reputation as a first-rate club spread. Teams traveled great distances to oppose them, and the Cuban Stars from Havana engaged the Giants in a three-game series in August and September 1911 for the semi-professional championship. On September 17, the Cuban squad won the deciding matchup 10–5 and captured the prize. In other contests, the Giants battled teams from New Jersey, Connecticut, Pennsylvania, and throughout the New York region. Notable delegations also represented the Cherokee nation and the New York fire and police departments.

Perhaps the finest aggregation to stand across the diamond from McMahon's club was the American Giants of Chicago. The *Indianapolis Freeman* reported that the Rube Foster–led team was victorious in 112 games out of the 132 they played in 1912, and it was generally believed they were the best African American franchise. In an attempt to prove otherwise, the Lincoln Giants entered into a best-of-12 series against Foster's men during the summer of 1913 and ended up with seven wins to their opponent's five. The final game, staged on August 13 in Chicago, was won by McMahon's team 4–1, thus earning the team the "colored championship" of the United States.

Things didn't always run smooth for the McMahons in the profession of promoting baseball. Not long after becoming manager of the Giants in 1911, John Lloyd abruptly resigned because he felt he wasn't getting the necessary respect from his players. Luckily for Jess and Eddie, they were able to convince him to return to the helm for the subsequent season. A separate problem related to what the *New York Age* newspaper called the "kidnapping business."

They were describing the practice of unscrupulous baseball leaders who coaxed players from rival teams to jump ship and join their club. The Giants lost several important athletes that way, and officials had to resort to similar tactics to keep pace.

In the realm of boxing, the McMahons continued to build their status. They became responsible for their third club in April 1912, when they worked out a deal to make matches for the St. Nicholas Rink, in a prime location on the Upper West Side of Manhattan. Months before, boxing had again been legalized in New York by the conditions of the Frawley Law, and the sport was experiencing unprecedented growth. When the Twentieth Century Athletic Club, which operated at the venue, failed to sustain itself in the high-volume environment, Cornelius Fellowes, the leaseholder, hired the McMahons, forming the St. Nicholas Athletic Club in the process.

Later known as the St. Nicholas Arena, the St. Nicholas Rink, at West 66th Street and Columbus Avenue, not far from Central Park, was a popular indoor stadium. Ice-skating and hockey were staples for Fellowes, and with the accomplished McMahons in charge, he expected big results. Things got off on the right foot when a sellout crowd paid to see featherweight champion Johnny Kilbane beat Frankie Burns on May 14—and hundreds were turned away. In a blockbuster move, Jess went to Chicago to sign African American world heavyweight champion Jack Johnson for a bout against top contender Joe Jeannette, putting up $5,000 as a deposit toward a $25,000 guarantee for the titleholder to appear. The *New York Times* stated it was the "greatest amount ever offered for a ten-round" fight.

The controversial contest, scheduled for the St. Nicholas Rink on September 25, 1912, received vocal criticism. Interested in learning more about the specifics of the bout, the New York State Athletic Commission requested the McMahon brothers appear before it on August 22, and, not so shockingly, once the meeting was over, the match was canceled.

"We've called the bout off for the good of boxing," Eddie McMahon announced. "Public sentiment is against the appearance of Jack Johnson here and that settles it."

"The McMahons called the bout off themselves," Frank S. O'Neil of the commission added. "But we were prepared to put a stop to it anyway. Johnson has been barred in England and in every state in the union except New Mexico. We have nothing personal against Johnson and we did not conclude to keep him out because of his color."

McMahon denied they were compelled to cancel the affair, but the question remained.

In 1913, an array of misfortunes capsized the McMahons' momentum. They received awesome fan response for a fight between Leach Cross and Joe Rivers on January 14, and allegations were made that they oversold the Manhattan Casino to make maximum dollar. It was also claimed that they boosted prices once they were aware of the massive audience trying to attend the show. As many as 600 patrons who had previously bought tickets were locked out by the fire department once the doors were closed, and the entire spectacle created an immense backlash.

State athletic commission secretary Charles J. Harvey told the press the McMahon brothers had greatly harmed boxing in New York. Additionally, the *New York Sun* asserted that the Cross-Rivers situation was, simply, a "disgrace."

Three months later, the offering of Luther McCarty against Frank Moran at the St. Nicholas Rink was a financial bust, particularly when counting the $5,000 cash guarantee given to McCarty. Attendance just wasn't where it needed to be, and the McMahons took a hit.

Their financial problems weren't limited to boxing. The Lincoln Giants were also facing a crisis, as revealed in August 1913. Players were not receiving their entire salaries, and the *New York Age*, citing a "number of judgments" against the McMahons in recent weeks, said the outlook was "not very encouraging" in its August 28, 1913, edition.

Trying to protect their boxing operations, the brothers implemented a new strategy to shield themselves from no-shows, which were a constant nuisance. The policy required all athletes to post an appearance bond beforehand as a display of good faith. The maneuver was an added level of defense against irresponsible fighters, whose nonappearances were damaging the McMahons'credibility.

But these changes, and any others, were too little, too late. Cornelius Fellowes decided to remove Jess and Eddie from their position, ending the McMahons' occupancy of the St. Nicholas Rink. Over at the Manhattan Casino, the Empire AC was faced with a wearisome year in the wake of the Cross-Rivers controversy. The club descended into inactivity, the lease expired, and on December 23, 1913, the athletic commission pulled its license. To make matters worse, the difficulties for the McMahons in the ownership of the Lincoln Giants were beyond repair, and their business with the franchise concluded not too long afterward.

The McMahon brothers were survivors, though, and in late December 1913, they were already rumored to be in discussion to lead a potential Federal League baseball club. They denied any interest in the outlaw organization, but it was clear they had options for a quick rebound.

Within weeks, the Empire Athletic Club was relocated to the Star Casino on 107th Street and Park Avenue, and the resourceful McMahons formed a ball team in place of the Giants, known as the Lincoln Stars. The transition was unpleasant, as they were stripped of all their top-caliber players, including John Lloyd and

Dick Redding. There was a glimmer of promise in their recruits, however, and pitcher Gunboat Thompson rose to glory by winning 16 straight games on the mound, according to the *New York Press*. Bill Pettus, Bill Pierce, and Guy Jackson led the team to a superior record, and the Stars were often billed as the champions.

Justifiably or not, the McMahon brothers' reputation was damaged, and the New York State Athletic Commission reminded the public of their various missteps in a peculiar way in 1915. The commission had received an application by the Manhattan Athletic Club of America to promote boxing, submitted by Edward Waldron of the Manhattan Casino. In rejecting the request, the commission automatically assumed that Waldron was working in cahoots with the McMahons, and, as the *New York Herald* put it, declined the application for the "best interests of boxing." In a summary analysis of Jess and Eddie, the commission cited their problems at the St. Nicholas Rink, trouble in maintaining contracts with fighters, and a deficiency in paying owed club taxes.

The McMahons claimed they weren't even a part of the new organization. Nonetheless, they were hammered for their presumed link. Accompanying the negative press was a huge opportunity for the brothers in the promotion of a title bout between heavyweight champion Jack Johnson and his Kansas challenger, Jess Willard. The bout wasn't slated for New York but Havana, Cuba, and the McMahons went into brief partnership with Jack Curley, who had yet to establish himself as a promotional entity in the East. On April 5, 1915, Willard made history and won the championship in the 26th round.

Over the next two years, the siblings faced a number of highs and lows at both the Olympic and Empire clubs, but they maintained their presence in the upper echelon of boxing promoters. Around August 1916, they were in the hunt to obtain the matchmaking position at Madison Square Garden, a coveted job, but didn't make the final cut. They supplemented their income by managing certain fighters, for instance, lightweight Eddie Dorsey and heavyweight John Lester Johnson, and were always searching for new blood to tout. On the baseball diamond, despite their best efforts, the Lincoln Stars unceremoniously folded in 1917.

Early that same year, boxing was again being vilified, and New York Governor Charles S. Whitman supported a repeal of the Frawley Law, a plan that would once again extinguish the sport in the state. He dismissed the chairman of the athletic commission, Frederick A. Wenck, under dubious circumstances and believed there was an abundance of crookedness in the sleazy underworld of the fight business. The Slater Bill passed through the legislature, and in May 1917 the governor signed the document banning big-time boxing. The law went into effect on November 15, and the old club membership system was revived in full force.

It was as if the clock had been turned back. On January 21, 1918, police infiltrated the Olympic club and arrested two fighters, the timekeeper and referee—all on the suspicion that they were breaking the law by presenting a boxing match for unaffiliated patrons. The next day, all four men were released, their charges dismissed.

The anti-boxing environment, in addition to the atmosphere created by the enveloping weight of World War I, caused the demise of the Olympic and Empire clubs almost simultaneously, in 1917–18. If any athletics were being staged, it was on a highly reduced scale, and they received little to no publicity. Considering the aggressive actions of law enforcement, secretive boxing events for "members" might have been more prudent, and these may have taken place far outside the radar of sportswriters and the police. There is a lack of verifiable evidence to confirm whether these types of shows were prevalent to any degree.

In their personal lives, the McMahon brothers were both family men. Eddie was the first to settle down, marrying around 1903, and had three daughters and a son. Later in the decade, Jess wed Rosanna "Rose" McGinn and named his first son, born on June 21, 1910, Roderick Jr. Second son Vincent James arrived four years later, on July 6, 1914, and their final child, Dorothy, was born in 1916. Jess settled on Dean Street in Brooklyn and religiously kept business hours at work to ensure he'd be home with his wife and children. He also cared for his mother until her passing in March 1917. With heavy familial burdens, the McMahons were excluded from wartime service, and as their promotional obligations diminished, they took straight jobs to pay the bills.

Eddie went to work for the railroad and Jess became a furniture salesman. The hiatus from sports was never supposed to be permanent. They just needed the conditions to improve, and in 1920, they finally did. New York Governor Al Smith signed the Walker Bill, legalizing prizefighting for the second time in nine years. Stressing the need to strenuously regulate pro fighting going forward, officials established a new licensing board and commission, and enthusiasts applauded the resumption of major league boxing.

The Dyckman Oval, a multipurpose outdoor athletic field in northern Manhattan, was where the McMahons reconvened their promotions in 1921. Jess soon gained a second matchmaking post at the Commonwealth Sporting Club on 135th Street in Harlem. Under his leadership, the Commonwealth featured "some of the finest exhibitions the grim game has witnessed and many ring celebrities were developed there," as Ed Hughes of the *Brooklyn Daily Eagle* explained. Guys like Mike McTigue, Charley Phil Rosenberg, and Tiger Flowers saw a career boost after appearing for McMahon, and while a number of his colleagues were unable to draw decent attendance, Jess was regularly packing his arena.

In a stroke of brilliance, McMahon organized a basketball team to represent the club on the hardwood, and his "Commonwealth Big Five" would become legendary. The squad, made up of Captain Frank Forbes, George Fiall, Hilton Slocum, Creed "Hop" Hubbard, and the Jenkins brothers, were the first team of African American professionals in New York basketball history. Often competing against white opponents, the experienced roster of skilled players was nearly unbeatable, running up a win streak of at least 28 games on their home court in 1922–23.

The Commonwealth Big Five engaged in grueling contests against world championship claimant Original Celtics, Perth

Amboy, and the Loendi Five of Pittsburgh. The latter beat McMahon's athletes for the undisputed "colored" championship in March 1923.

His endeavors at the Commonwealth elevated Jess to the top level of fight promoters. Not so surprisingly, when Tex Rickard, the unofficial chairman of all things boxing in New York City, was restructuring the executive composition of the new Madison Square Garden being built in 1925, McMahon was at the head of a short list to become matchmaker. Rickard's pet project, valued at $5.5 million and situated in Midtown Manhattan on Eighth Avenue, between 49th and 50th Streets, was expected to have the largest indoor seating capacity in the world. It was a momentous achievement, and Rickard was keenly aware that he needed a motivated innovator to manage boxing at the Garden day to day.

Based on his proven track record during a quarter century of sports promotions, the 43-year-old Jess McMahon was appointed Garden matchmaker on October 30, 1925. There wasn't a more valuable matchmaking office anywhere in the world, and McMahon took the importance of his duties incredibly seriously. However, with the ascension came a windfall of political scrutiny, not only from the Garden hierarchy but from the athletic commission and observant elected officials as well. All eyes were on the Garden, and the standard of matchmaking and promotions had to remain above board at all times.

McMahon was undeniably ethical. He was regarded as the right man to supervise the direction of boxing at the Garden and would comply with whatever oversight was necessary from outside entities. His real chore was personally customizing each show with precision, ensuring that the kind of fighters on display matched the first-class stage upon which they were performing. In effect, he was responsible for the box office attendance. At first people were going to be lured to the stadium out of curiosity, but after a short while, McMahon's matchmaking abilities were going to be tested. The numbers wouldn't lie.

After opening with a six-day bicycle race, the Garden introduced its first boxing program on December 11, 1925, and an estimated 20,000 people watched light heavyweight champion Paul Berlenbach beat Jack Delaney in 15 rounds. McMahon entered a never-ending process of negotiations with various managers, trying to arrange the popular fights people wanted to see. He worked to land Jack Dempsey, Jack Sharkey, Gene Tunney, Mickey Walker, Georges Carpentier, Young Stribling, Sammy Mandell, and scores of other recognizable battlers. He dealt with almost constant uncertainty as managers balked at the last minute, forcing McMahon to rework his booking design.

When he wasn't haggling with managers, he was coordinating with the athletic commission or Rickard. His attention was in constant demand, and he frequently attended shows from Boston to Philadelphia to gauge talent. In 1926, the Garden received two well-attended Tiger Flowers–Harry Greb fights. The first, on February 26, ended with Flowers winning the world middleweight championship. For the consequential world title battle between champion Jack Dempsey and Gene Tunney at Sesquicentennial Stadium in Philadelphia on September 23, 1926, McMahon did his part to help Rickard by booking the undercard. Over 130,000 people saw Tunney capture the heavyweight crown.

In 1927, McMahon arranged the show underneath the big Dempse-Sharkey contest at Yankee Stadium on July 21, and 80,000 spectators witnessed the outdoor spectacle. The next year, McMahon did likewise for Tunney's retirement bout against Tom Heeney at the same venue, and another 50,000 were present. At the Garden, McMahon was as productive as possible. Among his premier competitors were Paulino Uzcudun, Tony Canzoneri, Tommy Loughran, and Johnny Risko. Attendance was steadily impressive, and Rickard had reason to be content.

Though McMahon's tenure was generally successful, both in terms of the draw and the quality of fights offered, there were a few bumps in the road. A controversy arose in early 1927 over the contract for the Bushy Graham–Charley Phil Rosenberg fight, and the athletic commission punished McMahon, suspending him for nearly two months. Another notable issue was the cloud of suspicion that hovered over the first-round knockout of Delaney by Sharkey in late April 1928. Rumors of gambling influences, drunkenness, and general indifference were prominent after the drubbing by Sharkey, and none of it reflected well on promoters.

On the evening of September 5, 1928, McMahon resigned as Garden matchmaker to assume the same role at the New York Coliseum, a newly constructed stadium in the Bronx. The following January, his longtime friend Tex Rickard passed away.

The boxing scene in the New York metropolitan area underwent a massive transformation, and the loss of Rickard was immensely disruptive. Whereas McMahon's jump to the Coliseum had been accepted as peaceful by Rickard, it was now considered a hostile maneuver in a growing promotional war with Garden officials. In June 1929, McMahon expanded his operations by aligning with Humbert Fugazy to run boxing at Ebbets Field during the summer. He also formed a strong relationship with Cuban featherweight sensation Kid Chocolate and his manager Luis Gutierrez, and he promoted a bout in Havana between the Kid and Chick Suggs. Chocolate would become a major fixture at the Coliseum after it opened on April 12, 1929.

McMahon experienced a tumultuous 1929, and before the end of the year he resigned from the Coliseum and was linked to a Jack Dempsey promotional enterprise at the Polo Grounds baseball park. Other ventures were lined up, but not all flourished. He worked to arrange several major Ebbets Field programs in 1930, including one featuring Primo Carnera, but things fell through. Out at the Coney Island Stadium, his brother, Eddie, teamed up with Arthur Yende, a longtime assistant of the McMahons, to give local enthusiasts regular boxing entertainment, and Jess ran the Playland Arena at Rockaway Beach, Queens. Eddie would phase out as a major entity in sports promotions and pass away following a protracted illness in 1935.

Rockaway Beach was the residence of the McMahon family by 1930, and his oldest son, Roderick Jr., was employed in an office and as a lifeguard along the local shoreline. His other two children were devoted students, as he expected, and his commitment to discipline and education was never in question. With the extraordinary success of pro wrestling in the New York City area, Jess was compelled to enter the grappling business in 1931 at the Broadway Arena as a member of the Bowser troupe. Although his connection to wrestling at the arena was brief, he was unwilling to give up the prospect completely. There was simply too much money to be made in what was amounting to be the hottest time in wrestling history.

McMahon was no dummy. He brushed up on the lingo and fundamentals of pro wrestling, learning from a "stack of books he borrowed from a friend of Jim Londos," according to William Morris of the *New York Evening Post*, and declared allegiance to an old acquaintance, Jack Curley. Gaining a running start, Jess propelled himself into wrestling full force, but little did he know at the time that he was initiating a family legacy in the industry that remains active more than 80 years later.

(4)
CLASH OF THE
SYNDICATES

The popularity of professional wrestling was remarkable in the early 1930s. Despite cynical sportswriters relentlessly calling the sport's validity into question, fans were happy to suspend disbelief and just enjoy the show. Sure, the mechanisms of wrestling were questionable, and it was evident that scripted or "worked" matches were being acted out by friendly competitors from the same syndicates, but the athletic presentation was excellent and enthusiasts responded in record numbers.

In Los Angeles, the local affiliate of the Paul Bowser group, promoter Lou Daro, was featuring many of wrestling's greatest stars at the downtown Olympic Auditorium. The new heavyweight champion of the outfit, Ed Don George, was full of promise, and expectations were high. Daro, a shrewd 47-year-old Hungarian, booked the titleholder against the legendary Ed "Strangler" Lewis for an outdoor program at Wrigley Field and spent months laboring on the details. According to his optimistic predictions, the event had the possibility to draw 25,000 fans and the sport's first $100,000 gate.

Lewis was a bigger-than-life character outside the ring, and inside the squared circle, he carried enough name value to remain a top box office attraction. He wasn't, however, the wrestler he used to be. Weighing more than 230 pounds, he was out of shape and the eye disease trachoma was a constant affliction, leaving him nearly blind at times. George, on the other hand, was in the prime of his career. He was a former Olympian, adept in all of the holds and counters, and nimble enough to escape anything the sluggish ex-champion could throw at him. These aspects were apparently convincing enough for Bowser and Daro to approve the match and overlook the fact that Lewis was in vengeful spirits.

For the Strangler, there was no getting over Bowser passing the title from Gus Sonnenberg to George and breaking their 1929 agreement. The Wrigley Field matchup was an ideal opportunity for a nice payday and some much-needed retribution. On April 13, 1931, Lewis toppled George in two straight falls and won the world heavyweight championship. The result was unplanned, akin to the Wayne Munn fiasco, and sent a knife deep into the heart of the Bowser syndicate. The double-cross wasn't unanticipated, but Bowser was a little too confident in George's ability to ward off an ailing old-school shooter like Lewis. George couldn't manage it, and Lewis was successful in ripping the crown from Bowser's clutches.

The title switch had major consequences and embarrassed Bowser. To save face, he quickly etched a manageable plan to sandbag Lewis and regain his valuable championship. Exactly three weeks after the Los Angeles affair, Lewis went to Montreal and wrestled Frenchman Henri Deglane, ironically another former Olympian and a mainstay of the Bowser troupe. This time, Lewis was the one either overconfident or ignorant of the potential of a betrayal, and his foolish disregard left him susceptible to an underhanded ploy. Deglane, following a first fall victory, claimed he was bitten in the second, and upon inspection, officials disqualified Lewis and gave the challenger the title. The finish was unorthodox, but Bowser was desperate, and desperate measures were necessary to preserve the honor of his promotion.

While Bowser was occupied with these shenanigans, Jack Curley in New York was counting his money. He didn't have a problem with his heavyweight champion because, in fact, Jim Londos was the biggest superstar in the business. Curley, along with the rest of his office crew, were capably building up challengers, one after another, and fostering a reliable system of exhibitions with Londos always the prevailing hero. In February 1931, more than $54,000 was taken in at a Madison Square Garden program headlined by Londos and former collegiate football star Jim McMillen. Sandor Szabo joined the Greek champion in drawing 18,000 people to the Garden a few months later, but all shows were topped by Londos's summer spectacular at Yankee Stadium against Ray Steele.

Steele, who was born in Russia and grew up in Lincoln, Nebraska, was a student of Farmer Burns and one of the best wrestlers of the era. He developed from a light heavyweight to a 215-pound scientific marvel. He was as quick as they come, and because of his value to the Curley tribe, he was designated Londos's "policeman." On the evening of June 29, 1931, center stage at Yankee Stadium in the Bronx, the two did battle before 30,000 spectators in a benefit for Mrs. William Randolph Hearst's Free Milk Fund for children. Londos was victorious in an hour and nine minutes and retained his championship. Arthur Rhodes of the *Brooklyn Standard Union* called it a "perfect night" and said that it was "altogether the most favorable setting a wrestling exhibition has ever received in this city."

Having severed his ties to Paul Bowser after the washout at the Broadway Arena, Jess McMahon realigned himself with Curley and arranged a benefit event at the Coney Island Velodrome for July 30. In the main event, Londos defeated former baseball and football player Al Pierotti in 17 minutes and five seconds, and an estimated 8,000 people were in attendance, paying upward of $12,500. Another 2,500 were present for McMahon's offering two weeks later at the Coney Island Stadium, when Londos was again triumphant against Kola Kwariani. Bewhiskered Sergei Kalmikoff, fast becoming one of the most entertaining grapplers on the circuit, performed a "comedy skit" with Toots Mondt on the undercard. Rhodes of the *Standard Union* said their match was "highly hilarious and sublimely ridiculous."

The mixture of pure wrestling, occasional brawling, and humorous antics were cornerstones to any enjoyable program, and fans expected nothing more or less. It was crucial for matchmakers to represent these elements and to be aware of any upsurge in the audience's sentiment—including irritation from being overexposed to particular grapplers. The constant rotation of wrestlers from city to city went a long way to keep the latter from occurring.

Londos was the driving force of Curley's operations, but he wasn't limited to appearances in the New York area. He barnstormed across North America and became associated with the heavyweight wrestling title more than any other claimant. In St. Louis and Philadelphia, he found two faithful supporters in promoters Tom Packs and Ray Fabiani, but New York remained a tremendous source of wealth. During late 1931, Londos defeated George Calza at the Garden on two separate occasions, drawing no less than 15,000 people each time and a similar number versus Steele on December 21. New York area enthusiasts also witnessed Londos turn back the challenges of Gino Garibaldi, Renato Gardini, Dick Daviscourt, and Matros Kirilenko.

The tranquil success of the Curley-Londos partnership ended up on the rocks in April 1932, and the problems that instigated the mess had likely been building for a long time. But to wrestling aficionados outside the inner circle, the report of Londos jumping from the Curley camp to independence was completely earth-rattling. Why would anyone leave Curley's huge moneymaking empire? It wasn't like there were other opportunities the size of his New York interests, and no arena in the world was packing wrestling fans in like the Garden. Londos was walking away from hundreds of thousands of dollars.

According to Jack Kofoed of the *New York Evening Post*, Curley "made a millionaire of Jim Londos," the first wrestling millionaire in history, and that certainly was nothing to scoff at. The question remained: Why was Londos dissolving such an important business relationship? Was it because he was retiring from wrestling?

That answer was simple: Londos still had plenty of gas left in his tank and wasn't leaving the limelight anytime soon. The choice to break from Curley was entirely personal, and there were likely a handful of specific reasons. For one, the dominant shares of his income being split among varied Curley operatives, minimizing his actual compensation, was aggravating to say the least. Another factor was the simple notion of being so closely managed by Curley and Toots Mondt that his every move was precisely dictated. Londos was his own man, and the constant manipulation from "New York" was infuriating. Even without the Garden and Curley's venues, he'd be able to make a good living in his other cities and would be rid of the irritation.

William Morris, when he wrote his column in the *New York Evening Post* on April 6, 1932, might have tapped into another significant but heavily shrouded facet of the difficulties between Londos and Curley. He stated that "no end of concern" was being created by Londos's yearning "to return to Athens to be married while being hailed as champion." If Morris was correct, who could blame Londos for wanting to take some time off from his laborious schedule to visit family and perhaps wed in his native Greece? Curley's anxiety over such a vacation related to all the box office gates that would be missed during his absence, especially during the competitive wrestling war. Curley needed his heavyweight champion to be available whenever and wherever he beckoned.

Appearing sympathetic to Curley, Morris said Londos "hardly could have reached his eminence without sacrifice on the part of others." He added that a lot of "patience and time" went into fostering the belief that Londos was the greatest wrestler in the world. Undoubtedly, Curley helped propel him into the stratosphere, but the natural magnetism of Londos was just as responsible for his success. It was a combined effort of brilliance both in the ring and on the promotional end.

At the very least, the disagreement boiled over because Curley wanted everlasting loyalty for everything he'd done for Londos, and Londos wanted a little consideration to visit family. There was no compromise. By the end of April 1932, their working relationship was over. Notably, when Londos did finally enjoy a three-month trip home to Athens in 1933, he did so free of guilt and pressure.

In the 1937 book *Fall Guys: The Barnums of Bounce*, Marcus Griffin covered the split from a different angle. Like Morris, Griffin extolled a pro-Curley perspective, claiming Londos was facing a decline in popularity in 1932. The worrisome staleness and overexposure of their Greek champion had come to fruition, and Curley and Mondt were considering Dick Shikat as a replacement titleholder. Londos flatly declined to meet Shikat and that was his motivation for leaving the syndicate. The misleading tale only gave one side of the story and dismissed any other relevant information.

As might be expected, the break of Curley and Londos initiated the most fascinating period of backstage maneuvering professional wrestling had ever seen.

Curley made the first major move. Slightly unhinged by the early rumors that Londos was siding with his enemy, Paul Bowser, he reached out to his Boston adversary and began the process of smoothing things over between them. Although they had been at war for years, their reconciliation went surprisingly well as they realized Londos wielded a staggering amount of power. His accumulation of wrestling stars and allies could easily provide opposition in Boston and New York, forcing Bowser and Curley to defend their territories with everything they had. However, neither had anyone as popular as Londos, and Curley didn't have a champion at all.

Along with Mondt, Rudy Miller, and Jack Pfefer, Curley and Bowser formed a new alliance—one that never seemed possible. To replace the talent aligned with Londos, Curley was going to book Bowser's forces and anticipated Shikat to be a top headliner. Next, Mondt went to Wisconsin and spoke to Ed "Strangler" Lewis about making a comeback in New York. The tactic was questionable. Lewis's physical condition was poor, and although he possessed the heart, he was in no shape to return to the heavyweight throne. That's not how Mondt saw it. He felt Lewis was capable and recognizable enough to discredit Londos as champion and knew Londos would repeatedly back away from a match against the Strangler, which would ultimately taint his reputation.

Lewis agreed. Public relations wizards went into full spin mode to color things the way the bosses wanted, but it was a unique chore. Curley was known for putting Lewis down and touting Londos, and now it was the reverse. Morris of the *Evening Post* was bold enough to say that it was an "insult to public intelligence" to "attempt to discredit the man they so recently were lauding."

Westbrook Pegler added that Curley used to call Lewis a "great big hairy ham" but now was complimenting the Strangler as the best in the world. The turnaround in opinion was obvious to those who paid attention, but some New York fans could care less. They welcomed a different cast of characters on their wrestling mats.

The new syndicate organized an outdoor program at the recently built Madison Square Garden Bowl in Long Island City, and more than 25,000 attended the June 9, 1932, festivities. Lewis wrestled and defeated Shikat in the main event, becoming the top contender to Londos's title. Prodding the athletic commission to lock in the contest for later in the summer, Curley played his political cards and knew it was just a matter of time before the yellow streak down the back of Londos became apparent to all. It wasn't an ideal situation, but Curley was making the best of the circumstances. What he really needed was official commission sponsorship of a heavyweight titleholder, and that was only going to be available once Londos was discredited and stripped of recognition. He had to wait and watch things develop in due time.

Londos was taking action of his own. He settled into a comfortable circuit of supportive towns, strengthened his core of friendly promoters, and sought to expand. Since he was accompanied by nearly all of his top ring foes to the new outfit, he already had a huge advantage. His roster included Garibaldi, Szabo, Steele, John Pesek, and Everette Marshall. Behind the scenes, he was aided by

Packs, Fabiani, Lou Daro, and the ex-manager of Ed Lewis, Billy Sandow. The Dusek brothers were also immensely important, and brother Rudy was going to play a significant role in Londos getting back into New York.

An artistic grappler, Rudy Dusek gravitated toward promotions and matchmaking and wanted to dig into the New York scene with some level of importance. When Londos formed the new clique, Rudy found an opening to become the local booker for the champion's forces and assumed the post. He associated himself with another important sporting family, the Johnstons, who were considered boxing royalty after decades of managing and promoting in the New York City area. Of the four Johnston brothers, James was the most influential, having managed scores of champions and worked as a matchmaker at Madison Square Garden. Brother Edward, also known as "Ned," was a capable fight trainer, and William and Charles combined to promote shows at the St. Nicholas Arena and other venues.

Affiliated with the Bowser group for months, William and Charles Johnston adjusted their business strategy in the fallout of the 1932 turmoil and sided with Londos and Dusek. They figured on better returns under the new arrangement and placed Jimmy Johnston Jr., the 26-year-old son of James, in the pilot seat of the St. Nicholas Arena beginning on October 26, 1932. A short time later, the Londos-Dusek-Johnston clan opened up the Broadway Arena in Brooklyn under the auspices of Jack Clifford's Broadway Sporting Club, and their brand received a stellar response.

Meanwhile, Curley successfully coerced the New York State Athletic Commission into following his orders. The governing body dutifully directed Londos to sign for a match against Lewis, and when he failed to do so, he was stripped of all local title recognition on September 30, 1932. It was soon announced that the next champion would be produced from a bout between Lewis and Yugoslavian tough guy Jack Sherry at Madison Square Garden on October 10. The addition of Sherry into the spotlight was an interesting twist. For years, he proudly wore the badge of an independent and claimed to be the uncrowned heavyweight king. He gave up his status as an outsider and joined the Bowser troupe, but to fans, he was considered a threat against Lewis in what was perceived to be a shoot match.

But many New York enthusiasts were not interested. The pre-match hubbub was thick with talk of a genuine contest, and to purists that was an exciting notion. In contrast, casual fans wanted to be entertained by the usual folderol and were more likely to be repelled by such legitimacy. Lewis and Sherry followed through on the promise, and for about an hour, went through the sluggish motions of a real contest. They worked together to give the appearance of an "on the level" battle and neither gave an inch. Attendees who expected the routine rasslin' they'd come to love walked out in a huff. The rest remained and witnessed history as Lewis pinned Sherry and captured the vacant New York championship in an hour and 24 minutes. The disappointing crowd was somewhere between 5,000 and 8,000.

Despite his best efforts, Curley wasn't able to hurt Londos in the long run. New York fans held him in high regard and still acknowledged him as the unbeaten champion. To truly achieve the results he wanted, a sinister plan was required, and Toots Mondt was the perfect man to figure out a way to get it done.

A memorable year, 1932 couldn't end quietly. The New York commission strayed from the Curley playbook and sanctioned a dangerous match between Lewis and Ray Steele in what was going to be an authentic shooting affair. The Lewis-Sherry bout was child's play compared to the legitimate heat between Lewis and Steele and what the match represented as a whole. Reputations, future earnings, and leverage in the grappling war were all on the line at the Garden on December 5, and the unruly bout did anything but clear up questions of genuine supremacy. A frustrated Steele, weighing 25 pounds less than his rival, resorted to punching Lewis several times in the face and was disqualified. In the ensuing chaos, Curley was knocked out from a blow by ex-boxer Tommy Marvin and fans littered the ring area in disgust.

It wasn't ironic that Londos's return to New York coincided with a Garden program on January 23, 1933. Curley knew the

Greek champion wanted to divert attention from his show, and, to ensure a dominant victory in the head-to-head matchup, he slashed ticket prices. However, only about 7,000 fans paid to see Lewis successfully defend his title against Jim Browning. On a good note, people were starting to take notice of Browning, the up-and-comer in the Curley-Bowser syndicate. Alfred Dayton of the *New York Sun* made a point of saying that Browning "was marvelous in defeat." Originally from southwest Missouri, Browning was a 6'2", 240-pound sensation. He owned all the tools to be a great wrestler and was being primed for a championship reign.

New York American sportswriter Sid Mercer addressed a piece of prominent gossip when he mentioned that the Londos group was going to take over the Garden, probably because of the lackluster reception to Lewis. A change was necessary, and Curley made the right preparations for Browning's rematch. On the night of February 20, 1933, he was going to win the New York heavyweight crown.

The major downside to Browning was that he had yet to prove himself as a consequential box office attraction. He'd impressed his promoters, peers, and pundits, but the fans had not been overwhelmingly supportive. Nevertheless, Curley encouraged the title switch. Before a mediocre audience, Browning used his airplane scissors hold to beat Lewis and become champion. Fans heavily applauded the victory, and in the following days and weeks, a noticeable increase in attendance proved the wisdom of Curley's decision. Browning improved the draw at the New York Coliseum, Ridgewood Grove, and then drew upward of 12,000 for the rematch against Lewis on March 20. He took a number of popular victories from the former champion, Nick Lutze, and Sammy Stein.

Londos had no reason to worry. He was still wrestling's most valuable commodity and his syndicate was thriving. One of the leading youthful members of his troupe was "Jumpin'" Joe Savoldi, a former All-American football star at Notre Dame and a prodigy grappler. His athleticism earned praise, and his flying dropkick was fast becoming a staple on mats across the country. A Chicago promoter felt the time was right to capitalize on a Savoldi title match against Londos and booked the Stadium for April 7, 1933.

Going into the bout, there was an unusual amount of buzz from ringside analysts and insiders. Toots Mondt was the reason. He'd finally arranged the deck against Londos, and all of his patience was going to pay off. It was payback time, and Londos was walking blindly into a trap. Rumors and innuendos were flying in all directions, but all that mattered was what was happening in the squared circle, where Londos believed he was safe against a relative newcomer to wrestling like Savoldi. He didn't fear a double-cross by way of a sudden attack on the mat because he could defend himself, but he did ignore the possibility of being blindsided by a crooked referee.

Bob Managoff, a 50-year-old former wrestler from Turkey, was the assigned official. An old-time ruffian, he was familiar with all the tricks of the trade and was not naive to the underbelly of pro wrestling. He performed in a journeyman-type capacity for more than 20 years, appearing in carnivals and big arenas all over the map. In 1916, he participated in an exhibition against undisputed champion Frank Gotch in Wisconsin, and during their session, Gotch suffered a broken leg. The injury canceled a potential record-breaking match against Joe Stecher and altered the course of history. Managoff's actions at the Chicago Stadium, while not as drastic, had a similar effect.

Twenty-five minutes into the entertaining match, Savoldi found himself trapped in Londos's Japanese jackknife. He managed to get to his feet, and with Londos underneath him, briefly had the champion on his shoulders in a pin position. Managoff broke the hold, for what reason it wasn't immediately known, and spectators anticipated a continuation of the match. But Managoff shockingly raised Savoldi's hand, declaring him the victor, and quickly left the ring and building, as if he was running for his life. George Strickler of the *Chicago Daily Tribune* wrote that Savoldi initially seemed surprised by the ruling and Londos protested since there hadn't been a three count to score a successful pin.

According to Strickler's report, the audience "cheered long

and loud for Savoldi" in the aftermath of the match, and although it cannot be said for sure, it is probable that Mondt and Curley acted likewise. For the first time, one of their tactics hurt Londos's reputation and wallet, and they savored the moment.

Savoldi jumped to the Curley organization with the double-cross and went to New York for a Garden contest against Strangler Lewis in May. News of Londos's defeat spread far and wide, but Savoldi had trouble gaining traction as a heavyweight title claimant, especially after National Wrestling Association president Colonel Harry J. Landry announced that Londos was the rightful kingpin. The Chicago result was an impressive accomplishment for Savoldi and Mondt, but how it translated at the box office was most important. Once again, most New Yorkers yawned at the so-called significance of anything having to do with Lewis, and attendance for their May 15, 1933, match was either 6,000 or 9,000, depending on the source.

Frank Reil of the *Brooklyn Daily Eagle* lauded the "exciting finish," which saw Savoldi miss a dropkick and land outside the ring. He was eventually counted out. It was hard to dislike Savoldi as a performer. In terms of looks, he was the exact opposite of the Strangler, fit and athletic, and he was the kind of showman people enjoyed. Savoldi beat Lewis in a rematch and then was booked to face the New York champion, Browning, at Yankee Stadium on June 12. *New York Evening Post* sportswriter Jack Kofoed hinted at the unpopularity of the reigning champ and said that if the choice was his, he'd prefer Savoldi as the titleholder over Browning.

Logically, Savoldi made more sense if he was the better entertainer and bigger draw. But with the war still at a fever pitch, Curley retained the better legitimate wrestler to protect his title, and Browning went over. After nearly two hours, the bout was stopped at the curfew and the champion was given the decision. The bad news for everyone involved was that only 5,000 fans turned out for the show, and stormy weather was blamed. Savoldi and Browning actually wrestled in the rain throughout, but to sum it up, Ed Hughes of the *Brooklyn Daily Eagle* called the affair a "very dull and dreary exhibition." For everything they'd poured into Browning and Savoldi, Curley and his workers expected much, much more from their top two performers.

The Yankee Stadium event racked up painstaking losses, and Curley was in disbelief. All of his attempts to energize fans had failed, and it was clear that he needed a complete upgrade of talent to attract larger audiences. Despite earlier assumptions, the wrestling war was seemingly unwinnable and a tremendous nuisance. The next step was a possible compromise with the Londos group. The time was right, and all of the promotional heads from Los Angeles to Philadelphia were ready to tear down their syndicate walls to produce joint ventures.

In late November 1933, handshakes at the completion of a covert meeting at the Hotel Pennsylvania in Midtown Manhattan marked the formation of the "Trust," which was, until 1948 and the charter of the National Wrestling Alliance, the grandest organization of promoters in wrestling history. Involved in creating the remarkable treaty were Curley, Londos, Bowser, and Mondt, and their achievement meant peace for a majority of the grappling world. The bad feelings that had dominated for years were suppressed as the focus turned to making incredible amounts of cash.

Not everyone was pleased with the formation of the Trust. Jack Pfefer, who'd long been one of Curley's most valuable aides, had maneuvered himself into a position of power in 1933. But in doing so, he rattled a few cages and made some enemies. Pfefer was locked in as the matchmaker for the Johnstons, running a staggering number of venues, including the St. Nicholas Arena, Ridgewood Grove, New York Coliseum, and Broadway Arena. Already temperamental, Pfefer was enraged by the composition of the new organization and took the slight personally.

His instinct was to attack his foes where it would hurt them the most—in the eyes of the public. He went to a well-known sportswriter for the *New York Daily Mirror*, Dan Parker, and broke the unwritten rules of professional wrestling by revealing insider secrets. He overlooked that he might also be hurting his own business by disclosing such information in his haste to injure his adversaries, and the exposé instigated athletic commission meetings into the validity of his statements in January 1934. Those affiliated with the Trust vehemently refuted all of Pfefer's allegations.

Dr. Carlos Henriquez and Jess McMahon were on the periphery of the Trust when it was developed. The two were friends going back to the turn of the century, when both were involved in amateur and semipro football and baseball. Henriquez wrestled while at Columbia University and earned a degree in medicine. His son, Carlos, followed in his footsteps at Columbia but then turned pro wrestler around 1928 under his father's tutelage. A few years later, the elder Henriquez began promoting in Yonkers, but he found himself pushed out by a Curley initiative to take over the city's wrestling scene.

Henriquez bounced back in 1932, siding with the Bowser troupe during the grappling war. His negative feelings for Curley increased when it became apparent that Curley and his allies were ignoring the steady growth and potential of his talented son. Carlos Jr. went unbeaten in hundreds of matches and built a nice following of supporters, but he could never get a shot in high-profile bouts in New York City. Curley was blamed. In December 1933, Henriquez and McMahon launched a promotion from Sokol Hall in Yonkers, but their enterprise was brief. A few weeks later, McMahon opened up the Hempstead Arena on Long Island and was allied to the Curley regime, featuring the likes of Gino Garibaldi and Hans Steinke.

McMahon was settling for a permanent future in wrestling. He was presented with an opportunity to promote outdoor boxing events at Ebbets Field during the summer of 1934, but he declined because the sport was a weak draw. He instead staged grappling shows at the Municipal Stadium in Freeport, where he first operated in 1932. Following the decline of his alliance with Henriquez in Yonkers, McMahon signed to administer wrestling from Sokol Hall on his own, giving him three different business ventures. Although he was making headway and had been a significant leader in the fight game, McMahon was still at the bottom of wrestling's hierarchy.

As anticipated, the Trust led the sport into another golden age. Curley was so confident in the forward progress of wrestling that he predicted a universal $4 million intake at the box office between 1933 and '34. He was doing his part to sell tickets, exhibiting the benefits of the new syndicate by booking Ray Steele against Jim Browning for the heavyweight championship at Madison Square Garden on January 8, 1934. The crowd reacted in a very telling manner, booing Browning heavily and cheering Steele. Alfred Dayton of the *New York Sun* noted that when Browning had become champion, he was "tremendously popular." Ever since, his stock had crashed, and the audience was less than thrilled when he beat Steele to retain his title.

To send the crowd home happy, Curley brought out Londos, the real icon of wrestling at the Garden, and the throng of spectators reacted wildly to seeing the legitimate champion back on the main stage. A unification match between Londos and Browning was guaranteed.

Elsewhere in the business, Bowser had shifted his Boston-based American Wrestling Association (AWA) heavyweight title from Henri Deglane back to Ed Don George in February 1933, and George was a rewarding claimant wherever he performed. In St. Louis, as a result of the formation of the Trust, local interest skyrocketed for promoter Tom Packs. He staged a rematch between Steele and Strangler Lewis in December, without the fireworks of their New York contest, and drew over 9,000 fans. On February 2, 1934, the dream match between Londos and Gus Sonnenberg lured an extraordinary 15,666 people to the St. Louis Arena. Promoter Lou Daro, out in Los Angeles, was also seeing an improvement. Wisely, he was building up several key challengers for Londos, including the mammoth 300-pounder Man Mountain Dean.

At the weigh-in for his match against Browning on June 25, 1934, at the Madison Square Garden Bowl, Londos was a conditioned 195 pounds, well under the typical heavyweight. Browning was 38 pounds heavier. But part of Londos's appeal was his craftsmanship in the ring, dismantling larger opponents with speed and science, and often coming back from being down to win in underdog fashion. The New York State Athletic Commission added to the importance of the unification bout by giving its blessing to Curley to advertise the contest as a championship affair. Usually, it only recognized wrestling matches as exhibitions.

Browning employed all the right moves, using his size advantage to tire Londos out. It appeared that he was on his way to the winner's circle when Londos turned the tides, slamming his rival eight times in succession before successfully achieving a pinfall. The result was received with approval and applause, but again Curley was disappointed by the attendance. He wanted to double the 20,000 spectators and reach a gate of $75,000. The final amount was in the ballpark of $40,000.

Londos added title recognition in more than 20 states by his defeat of Browning. His victory stirred immensely favorable attention across North America, and he was as popular in the Midwest and on the West Coast as he was in the East. In Chicago, this fact was demonstrated by his long-awaited match against Ed "Strangler" Lewis on September 20, 1934. A crowd of over 35,000 set a new national gate record of $96,302 for the Wrigley Field spectacular. At the Los Angeles version of Wrigley Field, the imposing Man Mountain Dean challenged Londos on October 10, and another 23,765 paid $41,000. Daro, trying to be slick, announced the attendance as 38,000, probably because he wanted to outdraw the Chicago bout.

Of course, Londos was victorious in both matches. He entered a long-running feud with Everette Marshall, a 29-year-old from southeastern Colorado. Marshall had taken the legendary Billy Sandow as his manager and was a crafty veteran of five years on the mat. In February 1934 at Philadelphia, he extended Londos more than three hours before the Greek champion beat him, and he received another shot at the crown on November 19, 1934, at Madison Square Garden. This time, Marshall was the hero and Londos was hissed. It was a unique reversal of heat, perhaps unexpectedly, and proved that the audience wasn't always solidly behind Londos.

The champion's popularity was sustained, nevertheless. But the masterminds behind the Trust were plotting and planning, especially the "brain," Paul Bowser. With Londos and Ed Don George, the organization still recognized two different heavyweight champions. Bowser wanted to carefully establish an undisputed titleholder, a solitary kingpin recognized by all promoters. It was an exciting idea, one that was many years in the making, and the Trust had to locate and agree on a worthy candidate who'd pad all of their bank accounts evenly.

Respected and convincing, Bowser sold his peers on Daniel Aloysius O'Mahoney, known as "Danno," a flashy young man from Ireland. Tall and quick, O'Mahoney was touted, pushed, and promoted to the heavens from the moment he arrived in the United States. Wrestling had never seen such a unified effort to establish a credible contender, and he scored win after win over athletes of far greater talent and experience. O'Mahoney, with his entertaining Irish whip finisher, was impressive, and he lived up to the hype. He was only 22 years of age, and within a few brief months, he'd become the most talked about superstar on the circuit.

The plan was simple. Danno was going to face Londos and George, unify the titles, and travel the wrestling landscape as the unconquerable ruler of the heavyweights. In theory and on paper, the scheme was perfect. The brilliant minds who'd agreed to the operation failed to reflect on their recent history and ignored one possible outcome. A few years earlier, a prominent ex-champion had been scorned in a backstage double-cross. He hadn't forgotten, and if he had his way, O'Mahoney, the pride of the Trust, was going to rue the day he ever stepped into a wrestling ring.

(5)
ONE TOO MANY
CHAMPIONS

The combination of lackluster enthusiasm for champion Jim Browning and the backlash stemming from the Jack Pfefer revelations left New York City nearly in ruins. For the first half of 1934, business was horrendous, and the draw at Madison Square Garden declined to under 3,000. Outside the occasional bumps in attendance, the situation looked bleak, and regardless of the innovations or newcomers, nothing seemed to provide the sustainable boost promoters sought. Joe "Toots" Mondt, the foremost matchmaker in the country, saw the writing on the wall. Rather than help Jack Curley stop the bleeding, he departed the territory. His motivation might have been solely to make more money.

Toots loved the almighty dollar. His perceptive booking had contributed greatly to the success of wrestling in the metropolitan area, but in recent years, his personal wealth had exited nearly as quickly as it had arrived. The receiver of his funds worked the ticket counter at Belmont Park or the Aqueduct Racetrack in Queens. It was no secret that Mondt had a proclivity for gambling. Curley shared the same affinity and once admitted he'd sooner attend a race than either wrestling or boxing.

Mondt relinquished his influence in the New York region to Curley and Paul Bowser and pursued other opportunities. One of nine children, Toots was born in Iowa in 1894 and grew up in Weld County, Colorado, near Greeley. He was a bullheaded athlete, willing to grapple and fight in the schoolyard and then graduating to carnivals and improvised rings across the Rocky Mountain area. He also developed his personality and became quite the performer, able to entertain and con rubes during athletic shows. In his heart, he was a rebellious soul and often went against the grain. When it came to gambling, he liberally spent his own money, and his ethics were tested if he was at the helm of a promotion's cash box. He'd demonstrate time and again that it was best he handle only the matches and not the business end of any enterprise.

Given his reputation in 1934, Mondt was practically free to join any promotion in the country. He settled in Los Angeles and was welcomed with open arms by the Daro brothers. Still attached to the Trust, he continued to mentor up-and-comers and manipulated the booking scheme to increase the profile of challengers to the heavyweight title. His main new protégé became Ventura "Benny" Tenario, a fellow Coloradoan. Tenario, a Navajo, hailed from Trinidad, in the southern part of the state, and played football at the Haskell Institute. He ventured into the world of grappling, and over a period of five years, he blossomed from the welterweight division into the heavies, becoming 220 pounds of muscle. Mondt was confident that he had a star in the making.

Mondt's presence in New York was certainly missed. In acknowledging the current depression of wrestling after a small crowd turned out for a Garden show on January 28, 1935, Pat Rosa of the *New York Post* couldn't help but wonder if Curley just needed "the magic hand" of Mondt to restore grappling locally.

In spite of Curley's difficulties, the Trust orchestrated the meteoric rise of Danno O'Mahoney flawlessly. Irish enthusiasts were splendidly supportive of their countryman, but the groundswell of enthusiasm wasn't limited to any specific group—it was widespread. He was lauded for his athleticism and nonstop energy. A *New York Sun* sportswriter called him an inspiration and explained that he was the "most refreshing" grappler "in wrestling in many a day." Likened to Gus Sonnenberg and the invigorating atmosphere he created, O'Mahoney appeared destined for the heavyweight championship. His style wasn't like Sonnenberg's or that of other recent stars, and he exhibited a natural gift for performance, delivering a variety of speedy maneuvers and flashes of powerful strength. His Irish whip finisher was an enjoyable addition to the wrestling lexicon.

Only months before, Jim Londos had been quoted as saying he could hold the heavyweight crown for the next 10 years. But by April 1935, rumors and speculation were rampant that the Greek star was going to be replaced by O'Mahoney during the summer. The leaders of the Trust made their decision and happily watched from ringside seats as their prodigy went undefeated leading up to his fated June 27 match against Londos in Boston. Before more than 25,000 adoring fans, O'Mahoney scored a dramatic pinfall and captured the world title. A month later, he toppled Ed Don George for his claim, and O'Mahoney boasted the first undisputed championship in years.

Shifting Londos out of the title picture was ending an important era of wrestling history, but the members of the Trust were convinced they were instigating another period of achievement. That assumption didn't bear out for O'Mahoney's successful defense against Chief Little Wolf at Yankee Stadium on July 8, 1935, when only 12,000 spectators turned out—half of the expected number. At the Garden, the new champion drew decently against Browning, George, and Joe Savoldi, but the crowds in Boston routinely doubled, and sometimes tripled the attendance of New York shows to see O'Mahoney. His faithful followers were enjoying every minute of his reign.

In December 1935, syndicated sportswriter Harry Grayson painted a not-so-favorable portrait of O'Mahoney's tenure as heavyweight titleholder. He mentioned that he "does not look the part of a champion" and had "lost appeal with each appearance."

Grayson recited the derogatory comments from columnists in New York and San Francisco, including the statement that O'Mahoney "represented, in the crudest pattern, the fraud of wrestling."

On occasion, O'Mahoney was booed for his inexperience or mediocre performance, and other times simply because fans wanted a new champion. In O'Mahoney's defense, fatigue was a major factor. The young man was being pulled in every direction by promoters all over the map and meeting as many of his obligations as possible. But he was still a relative newcomer to the business, and even grizzled veterans were easily burned out by a similar schedule. Representing the entire Trust was an unrealistic job, and the wear to O'Mahoney's body and mind were apparent—fans could see it from appearance to appearance.

Too much was being asked of him. When he was feeling good, he was capable of going over an hour and delivering a memorable show, but in other instances, he was in and out of the ring in less than 20 minutes. On October 28, 1935, at the Garden, he delivered a knockout punch to Ed Don George in just over five minutes, and the sudden finish sent the crowd home angry and confused.

The complaints about O'Mahoney spurred talk of a successor, and Rudy Dusek pushed for his brother Ernie to replace Danno as the Trust's champion. Grayson covered this angle in his column in early January 1936, and he said to not be surprised if Ernie won the title in Pittsburgh on January 6, when he battled O'Mahoney at the North Side Arena. From Grayson's account, the powers that be had agreed to give Ernie the championship, noting that "Dusek really can wrestle. O'Mahoney can't." There is not enough evidence, however, to say whether or not all the leaders of the syndicate supported Dusek to win the crown. There might have been one major holdout: Paul Bowser, who not only had the most stock in O'Mahoney but had a shining star in the wings, Yvon Robert.

The hyped bout in Pittsburgh didn't end with a title switch. The competitors, instead, brawled outside the ring and were counted out after 45:10. While it was unlikely an attempted double-cross, it was an unusual finish and was probably, considering the attention it received, setting up a rematch.

A nightmarish scenario occurred during O'Mahoney's tour of Texas a few weeks later, and, because of his recent scheming, Rudy was rumored to have been involved. It revolved around a central plot to betray O'Mahoney in the ring and lift the title. In Houston on February 7, the champion faced off with the unorthodox Leo "Daniel Boone" Savage, and the latter's aggressiveness was cause for concern. After nearly 22 minutes, O'Mahoney threw Savage over the top rope, and the bout was stopped because the challenger was injured. Officials ordered a rematch to clear up the controversy, but the news was quickly dwarfed by reports out of Galveston the next day. O'Mahoney, it was said, had run out on his scheduled contest against Juan Humberto and left the state with his engagement unfulfilled.

The reason for the sudden departure was attributed to overheard whispers that Humberto planned to double-cross him and forcibly win the championship. O'Mahoney didn't want to go down that road and made his escape without further incident. It was somewhat far-fetched to propose that Dusek was the mastermind of the happenings in Texas, but in wrestling, anything is possible.

Replacing O'Mahoney with a unanimous decision was going to be problematic for the Trust. Each of the leaders needed a readily available champion, but they also needed someone who appealed to local enthusiasts. This was a significant issue for members. It was obvious that one candidate might be highly appealing in the Northeast but disliked in St. Louis or Los Angeles. Another type of wrestler was popular in parts of the South, and he too had to be contemplated. There was no way to resolve the dilemma, and the safest answer was to admit that it was impossible to have one man run the entire wrestling circuit as champion and try to satisfy everyone.

The power plays and politicking continued as newer championship aspirants were built up from the mechanisms of Toots Mondt. Out in Los Angeles, he fostered a grand international tournament at the Olympic Auditorium, running from April to July 1935. In the center of his promotions was Vincent Lopez, a skilled amateur wrestler from the University of Idaho. Lopez, born Daniel Vincente de Vinaspre, was billed as a native of Mexico, although he was actually born in Meridian, Idaho, and his parents were from Spain. A student of Strangler Lewis, he needed only two years to achieve headliner roles in Southern California at the helm of the Daro organization. On July 24, he beat Man Mountain Dean in the tournament final to win the local heavyweight championship, and throughout this time frame he routinely drew sellouts.

Mondt contributed to a second international tournament, this time in Philadelphia between November 1935 and February 1936. Promoted by Ray Fabiani, the event was framed to position Utahan Dean Detton as the top contender to O'Mahoney. Detton, 27, was a product of the Deseret Gymnasium in Salt Lake City and a champion amateur grappler. Mentored by the great Ira Dern, an ex-middleweight champion, he entered the pro ranks in 1931 and was fast-tracked by Mondt. During the tourney, he beat Jim Browning, Hans Steinke, Sergei Kalmikoff, and then Ed Lewis in the final on February 28, 1936, earning a contest versus O'Mahoney on March 9. His status as a future champion was confirmed.

In the aftermath of the Texas controversies, O'Mahoney was stripped of his National Wrestling Association recognition, and the press was having a field day with his reputation. The end of his reign was near, but no one, from his personal manager Jack McGrath to Bowser, knew exactly how near it was. On March 2, 1936, at Madison Square Garden, Dick Shikat violated the code of professional wrestling by winning a match he was told to lose. He applied a hammerlock submission and forced O'Mahoney to submit away the precious championship of the Trust, thereby altering history and establishing a new trajectory for the entire business. Rather than maintain a positive direction for wrestling and keep things stable, Shikat's move created nothing but chaos for promoters, who were banking on alternate schemes.

Shikat definitely had his reasons. Four years earlier, he had entered into a secret partnership with Curley, Mondt, Bowser, and Ed Lewis following the defection of Londos from the Curley organization. He was told that after losing to Lewis in June 1932, he'd be given a return bout victory, but the match never came about. Growing antsy, he was pacified by another promise and put up $12,000 of his own money in a deal that was supposed to assure him the championship. Again, he was swindled when Lewis dropped the title to Browning. Shikat was furious when he met with Mondt and Lewis at the Warwick Hotel, and his temper gave way to fisticuffs. He was a tough guy but no match for both Lewis and Mondt. He was pummeled.

With little choice, Shikat immediately jumped to the Londos group but was merged back into the mainstream with the formation of the Trust in 1933. He kept his mouth shut and played ball with the men who had cheated him, but he didn't forget what had occurred. On April 1, 1935, he wrestled O'Mahoney in New York, and as the two exchanged a number of legitimate blows, Shikat's bitterness increased. He realized he was being forced to stand idly by as a less-than-worthy wrestler was given the championship he himself deserved. He had put up the money and, for years, had been patient. But on March 2, 1936, Shikat saw his opportunity—the opportunity of a lifetime to get payback—and seized the moment.

The members of the Trust were blindsided by the betrayal, but all things considered, maybe they shouldn't have been. Their established scenarios were uprooted by the double-cross, and promoters were left scrambling for not only an explanation for the mess, but an easy solution. Bowser and O'Mahoney made up a series of excuses, blaming a difficult recent match against Yvon Robert for Danno's inability to beat Shikat, and then claimed the title couldn't change hands since championships were not recognized by the New York State Athletic Commission. Additionally, the bout was only one fall and title switches required three. These distractive rationalizations were weak and didn't go very far in strengthening O'Mahoney's claim to still be champion.

But Bowser was in charge in New England, and he continued to recognize O'Mahoney as his world titleholder. As for Curley, he told Eddie Wade of the *New York Post* that he was altogether done with champions, admitting there were far too many wrestlers claiming to be the best heavyweight. He wanted to stick to what he knew best, and that was staging high-profile shows for his loyal fans.

Mondt tried to make amends with his former pupil, tempting Shikat with a big-money offer to lose to Vincent Lopez in Los Angeles. Other deals also presented themselves, but Shikat was fed up with the ludicrousness of his former cronies. He wanted no part of them. He chose to side with a smaller conglomerate based out of Columbus, Ohio, and made up of local promoter Al Haft, Detroit impresario Adam Weissmuller, and the venerable Billy Sandow. The combination, acknowledged as the "Little Trust" because of its secondary status to the major syndicate, operated a circuit that primarily featured non-heavyweights. Everette Marshall was a major exception. He remained Sandow's prize and was recognized as a regional "world" champion stemming from a win in Denver over Young Gotch in 1935.

The plotline called for Shikat to be defeated by Marshall for the championship on May 22, 1936, in Denver. In the interim, Haft and his partners had to fight off a federal court lawsuit challenging their legal rights to Shikat's management. It was a desperate ploy by Bowser to encumber the new champion, and many of the promotional heavyweights appeared in court to testify about various aspects of their dealings. It was a fascinating spectacle for enthusiasts with an interest in the inner workings of pro grappling, but to most regular fans, it was an embarrassment and completely took the fun out of what was supposed to be a fine brand of entertainment.

But those in charge, with their grandiose egos and blood in their eyes, didn't seem to care that they were hurting their own businesses, and they fought with the public watching. The barrage of news reports out of the courtroom in Columbus was destructive, and the madness needed to stop. The quickest way was to separate the champion from the championship, leaving Bowser to contest the rights to Shikat even though it was a pointless argument.

That's exactly what happened. In Detroit on April 24, 1936, Shikat was dethroned by the 5'6" Ali Baba, an unexpected temporary champion. Baba, who was born in Kurdistan in 1901, was a veteran of the U.S. Navy and had been a pro wrestler for about 12 years. With his unique physical appearance, short and squat with good muscle development and a pointed mustache, he was a standout performer but an unlikely titleholder. He had impressed Weissmuller and local fans in Detroit in previous months, and the promoter considered him a logical replacement for Shikat under the circumstances. As predicted, the court case for Shikat's contract became irrelevant and was dismissed in May.

In yet another attempt by the New York State Athletic Commission to appear principled, it denied Baba's rights to the championship, citing controversy in the Detroit contest, and demanded a rematch at Madison Square Garden. The required bout was incredibly favorable to Baba and his handlers because it introduced him to the market and established his credibility as a legitimate grappler. The New York representative of the Little Trust was Jack Pfefer, and his bad feelings toward Curley hadn't subsided in the least. He pulled off a wily political play through his allies, the well-connected Johnston brothers, for whom James was the official promoter at the Garden. Basically, Curley was ousted from his matchmaker role and the undercard of the Baba-Shikat show on May 5 featured all Pfefer workers.

While Shikat was in New York to drop the rematch to Baba, he received awful news from Columbus that his wife had been in a serious car accident and severely burned. If Haft, Sandow, and Weissmuller originally wanted Shikat to regain the title, the unfortunate accident canceled those plans. His big match against Marshall in Denver was also abandoned. Shikat, completely distraught, returned to Germany with his wife's body following her death on May 14.

The bizarreness of pro wrestling continued. Pfefer, a highly suspicious and distrusting man, came to the conclusion that he was about to be double-crossed by the Haft group and made a preemptive strike. He went to Toots Mondt and buried the hatchet, and together they concocted a double-cross of their own, targeting Baba on a program Pfefer was running in Newark.

Baba thought he was on friendly turf and presumed he was going to leave Meadowbrook Field on June 12, 1936, the same way he had entered—as champion. After the match, however, he told a *Newark Evening News* reporter that he had been robbed when the referee disqualified him for an alleged kick to the groin of challenger Dave Levin. Levin's contract was sold to Mondt in a deal reportedly valued at $17,000, and with his victory over Baba, he was a claimant to the world title.

Known as the "Butcher Boy" for his five years toiling in that occupation, Levin was born in Brooklyn and attended Bushwick High School. He trained at George Bothner's Manhattan gymnasium and rose up the ranks under Pfefer's watchful eye. Once under the thumb of Toots, Levin went to Los Angeles and, in a match that received a great deal of publicity, faced off with Vincent Lopez in a unification contest at Wrigley Field on August 19, 1936. Promoters were far too optimistic with their attendance projections, believing the affair was going to draw over 40,000 people. The excitement they banked on was not there. Only 15,321 saw Levin beat Lopez in three falls and win the latter's championship, becoming wrestling's leading claimant. Levin's next major match was going to be against the popular Dean Detton in Philadelphia.

Detton was groomed to win the title by a budding new organization led by Mondt and Fabiani and was acclaimed for his legitimate wrestling skills. In the 1937 book *Fall Guys*, Marcus Griffin explained that Detton was tested in a workout session by seven "of the toughest wrestlers the game knows," and he beat them all "in short order." It was a trial, of sorts, arranged by Mondt to see how much of a shooter Detton was, and he passed with flying colors. One of his seven opponents was none other than Ed "Strangler" Lewis.

On September 28, 1936, Detton went over Levin in a match lasting a little over two hours. His victory was acknowledged all over the country, and Griffin felt a "growing confidence" was sparked among spectators with him as the supreme titleholder. All was well within the Toots Mondt tribe.

For all the so-called "shoot" matches that were really prede-termined fakes, the summer of 1936 actually featured one legiti-mate main-event contest. The bout was staged in the New York Hippodrome by Jack Curley on August 13 between Strangler Lewis, 46, and Lee Wykoff, 38, rivals of the Mondt-Detton and Sandow-Marshall syndicates, respectively. In the press, sports-writers explained that the athletic commissioners of four states, New York, California, Illinois, and Missouri, were sponsoring the genuine competition to produce a single champion. Fans were weary of the proposition and all the hype.

When Curley threatened to exhibit a shoot match in June 1932 between Lewis and Shikat, a columnist for *The Daily Star* of Long Island City asked, "Who wants to see that sort of thing?" The writer went on to explain that Curley ran "the risk of losing the faith and trust of his followers" by presenting a colorless bout since enthusiasts relied on him for "hilarious tomfoolery." Any deviation from the anticipated monkey business and clownery was poison to the audience, but it was music to the commissioners' ears. Curley had to ask himself, which was more important?

Apparently, the legitimate match happened, and the Lewis-Wykoff bout was as boring as it was predicted to be. Eddie Wade of the *New York Post* remarked that it "did not meet with the favor" of the "small" audience. He added that nearly 90 min-utes went by before the two even went to the mat, and that was because Wykoff accidentally fell. The finish saw both wrestlers stumble from the ring and counted out. A brutal two hours and 15 minutes had elapsed, and the match was a disaster by all accounts.

The decline of wrestling's popularity in New York was steady and unrelenting. After a four-month hiatus, the doors of the Garden were opened for a September 29, 1936, presentation, and newly crowned world champion Dean Detton, as well as Levin and Chief Little Wolf, represented Mondt's reemergence at the venue. The fresh batch of marquee names drew fewer than 3,000 people. Detton and Levin returned for a head-to-head matchup on November 18, and the crowd was a little larger. *New York Sun* sportswriter Edward Van Every remarked that it was "one of the finest bouts seen in this city in many a day." Levin missed a flying tackle a half hour into the battle and sailed from the ring, where he was counted out. Van Every said it was a "thriller" of a finish.

Steve "Crusher" Casey, a newcomer to the American scene from Ireland, also benefited from favorable press prior to his February 8, 1937, debut at the Garden. Imported by Bowser, he owned considerable ring experience both as a fighter and wrestler. The *New York Sun* indicated that Casey was, appearance-wise, the "most formidable" grappler since George Hackenschmidt, and his popularity was up there with Jim Londos. Bowser was certainly hoping that was the truth, and, of course, his Boston faithful were supportive of Casey's push to the top of the heap. Unlike Danno O'Mahoney, Casey was a tough veteran of the squared circle and was going to be mighty difficult to double-cross.

The far-reaching sphere of Bowser's enterprises extended to San Francisco and Montreal and included many smaller cities and territories. He was both a promoter and matchmaker, and with Curley's visibility reduced, he was the closest to being the real czar of wrestling. But in the days following the O'Mahoney incident in New York, many doubts were cast about his ability to pick a creditable heavyweight titleholder. He was humbled by the double-cross and forced to recoup the integrity of his promotion while under the umbrella of a damaged champion. O'Mahoney had to step aside immediately to recover the lost ground, and on July 16, 1936, in Montreal, Yvon Robert, a French-born athlete, captured the AWA crown.

Various backstage promotional agreements were fostered in the turmoil during the late 1930s. One of the new alliances was created around October 1936, between Tom Packs and Billy Sandow, and cleared the way for champion Everette Marshall to headline in St. Louis. In June 1936, Marshall beat Ali Baba for whatever claims the latter had despite his loss to Levin in Newark, and he tried to garner further recognition around the country. In December 1937, the empire of Packs and Sandow expanded measurably when they were joined in a talent partnership by Bowser, sending workers back and forth from Boston to St. Louis. The trio decided that a single champion was needed and settled on Casey.

But Sandow didn't want Marshall losing to Casey straight, imagining a payoff down the line for their feud. So they needed a transitory titleholder, and Packs recommended a fan favorite from St. Louis named Lou Thesz. Thesz was in his third year as a pro and had shown outstanding development through his travels across the central states, California, and parts of Texas. In late 1935, he made two appearances in Philadelphia, but otherwise he was an unknown commodity in eastern cities. Packs believed in him, as did shooter extraordinaire Ad Santel, Ray Steele, and many other reputable wrestlers who'd come into contact with the youthful prodigy. Thesz, only 21, was a star in the making, but in 1937 he was a pawn in the shuffling of the title.

Extremely protective of Marshall, Sandow refused to give Thesz anything but a count-out victory, and that's what occurred in St. Louis on December 29, 1937. Bowser added to the credibility of Thesz's championship by stripping Robert of his AWA belt and awarding it to him, all building up to a bout against Casey at the Boston Garden. On February 11, 1938, Casey captured the second and third falls from Thesz before more than 12,000 fans and captured the prize. It was a convoluted scenario, but the Bowser-Packs-Sandow group accomplished their mission. The challenge now was for Casey to live up to his expectations and draw big numbers to satisfy his management's monetary hunger.

Over in the camp of Toots Mondt, Detton proved to be an outstanding defending champion, but as a one-of-a-kind box office attraction he was falling short. Mondt realized that the best way to achieve greater attendance was to spotlight a name people were already familiar with. Add an unorthodox wrestling style, great strength, and a tremendous athletic background, and Mondt had his distinctive champion. That man came in the form of Bronko Nagurski, the legendary member of the Chicago Bears football team.

Nagurski was as well-known in mainstream sports circles as

they came. He made his pro wrestling debut in 1933 under the tutelage of Tony Stecher of Minneapolis and took grappling seriously. He was far from a weekend ring warrior. Nagurski stepped onto the mat the same way he did the field, with an incomparable intensity, and people could see the look of determination in his eyes. His history of competitive achievements and the respect he garnered, Mondt felt, were going to do wonders for professional grappling. On June 29, 1937, he beat Detton and captured the heavyweight title.

In November, he made his first New York appearance as champion and delighted the Hippodrome audience by demonstrating much more than just flying tackles and brute strength. Nagurski was familiar with legitimate wrestling holds, such as the hammerlock and full nelson, and successfully turned back the challenge of Chief Little Wolf in 23 minutes and 20 seconds. Tackles, not so shockingly, were his pet maneuver, and he used them to knock his foe out of commission for the win, much to the thrill of the audience.

While new syndicates were rising to prominence, another faded with the sudden death of Jack Curley on July 12, 1937. Since the late 1910s, he had been the established leader of wrestling in New York and ably bridged the gap between the unscrupulous grappling scene and city politics. He was respected by nearly everyone, and if an organizer wanted to coordinate a charitable function with a sporting event, Curley always agreed to participate. By doing so, he earned wrestling goodwill with the city's elite and the press. Wrestling was not a joke to Curley. Sportswriters admired his work, extending friendship and, most of the time, favorable reporting. Wrestling in New York would never again receive such positive coverage.

In his place stepped his 24-year-old son, Jack Jr., who inherited his father's enthusiasm for promotions. He fearlessly attempted to continue the business and boldly held on to the Garden in the face of intense competition from the more experienced Mondt-Fabiani group. His challenges increased when Mondt and Fabiani allied with the new boxing promoter at the Garden, Mike Jacobs, and then gained the rights to the prized Monday night wrestling spot—for years held by Curley Sr. His father hadn't been dead a month when the New York State Athletic Commission made that controversial decision, and it was a harsh move to stomach. Curley Jr. laid to rest the rumors that he was severing all of his father's old ties and announced he was going to maintain matchmaking rights for Bowser's troops at the Garden and 71st Regiment Armory.

Curley made two attempts to run the Garden in September 1937, using talent from Bowser and Pfefer, but attendance was far from overwhelming, somewhere between 2,000 and 4,000 per show. His September 15 program featured O'Mahoney, Casey, Yvon Robert, and Ed Don George, and included a technical masterpiece from Billy Raborn and Jesse James. But the audience was stoic throughout the card with the exception of one match, a bout between two lesser-known gimmick wrestlers, Count Von Zuppe and Professor Pietro Marconi. According to Eddie Wade's account in the *New York Post*, the crowd came to life as soon as they exited the dressing room for the ring. Taken by their colorful appearances, people enjoyed their comedy antics during the five-minute bout, and it was the only lively moment of the evening.

Based on that reaction, promoters should have realized what New York fans wanted and given them more of the same. Instead, Von Zuppe and Marconi were not booked for the following Garden show, and the chance to capitalize on a potential money-maker was lost. The pressure from the New York State Athletic Commission on promoters to cut down on non-wrestlers and banish dramatic performers contributed to the loss of followers. It was as if the commission was doing exactly the opposite of what pro wrestling enthusiasts wanted, and in trying to abolish the colorfulness of wrestlers they destroyed the business in the territory.

There was a happy medium of understanding when it came to wrestling that worked in other states. Commissioners in those locations realized they played a very minor role in the regulation of the sport and left the management of wrestling to the promoters. When it came to punishing individuals for nonappearances or demanding all athletes be medically screened and licensed, they were on top of it. But in terms of the various wrestlers and styles of grappling in the ring, they watched from afar and collected their percentages from each show.

It was very different in New York. William Muldoon, General John J. Phelan, and other members of the athletic commission performed their duties by the book. They demanded that promoters present straight exhibitions of wrestling, and the oversight was without question the toughest in the country. An example of the commission's handiwork came in May 1937, when it decided to limit the number of matches a wrestler could perform per week in the state to three. And only two of those appearances could be in the main event. It was an upsetting decree that hurt grapplers and promoters in their effort to make a living.

The commission's rigid enforcement concerned the promoters who staged shows in the metropolitan area. One wrong move, they knew, could cost them their license.

Jess McMahon played by the rules his entire career. He was that kind of promoter at heart. He didn't tend to rock the boat or go out on a limb. While a venturesome entrepreneur, he knew not to invite controversy in an attempt to be successful. As wrestling's popularity hit a crescendo and then proceeded to drop into the abyss, McMahon was altogether resilient. Between 1935 and '39, he was constantly employed, operating boxing and wrestling at Queensboro Stadium, the Coney Island Velodrome, and the Hempstead Bowl.

On Wednesday nights, McMahon's Hempstead Arena shows were mandatory viewing for area grappling fans, and he spotlighted the Duseks, Garibaldis, Gus Sonnenberg, Crusher Casey, and many other established athletes. He also promoted the 102nd Medical Regiment Armory in White Plains on a regular basis. In November 1939, McMahon was designated by his compatriots to step forward and address a grievance before the athletic commission. Known for his persuasive speech and always influential, he requested the commission lower its minimum wage of pro wrestlers from $10 to $8 per bout, acknowledging the poor conditions of the sport in the process. The commission agreed.

The *New York Times* routinely commented on the annual status of various athletics at the end of the year. In December 1938, the paper remarked that wrestling locally had been "relegated definitely to the ranks of minor sport and no promotions of any size were attempted here." The next year, on December 24, 1939, the *Times* mentioned that the "mat pastime, once a cardinal part of athletic programs, did not attract to itself the interest or confidence of the public."

The death of Curley and overbearing supervision by the athletic commission were factors in wrestling's inability to regain footing. Elsewhere in the United States, grappling remained prevalent, and with standout talent like Lou Thesz, Bobby Managoff Jr., and "Wild" Bill Longson, plus outrageous characters such as the French Angel and Gorgeous George, the next decade was surely going to be a memorable one for pro wrestling. Unfortunately, the fans left in New York City were going miss out on most of it.

(6)
A TERRITORY IN RAPID DECLINE

The authoritative national organization known as the Trust was exploited successfully from 1933 to '36, and the unified system of promoters and matchmakers shared in riches, talent, and power. When the group dissolved into anarchy after the double-cross of Danno O'Mahoney, many of the leading promoters did something strange. They actually started thinking for themselves and listening to fans' reactions to particular wrestlers to see which was right to push. Rather than getting their marching orders from a matchmaker on the other side of the country and forcing an unpopular champion on their enthusiasts, they booked a title-holder who was already known and appreciated in local venues. It was a smart business move and helped foster the creation of wrestling's honored territories.

Toots Mondt, for one, enjoyed the structure of the Trust. He was always hungry for power and liked dictating champions. That was obvious by his selection of Chicago Bears football star Bronko Nagurski to ascend the throne in 1937 and the attempt to market him nationwide as the real world's titleholder. Nagurski delivered improved box office numbers compared to his predecessor, Dean Detton, and was a draw in parts of the upper Midwest, Philadelphia, and Los Angeles. But not all promoters bought into the hype for Nagurski, especially those who wanted nothing to do with Mondt.

By early 1938, Steve Casey was touring the Paul Bowser circuit as a rival champion, and "Tigerman" John Pesek carried National Wrestling Association (NWA) recognition with support from Al Haft. In other locations, like Montreal, there was a separate champion. Mondt still felt there was room to reconnect the promotions and book a singular kingpin across the wrestling landscape. The challenge was finding the right wrestler to lead the charge. Nagurski caught on in some areas, but he wasn't the universally beloved grappler Toots hoped he'd be. Perhaps the perfect man for the job was the guy Mondt had fought for years, Jim Londos. In the interest of making money, they signed a peace pact, with Ray Fabiani acting as the middleman.

Londos had been on the comeback trail for about two years and was in top shape. Having been popular nearly everywhere and dominating the most successful period in the sport's history, he was believed to be the best choice to become the supreme champion. On November 18, 1938, in Philadelphia, Londos, now 44, beat Nagurski and returned to the throne. While the title switch back to the old favorite caused some upsurge in attention, the massive tidal wave of curiosity was subdued by the general apathy of the wrestling-going public. Additionally, promoters like Bowser and Tom Packs in St. Louis steadfastly remained independent of a central union. The chance of Mondt or anyone else securing complete sponsorship for a single heavyweight titleholder was gone.

Packs maintained his relationship with Billy Sandow and Everette Marshall, and the latter was acknowledged as the new NWA champion at the organization's convention in 1938. The NWA as a whole was a rigid body of state athletic commissioners from all over the map, and through the years, their greatest attribute was recognizing championships in the various weight classes. From time to time, the NWA did offer a consequential decision, but it was more often than not ignored because it was outside the inner circle of promoters—wrestling's real decision-makers.

To Packs, the NWA was important for two things: name value and the bureaucratic support provided by athletic commissions in member states, which ultimately gave him the power he craved. He wanted to embrace the association as the main supporter of his championship lineage. Much like the American Wrestling Association (AWA) for Bowser or the Midwest Wrestling Association (MWA) for Haft, the NWA was going to be Packs's pet organization—and give him widespread influence far outside of St. Louis. In effect, by his agreement with the NWA, his champion already had far greater state commission acceptance as titleholder than Londos, and Packs's status as a wrestling czar superseded that of Mondt.

The NWA world heavyweight title passed from Marshall to Lou Thesz on February 23, 1939, and then to Nagurski in June following a bout in Houston. Nagurski's reemergence as champion was the result of a working agreement between Packs, Mondt, and the wrestler's manager, Tony Stecher of Minneapolis. Once again, there was a considerable effort to elevate Nagurski to box office superstardom, but the anticipated masses were missing. He was a capable and entertaining worker in the ring, but he was unable to rejuvenate the audience and become that must-see performer. On March 7, 1940, tried-and-true veteran Ray Steele beat Nagurski and captured the NWA crown.

Out in Los Angeles, Mondt found himself in deep trouble. For years he had run the local promotion in conjunction with the Daro brothers in a sketchy fashion, but as the head booker, his word was final. Lou Daro, the elder statesman of the group, was seriously ill and serving in a much-reduced capacity. He decided, along with his brother Jack, to relent to Mondt in many circumstances, leaving Toots to his own designs. That was a bad idea. If there was anything Mondt specifically needed, it was a strong-minded leader to run the show and provide supervision of sorts.

Whenever he was able to call the shots, without oversight, things usually went sour. Los Angeles was no exception.

One of the major complaints was a failure to pay wrestlers for matches they performed in. For a booking agent, that was a significant matter and reflected horribly on the promotion. Toots already had a reputation as a poor payoff man, and some grapplers hated to work for him. He seemed to have no conscience when it came to his employees, and, because of his position, wrestlers had only one option, and that was to leave the territory. Undercard grapplers weren't even paid livable wages, and in many cases they couldn't wait to venture elsewhere. Mondt was as uncontrolled with his money in Southern California as he had been in New York and spent a lot of time at the horse racetracks at Hollywood Park and Del Mar. Legend has it that he was gambling the money he siphoned from the pay of his workers.

Karma came around to bite him, though. The California State Athletic Commission, as well as the California State Assembly, ordered investigations, and between 1939 and '40, countless secrets were revealed. Allegations of assaults, threats, blacklisting, and payments to sportswriters and political figures well into six figures were disclosed. The outfit used their ties to officials, including members of the athletic commission itself, to prevent rival promoters and bookers from receiving licenses to compete against them. Grapplers knew they were powerless because Mondt was the only operator in town—that is, until the commission gave a booker's license to ex-wrestler Nick Lutze in 1940.

With another option for employment, the disgruntled wrestlers jumped ship, and as a final nail in the coffin, the Daroses lost the Olympic Auditorium to George Zaharias. In September 1940, Mondt sold whatever was left of his office to Lutze and found himself at his lowest point in pro wrestling since the beginning of his career. Few people lamented his demise.

Back in New York, the bureaucrats behind Madison Square Garden were fed up with the lukewarm reception to wrestling at the venue and refused to schedule any future programs. The final offering, on March 30, 1938, was staged by Stanislaus Zbyszko and drew in the neighborhood of 5,000 spectators. Jack Curley Jr., who was expected to rise to a prominent role in area promotions, also turned his back on wrestling. He retired to concentrate on the insurance business. Poor conditions continued, but the Johnstons, Rudy Dusek, Jack Pfefer, Rudy Miller, and Jess McMahon parlayed their experience into running manageable events and fought hard to keep the remainder of their audience.

A noticeable change in the evolution of New York wrestling was the lack of coverage in newspapers. Before 1937, the treatment of pro grappling was front of the sports page news in just about every major paper from the *New York Times* to the *American*. Some sports editors watched the free fall in popularity and declined to offer anything more than sporadic coverage. Others gave brief articles to promote live shows, but cynical commentary from columnists was the norm. All of the possible modifications that could have been implemented to avoid disaster were ignored, and the worst-case scenario was realized. By 1939, pro wrestling was completely insignificant in the territory and a resurrection seemed improbable.

Pfefer reacted by broadening his horizons. In addition to maintaining a strong presence in New York, booking at the St. Nicholas and Ridgewood Grove Arenas, he expanded to parts of New Jersey and Connecticut. He fostered a successful endeavor in Bridgeport and later sent workers to Alfred Aceto, a promoter in Philadelphia. Out of his Broadway office, he built up his contingent of wrestlers and relentlessly scouted for talent. A 1941 report claimed he traveled 12,000 miles in search of new attractions, and he sought anyone with a marketable appearance or personality, from college athletes to 600-pound behemoths. His roster included the likes of Dave Levin, Bobby Bruns, Michele Leone, and the Brooklyn sensation George Becker.

Displaying a distinctive creativity, he started to cast his performers into gimmick roles that nearly mirrored wrestling celebrities already on the circuit. For instance, in the case of the French Angel, Pfefer created the Swedish Angel, reinventing the career of Olaf Swenson and turning him into a star. Another early gimmick was Lou Kesz, whose name sounded a lot like Lou Thesz. Pfefer often gave his athletes unique and exotic backgrounds, such as billing Missourian Jack Claybourne as a product of South Africa, and his colorful characters gained great notoriety wherever they wrestled. Youngsters Billy Darnell, Angelo Savoldi, and Herman "Dutch" Rohde, soon to be known as Buddy Rogers, were members of his troupe during the first half of the 1940s.

Although Pfefer's Swedish Angel garnered a good share of attention, his success was dwarfed by the French version, whose real name was Maurice Tillet. Recruited into the business and trained by Karl Pojello, Tillet became a leading attraction in the early 1940s, mostly because of his otherworldly looks. He suffered from acromegaly, a condition that caused excessive enlargement of his bone structure, and scientists believed he closely resembled a Neanderthal. At 5'8" and over 250 pounds, he was incredibly strong, and it was hard for fans to take their eyes off his exceptional body form. Once the word got out, everyone wanted to catch a glimpse, and Tillet sold well all over the United States and Canada. In May 1940, he defeated Steve Casey for Paul Bowser's AWA world title and reigned for two years.

Of the other premier heavyweights on the rise, Frank Sexton of Sedalia, Ohio, was at the top of the list. He was tall, powerful, and a skilled pure wrestler. Mentored in the ranks of Al Haft, he went out to San Francisco and garnered fame under a mask, billed as the Black Panther, in 1941. He captured the Pacific Coast heavyweight title four times and feuded with Bill Longson, Bobby Managoff Jr., and Dean Detton. Sexton rose up the Bowser syndicate ladder, and in 1945 he conquered Sandor Szabo for the AWA world championship in Boston. Popular and acknowledged for bringing credibility to the sport, Sexton was titleholder for nearly 1,800 straight days—an amazing show of confidence by his promotional supporters.

Longson and Managoff Jr. followed a different path and became champions of the National Wrestling Association. The lineage of the National Wrestling Association world title continued from Ray Steele back to Bronko Nagurski in 1941 and then to Sandor Szabo and Longson in February 1942. Montreal favorite Yvon Robert briefly held the belt from October to November of that same year before being dethroned by Managoff in Houston. On February 19, 1943, in St. Louis, Longson regained the championship and began a four-year reign.

Longson, 37, was a veteran campaigner and a crafty heel, having made his pro debut in 1931 after a solid amateur run as both a boxer and wrestler. He once fought the legendary Jack Dempsey in an exhibition and won a slew of Intermountain AAU medals in his hometown of Salt Lake City. In 1937, his time in pro wrestling was prematurely halted when he was splashed by the mammoth Man Mountain Dean and suffered a devastating back injury. Told he'd never walk again, he defied the odds and resumed his remarkable career. Longson was the master of the piledriver and many of his foes were flattened by the colorful maneuver. In St. Louis, he was loathed and loved by the wrestling populace, and the local promoter, Tom Packs, served as his personal manager and booked him all over North America with great financial success.

Managoff Jr. played the hero. He was a second-generation star from Chicago, and his father was the contributing referee in the 1933 double-cross of Jim Londos. Stylish and slick on the mat, Managoff was impressive as a teenager, and by age 24 he was a claimant to the world heavyweight crown. He mixed brawling and scientific wrestling and was a perfect foil for Longson. In terms of achievements, he captured the National Wrestling Association and Montreal world titles, plus a variety of honors in California and Texas. Notably, Longson's back problems and family obligations and Managoff's double cataracts prevented them from serving in the military during World War II. They fulfilled a different role by entertaining in the squared circle.

The war forced many changes in professional wrestling and seized scores of athletes for duty. Ruffy Silverstein, the former NCAA and Big Ten champion, was rumored to have been in line to win the National Wrestling Association title when he was called to the U.S. Army. Lou Thesz was in the prime of his wrestling life, and had he not been called to service, there is no doubt he would have made an impact. The same went for Steve Casey and, to a lesser degree, Ede Virag, who was a regional champion for an organization known as the National Wrestling Alliance, based out of Wichita. The need for soldiers affected innumerable wrestlers, promoters, and their families.

On July 24, 1942, Vincent James McMahon, the 28-year-old son of Jess McMahon, entered the U.S. Coast Guard at Manhattan Beach, New York. He was an intelligent young man, and of Jess's three children, he had taken the most interest in his father's work. His fascination with sports promotions had developed when he was a boy, watching Jess masterfully handle the broad backstage responsibilities of boxing events. He was but 11 when his father became matchmaker at Madison Square Garden, essentially the pinnacle of the field, and was blown away by the spectacle. It forged an unforgettable memory.

Jess was guarded about his family. He took steps to protect them from the cruel side of his business and ensured his children had the best schooling options. Vincent attended Public School 69 in Jackson Heights prior to enrolling in LaSalle Military Academy on Long Island. During the summers, he was sent to camp to keep him busy. William Morris of the *New York Evening Post* mentioned on August 3, 1929, that Jess had sent Vincent to a location "overlooking Buzzards Bay in Massachusetts." Included in the column was part of a letter "Vince" wrote to his older brother, Rod, where he explained he "learned how to follow up a left-jab with a right-cross knockout punch." He specifically told him not to tell his father and followed up by saying, "for I want to surprise him one of these days."

Jess apparently disliked Vincent's early aspirations to become a fighter. However, Vincent wasn't close-minded and participated in numerous athletics, from baseball and hockey to running cross-country. He finished up his schooling at Far Rockaway High School, graduating in 1932, and helped his father in various promotional efforts whenever he could. Three years later, a strange incident occurred on a bus en route from Brooklyn to Rockaway Beach, and Vincent and a friend, Edward Sargent, made the neighborhood news.

The story goes that Vincent and his pal encountered two police officers in the back of the bus. After an inadvertent push when the vehicle made a sharp turn, words were exchanged, but nothing came of it. But as the officers were walking off the bus, something was said to incite their tempers. They returned and arrested both Vincent and Edward. According to the latter, they were physically beaten, and Vincent said his nose was broken. The officers denied the tale. In May 1935, the case was brought before the Rockaway Beach court and the charges of disorderly conduct against Vincent and Edward were dismissed. The audience in the courtroom applauded the decision.

Vincent labored in the office of a newspaper, running errands and handling general paperwork. In 1940, when the federal census was recorded, he was still living at home in Belle Harbor, Queens, and was unemployed. His enlistment in the Coast Guard took him to Sullivan's Island at the entrance of Charleston Harbor in South Carolina and also to Wilmington, North Carolina. While in North Carolina, he developed a serious relationship with a local girl named Victoria Elizabeth Hanner, and the two got married. Still tied to the military, he returned to New York City and was discharged from the Coast Guard Barracks on New Chambers Street on August 18, 1945. Exactly six days later, Vincent Kennedy McMahon, the son of Vincent and Victoria, was born in Moore County, North Carolina. Vincent was later divorced.

In the aftermath of the controversy in Los Angeles, Toots Mondt took a surprising job. Deposed from his office at the Olympic Auditorium, where he controlled the destinies of more than 50 wrestlers as matchmaker, he simply walked to another part of the arena and became a concessionaire. He peddled cold beer and hot dogs and made himself livable wages. Despite his efforts to clean up his act, his run of bad luck was not yet through. In December 1942, the United Press announced a huge Internal Revenue Service movement targeting individuals in the sports field and Hollywood for delinquent taxes. Not so shockingly, Toots was named. The staggering amount he allegedly owed was $18,000.

Mondt bolted for New York and was eager to get back into

the wrestling business, even if it meant becoming a minion for Jack Pfefer. He briefly acted as a road agent for the Swedish Angel and worked out of Pfefer's Times Square office in the Longacre Building. At his side was Alfred "Al" Mayer, an experienced French-born publicity agent with a gift for advertising the next big wrestling show or superstar. Mayer had entertainment and promotions in his blood. His father and grandfather were producers in Europe, and as a boy he had traveled with internationally renowned actress Sarah Bernhardt. He entered the newspaper field and was a correspondent for dozens of publications, from the *New York Times* to the *London Daily Mail*. In South America during the 1920s, he became a boxing manager for Luis Firpo and Paulino Uzcudun prior to working for Jack Curley in New York. It was there he learned about pro wrestling.

With Pfefer looking to hit the road and become a national entity, Mayer and Mondt combined their interests and formed their own booking office. The maneuver put Toots back in the driver's seat. He immediately started doing what he did best, organizing promoters to expand his booking operations throughout the Northeast, and contracted a host of wrestlers. He was anxious to book a lot of his old friends like Chief Little Wolf, Man Mountain Dean, and Joe Savoldi, while at the same time propping up a relative newcomer, ex-football star Babe Sharkey, as a heavyweight title claimant. Born Charles Kemmerer, Sharkey stood 6'4" and weighed 250 pounds. He starred on the gridiron at Temple University and was a standout heel along the lines of Bill Longson.

Of all the wrestlers Mondt signed between 1944 and '46, none came close to being the box office attraction that Primo Carnera would become. The former boxing champion had recently escaped incarceration during the war in Italy and was assuming a second life in the public's eye as a professional wrestler. There was a running joke in sports circles about the number of people involved in the "management" of Carnera during his boxing career. He'd had a half dozen "managers" taking a percentage of his purse after each contest, and was considered a pawn or even a rube as countless people milked him into the poorhouse. Now he was involved in wrestling, and why would things be any different?

Mondt and his controversial Los Angeles boxing connection, Babe McCoy, roped Carnera into an ironclad contract, and in the summer of 1946, the latter ventured onto the circuit with Toots as his publicist, manager, and agent. Harry Grayson, sports editor for the Newspaper Enterprise Association, wrote a syndicated article about Carnera in August 1946, noting he had a "great future" in grappling. Mondt added that Primo was already "an accomplished wrestler," based on his previous experience in a circus. In terms of selling him as a viable and entertaining athlete, Toots would have said anything to sell tickets. After a session with Mondt, a naive sportswriter would have believed Carnera was the second coming of Frank Gotch.

It was all ballyhoo. Carnera was a huge, lumbering, visually impressive figure, but his physical prowess was limited. He didn't have to be adept at all the old catch-as-catch-can moves but simply put on a good show. His name value alone was going to lure them in, and Mondt knew he had a real winner on his hands.

Promotional alliances were still the fad in New York City, and the Mondt-Mayer agency held a strong territorial advantage over the Dusek tribe. Mondt booked to most of the major clubs, including the St. Nicholas, Ridgewood Grove, Jamaica, Queensboro, and Winter Garden arenas. The Johnstons and Rudy Miller were affiliated, and Pfefer maintained his friendly association with the group. Aside from Carnera and those previously mentioned, the roster was made up of Frank Sexton, Milo Steinborn, Kola Kwariani, Stu Hart, Sandor Kovacs, Ben Morgan, Paul Boesch, Bobby Bruns, and many others.

Rudy Dusek's main New York venue was the Broadway Arena in Brooklyn. He added the Sunnyside Garden in Queens under the management of Jess McMahon in 1947 and booked to numerous smaller arenas. Outside of New York, he sent regular weekly talent to Eddie Gottlieb at the Philadelphia Arena and continued his long-standing working relationship with Paul Bowser. Among the wrestlers aligned to this faction were the Dusek brothers, Yvon Robert, Maurice Tillet, George Becker, Bobby Managoff Jr., and Gino Garibaldi.

All bridges were not burned between Mondt and Dusek, and superstars like Carnera, Tillet, and Tony Galento were booked to arenas on both sides of the syndicate dividing line. In such instances, the bookers realized it was better to compromise and receive a piece of the cake than miss out entirely. Additionally, it gave their local fans a chance to see the top attractions who were making news elsewhere.

Although it was a slow build, the postwar years were rising to a boom period for pro wrestling. In fact, there was more optimism for the sport than there had been in more than 10 years. The central factor in the massive upturn of excitement surrounded the growing availability of television as an outlet. On January 6, 1947, Montgomery Wright of the *New York Sun* estimated there were only 5,000 television sets in private homes in the New York metropolitan area and another 3,000 nationwide. Prognosticators, envisioning the enormous rush to purchase TVs, believed as many as 500,000 could be sold around the country by the end of 1947.

New York already had three stations, NBC, CBS, and WABD (DuMont), and was making progressive moves to connect to a network of other Northeastern cities. Station officials at DuMont realized the importance of arena sports as part of their weekly programming and, in 1946, began featuring live boxing and wrestling shows. Arrangements were made through Sam Weiss, owner of Jamaica Arena, and his grappling impresario, Bill Johnston, to stage Friday night telecasts from the venue. The show was a pioneering effort for wrestling on TV, joining a similar endeavor in Chicago from the Rainbo Arena.

Promoters were unsure of TV's eventual impact, and there were early concerns that broadcasting shows would inhibit the arena-going public and hurt box office sales. Those worries were dismissed by DuMont executives as they added a Thursday night wrestling offering, initially from the Jerome Arena in the Bronx and later from the Park Arena. Over at WNBT (NBC), administrators took notice of the growing frenzy to produce live wrestling entertainment and realized it was a relatively cheap way to fill the nightly lineup. They launched a Tuesday night program from the St. Nicholas Arena featuring more of Mondt's wrestlers. WPIX, when it debuted as an independent station in June 1948, immediately included wrestling on Thursdays from the Queensboro Arena. WOR also got in on the act by presenting a Jamaica Arena program.

Wrestling on television in New York was plentiful, but the programming being filmed locally was not enough to satisfy the need. Using new technology, WATV imported a program from Turner's Arena in Washington, DC, beginning on Wednesday, May 19, 1948. On February 2, 1949, the ABC network debuted its popular Chicago Rainbo Arena wrestling series on WJZ. Then in September, DuMont expanded the reach of Chicago's Saturday night series from the Marigold Arena to New York on WABD. TV exposed the public to colorful characters and intriguing athletes, and an entire generation of new fans was hooked.

Gorgeous George, out in Los Angeles, was a headline attraction on television and used his masterful understanding of ring psychology to garner regional and national attention. It was all in the presentation, and George was a marvelous entertainer. He wore extravagant robes, commanded a dutiful valet, and looked down his nose at ringsiders. A product of the semipro circuit around Houston, he was essentially a journeyman light heavyweight most of his career. In Los Angeles, he perfected the "Gorgeous George" gimmick and became the signature performer of the era.

St. Louis was likely the most profitable wrestling city during the 1940s. The extraordinary success of Bill Longson created a mint for promoter Tom Packs and his supporting cast was always tops. With sizable payoffs due to the big audiences and the promotional staff's reputation for professionalism, the city was a joy to work for most wrestlers. Packs was a shrewd businessman and a hard-nosed veteran. Through his hard work, St. Louis enjoyed great success going back to the mid-1920s, but he didn't manage the entire operation alone. His assistant through 1941 was Sam

Muchnick, an ultra-wise former sportswriter who handled everything from public relations to matchmaking.

Muchnick was an invaluable employee, but his bad feelings for Packs led him to branch off and form his own promotion. Before he could get things stabilized, he entered the U.S. Army during the war and served for over three years. The time away didn't alter his mindset. Upon returning to St. Louis, he quickly sought a license and staged his first program in December 1945, using independent talent from Billy Sandow's organization out of Wichita. His enterprise was completely antagonistic to Packs, and their rivalry sparked a lengthy clash for the loyalty of wrestling fans.

But their wrestling war had larger implications in terms of which syndicate would dominate the landscape—Packs and his National Wrestling Association affiliates or Muchnick and his troupe of indie promoters. Muchnick made an important move in July 1948 by affixing his name to a new charter of booking agents. Their organization was dubbed the National Wrestling Alliance (also abbreviated NWA), the same designation as a regional promotion in Iowa managed by Paul L. "Pinkie" George. George conceived the idea of a legitimate "national" union of bookers, and although the National Wrestling Alliance was initiated with only members in Midwestern cities, it rapidly expanded to include representatives in Texas and California.

Muchnick's allegiance to the NWA and friendship with Jack Pfefer were factors in altering the momentum of the St. Louis wrestling war. Talent was the key. Because he was tied into Tony Stecher of Minneapolis, Max Clayton of Omaha, Orville Brown of Kansas City, Al Haft of Columbus, and George in Iowa, Muchnick was connected to a wider array of wrestlers—new names that would intrigue St. Louis enthusiasts. From Pfefer, Muchnick received one of the most talked-about youngsters on the circuit, the "Nature Boy" Buddy Rogers. Rogers had previously grappled for Packs and flipped sides on the whim of Pfefer to help Muchnick. That single deed catapulted Muchnick into the big time and changed the tides of the conflict.

The pressure got to be too much for Packs. In 1948, he was

bordering on bankruptcy and decided to call it quits. For a price in the ballpark of $37,000, he sold his St. Louis promotion to Lou Thesz, Bill Longson, Montreal promoter Eddie Quinn, and Toronto promoter Frank Tunney. The deal transferred booking control of the National Wrestling Association world heavyweight championship from Packs to the new outfit and put Thesz in charge of the local promotion. Unfortunately for Thesz, he inherited the same rivalry Packs was struggling against, and the war for the St. Louis territory continued.

The early progress of the National Wrestling Alliance was noteworthy, but not every booking agent saw its potential. Toots Mondt and Rudy Dusek in New York were both well aware of the NWA's budding influence, but neither wanted to submit to the oversight of what was basically a Western outfit. Mondt, specifically, was unwilling to conform to the bylaws of an organization founded by small-timers. He had more important dealings to worry about. His New York concerns were probably more valuable than all of the originators of the NWA put together, and they were not a threat to his business. There was no need for jealousy, concern, or interest in becoming a member of the Alliance.

Mondt was on a roll. Not only had he scored the contract of Primo Carnera and the lucrative box office earnings that went along with it, but he had finagled the rights to South American sensation Antonino Rocca from Kola Kwariani. The move was brilliant and his timing impeccable. Rocca, a nimble 28-year-old, resembled a tumbler more than a classically trained grappler, but fans wanted action, swift moves, and flashy tomfoolery, and Rocca was the total package. He was entertaining and instantly popular, and Mondt had no trouble filling up his calendar with bookings all over the United States and Canada.

The mood of the Mondt-Mayer office was usually contentious, and Toots's big personality was hard to cope with at times. It isn't known what specific incident ignited the quarrel that ended their partnership in 1948, but both men went their separate ways. Mondt wasn't without a headquarters for long. He quickly dug up two willing and able partners, Rudy Miller and Milo Steinborn, and formed the Manhattan Booking Agency. Most of the wrestlers he previously handled followed him over to the new organization, and he didn't miss a beat when it came to fulfilling the needs of metropolitan clubs with wrestling talent. He remained the sport's most successful matchmaker.

After leaving the bright lights of Broadway and taking to the road, Jack Pfefer was everywhere from Tulsa to Hollywood and Portland to Houston. He'd enter a territory with his mob of colorful characters and completely change the dynamic of the promotion. His workers were a little offbeat, but amusing nonetheless, and usually got the job done when it came to presenting a good show. His main star, Buddy Rogers, was a different beast altogether and, in some opinions, had already outgrown the smallness of Pfefer's carnival road show. Pfefer disagreed, and he grew increasingly suspicious that other promoters were trying to steal Rogers. He had a hot temper and seemed to enjoy adding names to his already long list of enemies.

Professional wrestling in New York City was in the midst of revitalization in 1948 and into '49, and promoters had every reason to be hopeful. There were endless TV programs to expose the variety of grapplers and a few top-tier superstars who carried the kind of magnetism that could lure thousands to sports arenas. It was the dawn of a new era, and the time seemed right to let bygones be bygones and forget the troubled past. Mondt, Rudy Dusek, Bill and Charles Johnston, and their contingent of partners and allies concluded that wrestling needed to make a high-profile return to Madison Square Garden. The Garden was, as everyone knew, the most illustrious setting for grappling in the world. Wrestling's return would signal the sport's rebirth.

Bookers, promoters, and other officials were ecstatic, and the renaissance meant tremendous sums of money. They could already hear the dings of cash registers as they collected the loot from a sold-out Garden, and Toots Mondt was the biggest dreamer of all. To ensure everything went perfectly, Mondt and his team worked overtime to prepare and booked the best show they thought possible. Imported from the West Coast was the one and only

Gorgeous George—the talk of all wrestling—and his opponent was the gritty veteran Ernie Dusek, who could play both the hero and villain depending on the situation.

Everyone was excited. Everyone, that is, except the New York wrestling public, most of whom shunned the February 22, 1949, show. Less than 4,200 turned out, and George failed to live up to his reputation as a supreme performer. He flopped and the local press made sure the entire fiasco was well reported. The hopes for a big-time homecoming at Madison Square Garden were dashed, and pro wrestling's anticipated renaissance in New York was on hold.

(7)
REVITALIZED BY TELEVISION

During wrestling's explosion in popularity in the early 1930s, promoters of all shapes and sizes designated a "home territory" and claimed exclusive rights, regardless of whether that was true. William Joseph "Joe" Turner planted his flag in his own backyard, Washington, DC, a city he had lived in since he was a boy. Already a celebrity through his two and a half decades of wrestling, including a stint as world middleweight champion, Turner was a favored son and his shows at the Auditorium and Griffith Stadium were well received. Following the end of his 1934–35 campaign, he received word that the Auditorium was no longer going to be available for his promotions. He immediately sought a suitable replacement.

In October 1935, he signed a multi-year lease for a structure on W Street in the northwest part of the city, between 13th and 14th Streets. The building, essentially a garage, was owned by Cresson E. Finch and had been since 1917, and according to the terms of the lease, broad renovations were to be completed before Turner staged his first program. Measuring 85 by 150 feet, the main part of the structure was to be accompanied by a front entrance hall, ticket booths, and concession plus a dressing room area. The overhaul was rushed and completed for the debut of grappling at "Turner's Arena" on December 5, 1935, and a capacity crowd of 2,500 watched undisputed world champion Danno O'Mahoney clobber Jack Donovan.

Turner's Arena was the heart of pro wrestling in DC, and all the greats appeared there in the 1930s and '40s. Turner was admired for his professionalism and philanthropy, and he had friends all over the sports world. He capitalized on his strong associations with leading matchmakers, such as Toots Mondt, and gave his local enthusiasts the best cards he could muster. At 62 years of age, Turner suddenly passed away in 1947, leaving a major question about the future of wrestling in the city. His widow, Florence, rather than end the celebrated Turner legacy, decided to continue the business with assistance from her husband's longtime booker, Gabe Menendez.

In 1945, Jess McMahon diversified his interests by going into business with German-born promoter Fred Kirsch, an agent for heavyweight boxing champion Max Schmeling in the 1930s. Instead of brokering a sports arrangement, McMahon and Kirsch dabbled in promoting concerts at the Constitution Hall in Washington, DC. They sold out the venue with the orchestra of Sigmund Romberg and featured Phil Spitalny and his all-girl musicians, known as the "Hour of Charm." Jess eventually got fed up with traveling to DC and passed off local responsibilities to his son Vincent, who moved to Washington in the middle of 1946.

An amazing networker, Vincent rapidly connected to his father's old acquaintances and had little trouble mingling with the social elite. He knew both Menendez and the late Turner, and on December 3, 1948, he was hired by the management of Turner's Arena to act as the venue's general manager. The job was a momentous opportunity, and McMahon, much like his father, took on the duties with complete enthusiasm. He wasn't afraid to put in hours late at night and develop relationships with political, union, and athletic groups in efforts to get them to hold their events at the arena.

McMahon was more than successful. He brought in basketball games, concerts, and dances, and in early 1949, the arena was so booked up that it sometimes had two different events a day. Over on the wrestling side of things, the sport was still a lucrative operation for the Turner-Menendez outfit, and grapplers were brought into the city from Mondt's New York agency. Spectators were regaled with world-class talent, everyone from heavyweight champion Frank Sexton to Antonino Rocca and Gene Stanlee. Shows were also featured on WMAL-TV with Jim Gibbons doing commentary.

Interestingly, before a widespread peace accord was made in 1949, Rudy Dusek invaded Washington, DC, and held Monday night programs from the Uline Arena. Dusek was resolute in his fight for the territory, , even finding a TV outlet on WTTG. Soon, the region was saturated by wrestling on television, including shows imported from New York facilities.

Nearly 10 months after the disastrous February 1949 return to the Garden in New York, Mondt and his allies tried it again. Having learned that Gorgeous George and the Duseks were not enough superstar drawing power to entice fans to buy tickets, they stacked a card on December 12, 1949, with Rocca, Stanlee, Primo Carnera, Kola Kwariani, Lord Carlton, Jim Henry, and old-time favorite Joe Savoldi. The strategy to load the bill worked wonders, and nearly 18,000 people paid $50,639.28 to attend the show. It was the largest Garden wrestling attendance since 1931.

Wrestling was back. Mondt, with Rocca as his primary catalyst, revived the New York audience and restored the Garden to the forefront of the business. Grappling drew more than 16,000 at the arena in March and over 14,000 again in May 1950, both times with Rocca, Stanlee, and Carnera in the top spots. Of the trio, Stanlee was the only man not born in Italy. He was reared in Chicago, had served admirably in the U.S. Navy during the war, and had made his wrestling debut around 1946. Possessing clean-cut looks and a brawny physique, he was known as "Mr.

America" and was a regular on TV. His popularity helped the Garden revitalization, but Rocca was the true star.

New York was considered a leader in the growth of wrestling on television, but it lagged behind Chicago in terms of overall influence. This was because New York lacked a pioneering promoter who had enough insight to revolutionize grappling on TV and could also factor in the national picture.

Chicago became ground zero for wrestling on television because of the forward-thinking Frederick Koch, a 47-year-old former grappler known professionally as Fred Kohler. Kohler was a Windy City native, and for years he had struggled to break into the big time, staging shows with a cast of non-heavyweight performers. Finally in 1936, he turned a corner as the local representative for the Al Haft–Billy Sandow combination, which assumed power in the aftermath of the double-cross of Danno O'Mahoney. Kohler soon partnered with Ed White, a veteran in Chicago wrestling circles, and successfully built his promotion into one of the premier organizations in the Midwest.

The war years were particularly harsh at the box office for Kohler, but he persevered. In July 1946, he introduced Chicago to grappling on TV in its most primitive form, but with his partners on the television end, he worked out numerous technical issues to improve the picture quality. Unlike many of his counterparts, Kohler took a serious interest in the production and promotion of his wrestling TV programs, and he became good friends with executives at WBKB, WENR, WGN, and at the DuMont Network. His first-rate offerings convinced station managers to broadcast his weekly shows from the Rainbo and Midway Arenas, the Madison Athletic Club, plus a Saturday night event from the Marigold Arena. His monthly, or bimonthly, International Amphitheater events were also telecasted either live or on tape delay.

Always contentious and involved in coordinating every facet to a T, Kohler was in a perfect position to take advantage of the expanding TV medium, and executives looked to him to provide wrestling content on both ABC and the DuMont Network. That meant the wrestlers he featured locally in Chicago were also being seen across the country. In turn, the promoters in the cities that received his TV programs were going to want to book those same wrestlers to appease fans. Smartly, Kohler signed many of his top stars to contracts to ensure he'd receive a percentage from every out-of-town booking. Because of his extensive control of talent and ability to affect box office receipts from Boston to St. Louis, he surpassed Mondt as the sport's most influential man.

Johnny Doyle in Los Angeles was not far behind Kohler, and his rise to the upper tier of promoters came as a result of many different factors. The son of a newspaperman, he was born in 1909 and grew up southwest of Chicago. He spent time in Seattle, where his father worked as the publisher for the *Post-Intelligencer*, and then settled in Pasadena, California, with his family. His initial foray into wrestling came as a subordinate in the Lou Daro–Toots Mondt group in Los Angeles, but he made his bones as an assistant in several eastern cities, including in Philadelphia as a pupil of Ray Fabiani. He returned to Southern California a much wiser man and secured management positions at the Eastside and Ocean Park arenas.

Doyle teamed up with an old Seattle friend, Musty Musgrave, bought out the booking rights for the entire region from Nick Lutze, who had succeeded Mondt, and together, Doyle and Musgrave rebuilt the territory. After Musgrave passed away, Doyle solidified his place as the top matchmaker, sending wrestlers to the Olympic Auditorium and numerous other venues in the area. His friendships with Mondt, Fabiani, and others in the East allowed him to regularly import key wrestlers like Carnera and Rocca. At the same time, he was the agent behind the rise of Gorgeous George and "Baron" Michele Leone, two of the era's most potent showmen.

Doyle was a regular at all of the popular late-night spots and made many friends in Hollywood, both in movies and television. He was carefree with spending money and and was often the life of the party. Backstage, he was generally respected, and he routinely invited wrestlers back to his home for a hot meal with his family. He made a number of significant strategic moves to ensure his power, and he was fierce during head-to-head rivalries against promoters. In 1950, he formed a four-way agreement with Olympic promoter Cal Eaton, Hugh Nichols of the Hollywood Legion Stadium, and Mike Hirsch of the Ocean Park Arena that transformed their businesses into a multi-million-dollar enterprise.

With expansive television outlets, their near-complete dominance of talent, and connections to the National Wrestling Alliance (NWA), the Doyle syndicate evolved into a remorseless monopoly. They manhandled outsiders and threatened to blacklist wrestlers who appeared for non-NWA affiliates. Additionally, the syndicate possessed strong political ties, up to the governor's office, and had longtime friendships with high-ranking athletic commission members. Between 1948 and '53, the Los Angeles office was one of the most fortified and successful wrestling organizations in history.

Television exposure turned many average grapplers into highly appreciated stars. It also made it relatively easy to build up a rookie as a potential future champion. In the postwar period, a slew of former collegiate amateur wrestlers turned pro, and they were a welcome addition to the TV universe. Mike DiBiase, Ray Gunkel, and Leo Nomellini were at the head of the class, and each was a splendid performer, combining legitimate mat knowledge and colorful mannerisms that appealed to audiences. But ahead of them all was Verne Gagne, perhaps the greatest newcomer on the wrestling scene since Lou Thesz. Gagne had it all—a profound awareness, natural instincts, and an ability to rapidly adapt to the pro wrestling mindset. He was a promoter's dream, being extremely marketable and extraordinarily popular.

Gagne turned pro in 1949 at the age of 23, under the tutelage of Joe Stecher and Joe Pazandak in his hometown of Minneapolis. He was already famous, having starred at the University of Minnesota in both football and grappling, and had won a handful of individual wrestling titles, including two NCAA championships. On top of that, he had served in the U.S. Marines during the war and had been an alternate at the 1948 Olympics. His life experiences and maturity gave him a leg up in his early professional endeavors, and he was a willing understudy of veterans like Paul Boesch during an early run in Texas.

Promoters made the most of his youthful star power, and in 1950 he was pushed to the world junior heavyweight crown, receiving sponsorship from high-ranking members of the National Wrestling Alliance. He handled the chore admirably and appeared for associates across North America with distinction. Ignoring his expanding fan base was an impossible chore, and there was no question that he was being positioned for a future bid for the Alliance's heavyweight championship.

The National Wrestling Alliance was growing by leaps and bounds and showed no signs of slowing. One of the organization's foremost accomplishments came as a result of the cessasion of hostilities in St. Louis. The Lou Thesz–Sam Muchnick peace accord brought a mass of new allies into line with the NWA and fostered the unification match between Thesz, the National Wrestling Association kingpin, and Orville Brown, the Alliance's representative. However, before the bout was held, Brown was critically injured in a near-fatal car accident and forcibly retired. Thesz was then unanimously backed as champion of the Alliance.

By September 1950, the National Wrestling Alliance had 24 members from Buffalo to Honolulu, and the group was expected to expand even more. But strange things were happening in the wrestling world, threatening the union's stability, and many promoters were furious. The problems stemmed from the help Alliance members were providing nonmembers, particularly in Chicago, where Fred Kohler was in the fight of his life against the owner of the Rainbo Arena, Leonard Schwartz. The two men had previously worked together, but their friendship ended when Kohler severed his ties with the Rainbo after a personal dispute developed over the cost of the rent. Schwartz, a 42-year-old property appraiser and businessman, held the vital national ABC TV contract and decided to continue promoting wrestling without Kohler's workers.

Schwartz was relatively impotent on his own. He wasn't a booking agent, nor was he completely wise to all of wrestling's inner secrets. He needed a trustworthy partner to supply grapplers for his weekly program, and because of his invaluable ABC television exposure, there was plenty of interest. Initially looking to Jack Pfefer, he soon worked out a deal with Al Haft of Columbus and began importing the latter's superstars, Ruffy Silverstein, Bill Miller, Frankie Talaber, and a young Johnny Valentine.

Haft was a member of the NWA, and it was against the organization's credo to assist an enemy of the union. Kohler raised a fuss almost immediately and wanted to end all support of Schwartz and run him out of the business. His goal became nearly impossible when Schwartz came to terms with the Manhattan Booking Agency to promote its roster of stars. That meant the Rainbo Arena would be the Chicago home for Rocca, Carnera, and Stanlee. The agency had also recently experienced a restructuring, and Toots Mondt was aligned with Ray Fabiani and none other than Jim Londos, the eternally young Greek legend. Londos returned to the Windy City for Schwartz, and Kohler fumed.

Kohler's plight got worse when Mondt was approved for membership in the NWA in October 1950. Admitting Toots didn't make sense to him. For months, Mondt had blatantly scoffed at the Alliance, almost mocking its purpose and potential. And now members welcomed him as he assisted his enemy in a promotional war in Chicago. Unless Mondt and Haft both pulled their troops from the Rainbo, the NWA was proving to be nothing more than a hypocritical social club, and he wanted nothing to do with it. The withdrawal never came, and in November, Kohler resigned from the organization.

The political gamesmanship was rampant, and it didn't seem possible for the NWA to regulate so many egos and personalities. Mondt by himself was a whirlwind capable of derailing a whole host of things, but Alliance president Sam Muchnick was confident the organization would not only survive the inclusion of overbearing characters but thrive. Muchnick just needed to get everyone in line, and the curious actions of the Manhattan Booking Agency and others in Chicago was something that had to be solved amicably.

Mondt and Kohler were essential to the future of the NWA. If either one stood as an independent entity versus the Alliance and tried to break up the union, they were influential enough to crack the foundation by encouraging allies to abandon ship. That was the last thing Muchnick wanted. He set up a meeting in Chicago in early February 1951 and attempted to pacify the various parties. He successfully mediated a truce, and the NWA came away from the conference with both Mondt and Kohler satisfied with the new stipulations in place. In certain areas, they'd agree to disagree, but generally, they were connected in the spirit of camaraderie and making money. With the quarrel behind them, they anticipated a landslide of positivity in their own promotional regions and for the NWA as a whole.

Due to the lack of publicity, the Alliance was a lot less prominent in New York City than in other parts of the country. Wrestling champions were forbidden by the state athletic commission, making world titleholder Lou Thesz inconsequential. Moreover, New York fans were often bored by colorless performers, and Thesz's virtuous style was too straight for their taste. Enthusiasts wanted a mix of wrestling and comedy, and Thesz was much more of an old-school tactician than a pure entertainer. His methods were considered to be far too serious. Rocca, on the other hand, delivered a dazzling routine that played to their emotions perfectly.

The value of the NWA was realized by Mondt and then by Rudy Dusek during the first part of 1951. Between the two bookers, New York City and the surrounding area were completely locked into a tight monopoly, and Alliance membership meant their businesses were protected. Wrestlers were expected to toe the line and adhere to the guidelines or face not only local banishment but a widespread blacklisting. For promoters, there was plenty of confusion when it came to the National Wrestling Alliance. The rise of a central sanctioning body with international associations and a real purpose to bring order to pro wrestling was an exciting concept. Promoters wanted to be involved but were left shaking their heads when their membership applications were denied.

As a rule, the Alliance only enlisted certified booking agents, but once the various territories were cordoned off and represented, there was no room for outsiders. Mondt and Dusek covered the New York region, and promoters, without exception, had to receive their talent from them. Al Mayer challenged the NWA's law by applying for his own membership, but he was promptly rejected. The Johnstons were in a similar situation. Charley Johnston and his nephew Bill were at the helm of their wrestling operations and found they had no voice in the realm of the NWA. It didn't seem fair. Already diminished following the May 1950 death of Charley's brother Bill, the expert director of grappling for the family, the Johnstons were left to cope with the harsh new realities of life under the umbrella of the Alliance.

Without Bill's influence and on the opposite side of the NWA, the Johnstons recoiled from wrestling, and Madison Square Garden once again went dark. Nephew Bill, the son of James Johnston, the legendary former boxing promoter at the Garden, maintained a small grappling interest in Kingston. In the summer of 1951, he announced an initiative to oppose the Alliance and declared 45-year-old Abe Coleman the world heavyweight champion of his new combine. Charles J. Tiano, sports editor for the *Kingston Daily Freeman*, noted in his September 12, 1951, column that Johnston planned to expand throughout the United States and also book his "50 leading grapplers" to international locations.

In theory, the unification of alienated promoters left out of the NWA was a smart move. The central problem was that the Alliance controlled all of the big-name box office talent. Johnston's troupe of Coleman, Lenny Montana, Ivan Gorky, and Lord Spears was an entertaining mix for one or two shows, but the rotation of wrestlers from outside areas was necessary to maintain a thriving promotion. If Johnston was actively contesting the power of the Alliance, he was going to receive zero help from Mondt and Dusek, regardless of their history together. It didn't take him long to realize there was no way to compete, and his idea for an expansive syndicate to challenge the NWA crumbled.

Other than a disappointing Yankee Stadium event, which

drew only 11,300 spectators in July 1950, big-time wrestling remained out of New York City until January 14, 1952, when the Garden was reopened for a special benefit program for flood victims in Italy, and Charley Johnston was back in his prominent role as promoter. The obstructions that had hindered cooperation were smoothed over, as Mondt desperately wanted back into the Garden. A crowd of about 9,000 attended the show headlined by Rocca and Carnera, while NWA champion Thesz beat Bobby Managoff in the semifinal.

The situation in New York appeared to be on track, but backstage, in secret, things were moving fast and furious. Days after the Garden program, Mondt and his partners sold the Manhattan Booking Agency to 36-year-old Pedro Martinez for $100,000. The deal called for all of Mondt's contracts to be transferred to the Rochester-based promoter, including the rights to Rocca, and Martinez immediately became the leading booking agent in the East. Since his time was going to be at a premium, Martinez hired Mondt to manage his agency, basically to fulfill many of the same duties he had performed previously. Mondt was even sold a minority percentage of the company. Although Martinez was in charge, he planned on holding Toots accountable for the success or failure of the business.

Mondt's gambling itch was still, and would remain, a problem. That alone was a concern when it came to leaving him unsupervised to operate the daily responsibilities of any company. Martinez was apparently convinced that Mondt had his head on straight and returned to his Upstate New York life expecting to make incredible riches from his investment.

Unfortunately, Martinez bet on the wrong man, and Mondt cost him a fortune. Toots played fast and loose with nearly every cent that touched his hands and was lackadaisical in his matchmaking, hurting a number of important towns on his circuit. As a result, Martinez sold 50 percent of his stock six months into the endeavor and awaited better news going into the winter. Their financial health was riding on the numbers at the Garden. In November 1952, their outfit drew an impressive audience of 18,000 and followed up with 11,000 in January 1953, but Martinez finally realized it was a losing proposition. He was finished with his New York City commitment and rid himself of his remaining shares on January 10, 1953. The buyer: Toots Mondt.

Jess McMahon, the old maestro, celebrated his 50th anniversary in promotions during the early part of the 1950s. He completed a stint at the Sunnyside Garden in Queens and maintained solid ties to clubs in Connecticut and Pennsylvania. In December 1952, his son Vincent was positioned in Washington, DC, to make his first big move into pro wrestling. For a reported $60,000, he bought the grappling rights to the city from Gabe Menendez, including a sublease to Turner's Arena. McMahon—along with his silent partners, Nat Proctor, Philip Gray, and Charles O'Connell—was fully intent on continuing the weekly wrestling shows and wanted to keep the arena filled with as many events as possible, athletic or otherwise.

The character of McMahon's business was evident from day one, and, like his father, he was known for his honesty and integrity. He inaugurated his promotion on January 7, 1953, and booked his talent from several sources, but mainly Mondt in New York. His cast of characters delivered all the various styles, from the overcooked heel to the collegiate hero. The Zebra Kid, Golden Terror, and Swedish Angel were right on the mark when it came to gimmicks, whereas clean-cut Rocca and Verne Gagne were definitely the most popular. McMahon featured women grapplers from the outfit of Billy Wolfe, brought in imitation performers such as Gorgeous George Grant and the Nature Boy, and staged wrestle royals and tournaments to provide enough diversity to keep patrons returning.

Gagne, to McMahon, represented a crop of important Chicago TV stars who had become the toast of the nation because of their prominent appearances each Saturday night on the DuMont Network. The faction was made up of such hotshot luminaries as Hans Schmidt, Pat O'Connor, Ray Gunkel, Sonny Myers, Bob Orton, and Art Nielsen, and promoters all over North America coveted members of the troupe. Later in 1953, Mondt realized their importance and pleaded with Fred Kohler for help to fulfill the needs of his arenas on a more regular basis. Washington, DC, was covered in the agreement, and McMahon benefited from the influx of celebrity talent funneled from Chicago through Mondt's agency.

During 1952–53, there were many notable happenings in wrestling. In Los Angeles, Johnny Doyle brokered the sport's first $100,000 gate, on May 21, 1952, for a show headlined by Lou Thesz and Michele Leone. Leone, incidentally, was remembered by many eastern fans for his villainous style, but out in California, he had adopted an entirely new persona—the Baron, an Italian nobleman. Very quickly, he transitioned from a background player to one of the biggest draws in the business, capable of selling out the 10,000-plus-seat Olympic Auditorium. He was an extraordinary showman, and Doyle maximized his potential. Audiences loved every minute of it.

The buildup lured 25,256 to Gilmore Field in Hollywood, and the gate tallied $103,277, outdrawing Londos-Lewis from 1934 by $7,000. Thesz beat Leone to unify their two versions of the heavyweight crown and strengthened his claim to the undisputed world championship.

No champion in wrestling history did more to reinforce the status and reputation of their title than Thesz did as the NWA world champion. Since 1949, he had appeared everywhere from Madison Square Garden to country fairs in the middle of nowhere, and he had met the best in the business night after night. He elevated the credentials of the National Wrestling Alliance by his hard work and travel, and his integrity as champion was unmatched. He enjoyed wearing the belt and had the dignity and awareness not to squander his special position. Without a credible heavyweight king, the NWA would certainly have failed. Thesz was the kind of wrestler who could meet all challenges and was trusted enough to turn down potential offers to double-cross the Alliance. In the ring, no one was getting the better of him. He was that good.

Roy Dunn and his backers figured differently. Nearly six years older than Thesz, Dunn had been an Olympian in 1936 and won a National AAU Championship. During the 1940s, he had claimed a regionalized version of the National Wrestling Alliance title based out of Wichita, and his status as one of the truly great independent wrestlers never diminished. That was the primary reason why outsiders of the NWA sought him as a practical alternative to Thesz. They knew that with his outstanding credentials, he could criticize Thesz as champion and potentially beat him in a straight match should it ever occur.

In early 1953, Dunn's services were called upon by Dallas promoter Ed McLemore, during a budding promotional war spanning most of East and Central Texas. The feud stemmed from a disagreement over the compensation of wrestlers for TV appearances, and McLemore, who produced a widely distributed program from the Sportatorium, was accused of failing to pay grapplers what they were owed. A conflict was sparked with his former allies, led by Morris Sigel of Houston, and turned all Alliance resources against McLemore's Dallas outfit.

McLemore immediately went on the offensive and tried to hurt Thesz's box office value. He brought in Dunn to castigate the titleholder, and various challenges were issued but ignored. Despite his fine resilience against long odds, particularly the fact that he was unable to promote any of the popular NWA talent, McLemore's effort to sway public opinion against the organization was ineffective. Generally, little favorable to wrestling's reputation was accomplished. That was made clear when McLemore's home arena was burned to the ground in an arson attack in May 1953. Many felt the incident was directly tied to the promotional conflict, but no proof ever turned up.

The problems in Dallas were exceptional because of the arson, but the ugliness surrounding the various promoters and their out-of-control egos was standard fare across the NWA. Billy Wolfe, in charge of women's wrestling, was notorious for his improprieties, including relationships with various members of his troupe even though he was married to world champion Mildred Burke. By 1953, the once happy couple had completely turned on each other, and Wolfe was using his NWA membership to hinder match opportunities for Burke. Desperate to clear things up, Burke negotiated a deal that would essentially retire Wolfe from the business for five years—and give her all rights to the booking franchise. Burke came up with $30,000, paid him off, and expected to recoup the money and more on the back side. She was, after all, the new head of the entire women's grappling domain.

But Wolfe represented the shadier side of the NWA, and even though he took her money, he decided to renege on the arrangement. He quickly jumped back into the wrestling world, managing June Byers, Nell Stewart, and other well-known attractions. Using his expansive contacts throughout the Alliance, he regained scores of premier booking opportunities that would otherwise have gone to Burke's syndicate. It was a terrible turn of events for the 38-year-old champion from Kansas City. Burke had reigned supreme since 1937, and her hard work had demonstrated that women's wrestling wasn't just a colorful sideshow but an entertainingly competitive spectacle. Her toughness was evident, as was her knowledge of wrestling, and when she was on the mat, fans knew which competitor was the champion.

After all she had done for the members of the NWA, boosting ticket sales and contributing to the personal wealth of all, Burke was now shunned. Most promoters were fully prepared to continue working with Wolfe and to accept Burke's blacklisting without question. But Burke fought back. She protested to the NWA leadership, sent letters to people she thought were friends, and yearned for an official resolution reaffirming her place as champion and booker for the women's wrestling tribe. At the annual convention in 1953, the Alliance did the opposite by refusing to get involved. A year later, rival champion Byers beat her in a controversial bout in Atlanta, and Burke's status as titleholder was completely tainted—just as Wolfe had hoped.

Burke went on to pioneer women's grappling in Japan and had already cemented her legendary status, but the way she had been schemed out of the picture by her ex-husband was appalling to observers. It was an example of the NWA boys' club and how they either directly backed a fellow member or sidestepped contentious issues to protect one of their own.

Fast becoming the most talked about wrestler on the circuit next to Thesz, Verne Gagne was a national superstar by 1953, and his promoter, Fred Kohler of Chicago, wanted to reward him with a special "sectional" championship known as the United States heavyweight title. The honor would be defended on Kohler's Saturday night DuMont telecast, and it was supposed to benefit the promoters in cities where Gagne appeared as champion. Thesz disagreed. He saw it as a deliberate maneuver by an NWA member to distort the championship hierarchy, leaving many fans to mistakenly suppose Gagne was the top heavyweight. Thesz complained to Muchnick, and shortly thereafter, Kohler was told to withdraw Gagne's recognition.

Kohler didn't budge. To him, Gagne was the rightful U.S. champion, and fans were responding positively to the recognition. He told Muchnick that his actions weren't prompted by any ill will toward Thesz and he personally had done more to promote Thesz as the undisputed world champion than any other member. Nonetheless, the grievance continued until November, when a special NWA meeting was held in Chicago. There, Kohler accepted a compromise and renamed Gagne's championship the "U.S. television title."

But there was an even bigger picture that has, through history, been overlooked. Thesz and Gagne were the top two wrestlers in the country for most of the 1950s. They were scientifically skilled heroes and immensely likable. Both were able to mix it up in the ring and even work as a heel if the situation called for it. The bankability of a match or series of matches between the two idols would have shattered the all-time gate record, especially if Gagne had won the world title and had a temporary reign. The promotion across television and excitement would have been immense. It would have rivaled Frank Gotch–George Hackenschmidt from 1908 and Jim Londos–Ed "Strangler" Lewis from 1934, two of the most important matches in history.

Thesz and Gagne had wrestled before and the box office numbers were decent, but in 1953–54, the conditions were unparalleled for a U.S. TV champion versus world champion title bout.

It didn't happen because Thesz (and maybe Muchnick) disliked Kohler and Gagne since Gagne was billed as a titleholder, plus the fact that Gagne was more popular than Thesz in certain cities. Jealousy may be too strong of a word, but there was bitterness that was far more personal than the average rivalry. It was also known that a secret ballot was taken by NWA members to find out who would succeed Thesz if necessary. Gagne won hands down. He was clearly on Thesz's tail for the NWA championship and had the boardroom support, but Thesz would make sure, at least as far as he was concerned, that Gagne would never succeed him. Gagne didn't.

The failure of promoters to produce a Thesz-Gagne match and a temporary title switch to capitalize on the excitement would be somewhat akin to WCW never pulling the trigger on a Bill Goldberg–Hollywood Hogan bout in 1998. All the fans wanted it and it would have set new records, but it never happened.

Gagne's career didn't falter because of the situation. He proved a better draw than Thesz at Madison Square Garden, headlining numerous programs between 1953 and '54, and also appeared for McMahon in Washington, DC. His stock skyrocketed, and it didn't matter if he was facing a fellow hero like Antonino Rocca or battling notorious heels Killer Kowalski and Hans Schmidt, he was a premier attraction. Unfortunately, the window for the electrifying matchup against Thesz closed as wrestling's popularity began to decline. Plus, the U.S. government was about to open a relentless investigation into the NWA's crooked practices. Maybe, for him, it wasn't a good time to be champ and representing the so-called virtues of the Alliance after all.

"Toots" Mondt was a colorful character in and out of the ring, and his imaginative vision for pro wrestling helped foster a new era of showmanship and creativity. (NOTRE DAME) ▲

In the 1930s, "The Golden Greek" Jim Londos was wrestling's biggest hero and box office sensation. The business thrived with Londos on the bill. (NOTRE DAME) ◄

Promotional mastermind, Jack Curley (far left) works out the details for an upcoming show as New York State Athletic Commission chairman William Muldoon (seated, middle) and others look on. (NOTRE DAME) ▲

Jack Pfefer (seated, middle) was a shrewd promoter and booking agent during a career lasting 40 years, and he was frequently embroiled in controversy. (NOTRE DAME) ▾

"Nature Boy" Buddy Rogers (left) and promoter Tom Packs enjoyed great success in the latter's St. Louis territory in the late 1940s. (NOTRE DAME) ▾

Kola Kwariani, a hulking wrestler from Eastern Europe, had a long career as a scout and booking agent and was a principal figure in the New York promotional wars of the 1950s. (NOTRE DAME) ▴

that my father and the Striblings had to sit on the steps in an aisle to make a bout. My father sat behind me with Pa Stribling, who managed Young Stribling, sitting next to me.

"Not many people know that Jack Dempsey and Gene Tunney were booked to fight in New York, which turned it down because Harry Wills, a Negro, said that Dempsey was ducking him. That's why the fight went to Philadelphia instead. Dempsey was not ducking Wills. Jack Sharkey had no trouble with Wills before winning on a foul."

These were some of the memories that McMahon can easily recall when talking about promotions and Madison Square Garden. He's had pleasant memories and sad ones, like the time last January when McMahon staged the last ring show in the old Garden, which featured Sammartino against Taro Tanaka.

"I was just about the last person in the place," he remarked. "All the front doors were locked and I had to leave by way of the employee's entrance. I just sat around thinking back. It felt eerie, thinking about the things that I saw there in the 42 years since my dad opened it."

Jess McMahon wasn't one of the Damon Runyon type characters that made up the fight game then. First of all, he was a graduate of Manhattan College, and how many guys along Jacobs Beach could make that distinction? Then Jess ran a

McMahon feared that the fans would miss the old Garden. "Fans don't like to change their routine."

McMahon practically grew up in the Garden on 49th St. His father was a successful promoter there years ago.

neat and proper office. His working hours were strictly from 9 to 5 and who ever heard of that among the cigar smoking, card playing characters who usually conducted their business in the back rooms of the many saloons along the way? McMahon himself didn't smoke and purposely kept proper hours in order to maintain a close family life in Far Rockaway.

In a tribute to his memory, The Garden moguls gave Vince the distinction of putting on the first ring show in the new Garden. McMahon came right back with Sammartino in the main event against Bull Ramos, a 325-pound Apache Indian. It was Sammartino's 55th main event appearance in five years in the Garden, and no athlete in any sport could come close to approaching such a milestone.

"He is the strongest man in the world," exclaimed McMahon. He can do a pushup with two wrestlers on his back. Most people don't seem to know it but Bruno outdid Paul Anderson, the weight-lifting champion, by 90 pounds in a tournament. Bruno began lifting weights in a Pittsburgh YMCA to build himself up after virtually starving during World War II when the Germans occupied his little town in northern Italy."

Although his office is located in Washington, D.C., McMahon's operations extend far beyond the eastern seaboard. He recently concluded a contract with Japanese promoters for a two-week tour by

53

A leading sports promoter, Jess McMahon paved the way for his son Vincent James and grandson Vincent Kennedy to thrive in professional wrestling. (NOTRE DAME)

Performing a dancer-type gimmick, Ricki Starr was actually a talented wrestler, having grappled as an amateur in his youth. Exceedingly popular, he was one of the biggest showmen of the 1950s and '60s. (NOTRE DAME) ▾

Dallas promoter Ed McLemore presents a women's championship belt to The Fabulous Moolah. Moolah dominated the women's wrestling landscape for several decades. (NOTRE DAME) ▴

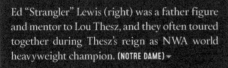

Ed "Strangler" Lewis (right) was a father figure and mentor to Lou Thesz, and they often toured together during Thesz's reign as NWA world heavyweight champion. (NOTRE DAME) ▾

Antonino "Argentina" Rocca was a high-flying tumbler and main-event attraction for years, not only in the northeast, but also across the wrestling spectrum. Few grapplers in history commanded audiences like Rocca. (NOTRE DAME) ▴

An Inside Look At Promoter Vince McMahon

Capitol Spells Capital For
"MR. WRESTLING"

By James L. Harte

An interviewer, sandwiching questions between constant telephone interruptions, which are taken two at a time with an instrument cradled on each shoulder (the twain seem always to ring simultaneously), watches askance.

His ears are attuned to the voice of its receiver, while the single central mouth of the busy head twists from one mouthpiece to the other, adeptly carrying on two simultaneous conversations. One would not be amazed to see the two hands of the fellow each making separate notes of the talks from its side of the head in like simultaneous action.

They do not. The hands are usually engaged in a third endeavor: digging through files for a bit of information for the interviewer; opening a batch of mail; initialing approval of an advertising poster; auditing a box-office report; signing checks.

The double-barrelled phone calls have been answered. The interviewer has time to blurt a query. The phones sound off again. With calls from every corner of the country, and overseas. And this is but a small part of the hectic workday that is every day, with time out on Sunday only for church, for Vincent McMahon, "Mr. Wrestling"* to all the professional practitioners of the sport today. Vince is wrestling's top promoter-matchmaker, and his empire extends not only into most major American cities but into Puerto Rico, Venezuela, Japan, Australia, and elsewhere.

On meeting him, no one would

*A title inherited from his erstwhile partner, Toots Mondt.

25

Most people don't realize it, but Buddy Rogers (right, seated) was also an astute backstage manipulator and businessman. Here he signs a contract to wrestle in Tampa for promoters Eddie Graham (standing) and Cowboy Luttrell. (NOTRE DAME) ▼

Unquestionably one of the biggest draws in wrestling history, Buddy Rogers was an exceptional performer, hated and beloved by audiences at the same time. (NOTRE DAME) ▲

"High Chief" Peter Maivia, the grandfather of Dwayne "The Rock" Johnson, was a successful grappler all over the world, particularly in the realm of Vincent J. McMahon. (GEORGE NAPOLITANO) ▼

Bruno Sammartino (left) was the predominant wrestler in McMahon's WWWF in the 1960s and '70s, and without his star power, the organization would never have succeeded. Larry Zbyszko (right), also from Pittsburgh, was mentored by Sammartino. (GEORGE NAPOLITANO) ▲

Andre the Giant was a one-of-a-kind legend and traveled the globe under the management of Vincent J. McMahon beginning in the 1970s. (GEORGE NAPOLITANO)

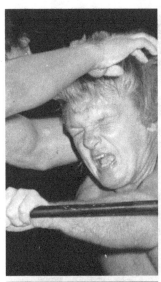

One of pro wrestling's great icons, Bobo Brazil was a fixture in the northeastern territory and was often billed as the WWWF U.S. champion. (PETE LEDERBERG) ▼

An entertaining tough guy, Johnny Valentine (right) was a four-time co-holder of the U.S. tag team championship in the northeast. (PETE LEDERBERG) ▲

Pedro Morales held the WWWF heavyweight championship from 1971–73, and was one of the most popular heroes in organization history. (PETE LEDERBERG) ▲

Texan Stan Hansen was credited with breaking the neck of Bruno Sammartino in 1976, setting up a high-profile match at Shea Stadium, which Bruno won by countout. (PETE LEDERBERG) ▼

A powerful heel, "Superstar" Billy Graham (right) was a tremendous box office draw for Capitol Wrestling and reigned as WWWF champion in 1977–78. Young Vincent K. McMahon is holding the microphone. (GEORGE NAPOLITANO) ▲

Bob Backlund, the all-American wrestling hero, was WWF heavyweight king for most of 1978–83. (PETE LEDERBERG) ▲

(8)
NEW YORK
IN A TOEHOLD

Early in his tenure as promoter at Turner's Arena in Washington, DC, Vincent McMahon was confronted by a problem he really didn't want to deal with: booking boxing matches. He actively shopped the position around, but the general sense was that live boxing at the arena was overshadowed by the more popular televised wrestling contests and that the enterprise was worthless. McMahon disagreed and decided to take on the job himself. In February 1953, with local featherweight Gene Smith as his principal headliner, he doubled up his promotional responsibilities and launched boxing from the arena.

McMahon was levelheaded in his approach and had minimal expectations. He featured the likes of Holly Mims, Tommy Thompson, Filberto Osario, and a young Floyd Patterson and brought in Jimmy Cooper to challenge Smith. The two had fought several years earlier, a bout Smith had won, and on June 2, Cooper gained a bit of revenge with a knockout victory in the sixth round. Their fierce battle gained national attention, and

McMahon saw the financial possibilities of an outdoor rematch later in the summer.

On July 21, 1953, before an estimated 7,500 spectators at Griffith Stadium, Smith beat Cooper by TKO, and the success of the show propelled McMahon into a more prestigious class of sports entrepreneurs. He soon worked with Ray Arcel, staging boxing matches from Turner's Arena on the ABC network, and offered a $25,000 guarantee for world featherweight champion Sandy Saddler to face Smith in a championship bout. McMahon's indomitable spirit shined bright as he challenged the five nights a week boxing television monopoly and demonstrated that arena shows could still be profitable in DC.

Heading into the winter of 1953, a firestorm unrelated to sports tarnished the reputation of Turner's Arena and forced McMahon to appear before a U.S. Senate subcommittee. The matter related to underage drinking and McMahon's Saturday night dance events. In fact, the entire neighborhood surrounding the arena was pinpointed as a haven for illegal liquor sales to minors. It was presumed that kids were stopping at area bars, buying whisky and beer, and consuming the beverages at the dance. McMahon forbid liquor at the arena and for a time, when not working with police, hired his own special officers to weed out violators. Over the course of a year, 138 individuals were arrested at Turner's for drunkenness, disorderly conduct, and public consumption.

McMahon was completely on board with any strategy to suppress juvenile delinquency at his facility, but other than hiring more security, there was little he could do. Teenagers weren't getting the liquor at his establishment because soda was all they sold. Nearby taverns apparently needed tighter regulations, but their devious practices were not his responsibility. McMahon went about his business, refocusing on his promotions.

Across the sporting landscape, people were noticing McMahon's exploits, and it wasn't difficult to comprehend that he was the son of the famous Jess McMahon. His father remained a staunch supporter and advisor, and when he needed counsels, there was nobody better to discuss business with. In November

1954, Jess went to Wilkes-Barre, Pennsylvania, to observe a wrestling program and became ill. His condition was diagnosed as a cerebral hemorrhage, and the 72-year-old died a few days later, on November 21. He was buried at St. Raymond's Cemetery in the Bronx.

The loss of the elder McMahon was a jolt felt across professional wrestling, as many members of the National Wrestling Alliance had worked with him to some degree. The NWA was still growing and nearing 40 members in total. The organization had branched out to include nearly every major promoter in the business, and its roster was more than impressive. Names such as Eddie Quinn in Montreal, Harry Light in Detroit, Joe Malcewicz in San Francisco, Paul Jones in Atlanta, Stu Hart in Calgary, and Mike London in Albuquerque gave the NWA extensive reach, and it seemed no corner of the wrestling world was devoid of Alliance influence.

Al Karasick in Honolulu, and his connections to Japan, added to the international flavor, as did Salvador Lutteroth of Mexico City. The open lines of communication between promoters made it relatively easy for wrestlers to venture from territory to territory, and when a member needed new faces to appease his local audience, all he had to do was contact a neighbor and make a swap. Alliance affiliation guaranteed appearances by the board-sanctioned titleholders, made up of the world heavyweight and world junior heavyweight champions. The world light heavyweight title was also officially sanctioned by the NWA, but it was mostly confined to territories that regularly featured non-heavyweight competitors.

Superstars Antonino Rocca, Primo Carnera, Verne Gagne, and the contingent of women's grapplers were available to Alliance promoters, but they had to be specifically booked through their designated administrator. The same went for the troupe of little people on the wrestling circuit. Little Beaver, Sky Low Low, and other popular performers were managed through the Detroit office by Bert Rubi and Jack Britton and appeared throughout North America. Lou Thesz, as the NWA world heavyweight champion, was booked directly through NWA president Sam Muchnick, who arranged the champ's schedule months in advance. Larger territories saw Thesz for longer periods of time, but mostly he made one to three appearances before shuttling to the next region.

The management of the various champions was one of the prized attributes of the NWA. From day one, members set out to consolidate the innumerable claims and ultimately sponsor a single titleholder in each division. While it took a few years, the Alliance did eliminate recognized heavyweight claims in Boston, Columbus, and Los Angeles and found a way to coexist with the Montreal championship. The widespread acceptance of the NWA brand and its titleholders was a gradual movement. Alliance rules and regulations were touted by members in their specific territories, and the NWA logo appeared on arena programs. Fans developed a strong association with the Alliance, recognizing its prominence and dedication to providing top-quality wrestling. To them, the NWA meant excellence.

But behind the scenes, there were a number of disgruntled individuals, and to them, the NWA meant a whole host of adjectives, none equating excellence.

Portrayed as a cohesive union of booking agents working to better pro wrestling, the NWA was an exclusive club with tremendous flaws. Its personnel crafted and guarded their power, keeping it at membership level, leaving wrestlers and affiliate promoters without a voice. The personal grievances of members against anyone, from a referee to a box office attraction, had the potential to develop into an Alliance-wide blacklisting, and everyone involved with the organization was aware of the ramifications of being an agitator. However, it was known that wrestlers who were able to draw money were given a pass. But journeymen and small-time promoters were cut little slack, and if they stepped out of line, their careers were in danger.

The NWA bylaws were universal, but other than that, members handled their businesses as they saw fit. They implemented policies, championships for their territories, and curtailed radicals by invoking their own system of discipline. Roy Welch and Nick Gulas, operators of a large territory extending from Tennessee to

Kentucky, Alabama, and Mississippi, were notorious for sending instigators on "gasoline runs," which took the wrestler upwards of 600 miles for a job paying less than $20. They purposely limited the pay of their athletes and then offered loans to make the wrestler beholden to them. These tactics were contentious at best, but for the grapplers on the circuit, it was the rule of law.

Members elsewhere were just as controlling. They were dead serious about the lines on the map delineating their territories, and their land was their land—no one had a right to interfere. That meant any other promoters, affiliated or independent, were absolutely forbidden from staging a program in their region. Plus, members acknowledged and respected their neighbors' territories. On some occasions, there was confusion about the ownership of specific towns, and an NWA mediation party had to be called in to intercede. But generally, the boundaries were pretty well established.

All over the country, veteran promoters were squeezed out of business by the member in charge of the territory in which their city belonged. It didn't matter if they had promoted there for two weeks or 20 years; they were at the mercy of the NWA affiliate in charge. In many cases, the member wanted to put his own man in the town to promote or just didn't feel it was necessary to supply the local operator with sufficient talent to present shows. The promoter had little recourse, and many times, they tried to use an outside booking office to get wrestlers. They were always denied and referred back to the office in charge of the city. It was a runaround that stripped individuals of their livelihood and was both frustrating and cruel.

Two years earlier, in 1952, an independent promoter in Iowa City, Iowa, had done the impossible by booking Antonino Rocca for a big show he had lined up. The authorization for Joe "Toots" Mondt to send one of wrestling's biggest attractions to a nonaffiliate either marked a decided change in NWA policy or was a significant blunder on Mondt's part. Already lambasted for his defective accounting, Mondt was scolded by the Alliance, and Pinkie George, who ran the Iowa territory, made a number of angry phone calls to organization leaders. George was finally able to persuade Rocca to run out on his date for the nonmember.

Ever since regaining control of the New York booking office from Pedro Martinez, Mondt had been slowly sinking the most profitable territory in the Alliance. His pride and joy, Madison Square Garden, was revitalized behind Chicago TV performers like Verne Gagne, Killer Kowalski, and Pat O'Connor and producing bundles of cash. For that reason, Chicago booker Fred Kohler wanted some oversight of Mondt's money management and sent his top aide, 29-year-old Jim Barnett, to New York to supervise. Mondt, nearing 60, didn't mind. He was much too busy with his extracurricular activities to care who was wandering around backstage. But his unreliability was well known, and Martinez was the latest unfortunate victim of Mondt's lackadaisical approach to money. Owed over $19,000, Martinez confronted Toots in the Garden dressing room in February 1954 and ended up socking Mondt for his indiscretions.

Mondt's work as a booking agent had also deteriorated, and that had usually been his saving grace. His talent roster didn't have the depth of previous years, and the majority of stars he was banking on were from Chicago. That left the rest of his territory, including a number of big Northeastern cities, hurting for an improvement in the class of wrestlers. Ray Fabiani of Philadelphia suffered as much as anyone else in 1953–54, despite being an old-time partner of Mondt, and he lost about $15,000 during the depreciation of the region. Weak attendance, as a result of the dismal offerings, forced him to abandon the Philadelphia Arena for a smaller venue because he was unable to guarantee the rent every month.

Fabiani knew promoters across Pennsylvania in the Pittsburgh area, many of whom were getting wrestlers from booker Al Haft, were having success, and Mondt was the only reason he wasn't drawing a profit. Ed Contos in Baltimore was in the same boat. Advertisers on his weekly television program were threatening to walk if he didn't improve the quality of performers on the telecast, and in his desperation, he pleaded with the Maryland State Athletic

Commission to intercede. Commissioner J. Marshall Boone stepped in and tried in vain to get in contact with Toots to work matters out. He then contacted Sam Muchnick and the NWA. Muchnick was receptive, but because of the organization's policy to protect members, he informed Mondt of the complaints and temporarily stonewalled the commission.

In April 1954, Mondt felt there was no other option but to declare bankruptcy. The decay of his territory, including Washington, DC, and parts of both Virginia and New Jersey, was too far along to mend. The Manhattan Booking Agency went under, but, as always, Mondt was personally untouchable and remained somewhat afloat. But athletic commissioners in Maryland and Pennsylvania saw Mondt's bankruptcy as an opportunity to start anew. They announced Baltimore and Philadelphia were "open cities," meaning that promoters were free to obtain talent from whatever booking agency they desired. Mondt was out of the picture, regardless of what he or the NWA claimed.

Later in the year, both Fabiani and Contos applied for membership in the Alliance and were rejected. From the perspective of the NWA, Philadelphia and Baltimore were still valuable towns. For that reason, they were going to be covered by existing members, whether it be Haft out of Columbus, Rudy Dusek of New York, or Jim Crockett in the Mid-Atlantic region. Also, abiding by NWA rules, neither Fabiani nor Contos were booking agents, negating any possible position in the organization.

The Mondt situation publicly shed light on the elite nature of the National Wrestling Alliance. Its recognition of exclusive territories and the demands put on local promoters was clearly unlawful. In a free-trade environment, Fabiani and Contos would have been able to obtain grapplers from any booker in the world, without having to fight to do so. The existing environment skewed the entire marketplace toward NWA members, and by the middle of 1954, outsiders were finally beginning to stand up and vocalize their grievances. The floodgates were open.

Surprisingly, Johnny Doyle was a major critic. For years considered a luminary of the NWA based out of Hollywood, Doyle had worked steadily to advance the cause of the Alliance. In January 1954, he unceremoniously sold his share of the Southern California monopoly and initially expected to take a job in New York City alongside Mondt. The opportunity evaporated when Mondt imploded the territory, and Doyle found himself unemployed. He returned to wrestling as an independent operator in Los Angeles against his former partners and experienced the tyrannical power of the NWA firsthand. Many of the grapplers Doyle used to book, and had remained friendly with, were intimidated to ensure they wouldn't appear for him, and although he was able to gain TV outlets, his endeavors were fading fast.

Doyle joined a growing list of individuals who spoke to antitrust investigators of the U.S. Department of Justice in 1955. He was in a unique position to divulge insider secrets and explain the operating procedures of the NWA. Many promoters formerly affiliated to the Alliance were open witnesses, but the closer the inquiry got to active members, the less candid the interviews became. Usually, comments were directed away from the Alliance or pointed toward Doyle as a significant instigator. The job of narrowing the scope of the investigation to certain particulars, then finding irrefutable evidence and witnesses, was a demanding chore for government officials.

That task was only made harder by the surreptitiousness of pro wrestling. While on the hot seat before an inquisitor, there would be pressure to speak bluntly about wrestling's underbelly. But the natural persuasion of a wrestler or promoter was to conceal information and evade the potentially damaging questions of authorities. Several of the people interrogated dodged sticky subject matter when they could have provided a breakthrough. For instance, Jack Pfefer, who infamously broke the unwritten rules of wrestling in the 1930s when he gave trade secrets to a newspaper writer, did just the opposite during the NWA investigation.

Of everyone involved with the Alliance, Muchnick believed in the union the most. Knowing that some semblance of prosecution lay ahead, he had two sincere concerns, not only for the NWA but for wrestling as a whole. First, he was worried the government would push for a complete and total dissolution of the organization. He wanted to see the Alliance continue and pushed for its survival in communications with investigators. Second, he figured a prolonged court case could damage the industry by confirming wrestling's inauthenticity. If people were, in a public proclamation, exposed to the truth of grappling being scripted and matches being faked, there was no telling if the audience would ever support the business again. It could be a deathblow.

Meanwhile, the popularity of wrestling began to wane, even without a climactic announcement or event. In fact, the downturn was probably spawned by a half-dozen or more reasons. Overexposure was definitely a problem. The scores of television shows in each territory, produced both locally and nationally, were tiring the audience. The excitement of grappling and its vast lineup of colorful superstars were fashionable during television's expansion, but the fad was wearing off. Fans had seen Gorgeous George, Verne Gagne, and Antonino Rocca, and the song was pretty much the same every match. Promoters needed something fresh to rekindle attendance.

The leaders of the Alliance figured it was time to revert to a proven booking formula, and that's what they attempted in 1955, when they pushed a football hero to the heavyweight championship. Memories of Wayne Munn and Gus Sonnenberg were dredged up when 30-year-old Leo Nomellini, a star of the National Football League's San Francisco 49ers, took a controversial victory over Lou Thesz, the longtime NWA champion. Their championship match occurred on March 22, 1955, in San Francisco and ended with Thesz being disqualified for kicking the challenger from the ring during the third fall. The finish was perfectly arranged, allowing both wrestlers to leave the arena claiming the title. In turn, Muchnick and his allies believed they'd benefit from having two champions on the circuit, building toward a high-profile rematch.

Nomellini's victory received national attention, and stories were printed in major newspapers from coast to coast. Promoters were optimistic, but the idea faltered from the beginning. Fans were only moderately interested in seeing Nomellini as champion, and the anticipated windfall was never realized. In all, Thesz and Nomellini did good business in San Francisco, but the feud stumbled elsewhere, and the entire angle was scrapped in St. Louis on July 15, when Thesz reunited the two claims.

Later in 1955, Vincent McMahon announced a future appearance by Thesz in Washington, DC, and launched a multi-week elimination tournament to locate the worthiest opponent. Yukon Eric, the Great Kato, and Antonino Rocca were in the running, but despite all the buildup, Thesz didn't enter the District even though he wrestled in Baltimore and New York City in October and November. The snub didn't make much sense, and matters became even more confusing when McMahon found out Ray Fabiani was expanding his Philadelphia promotion into DC—and advertising Thesz as one of the wrestlers he was going to feature.

If that occurred, McMahon would face considerable problems. He'd been led by the NWA to believe he was an affiliate in good standing and had spent considerably building things up for a Thesz title defense at his arena. These difficulties couldn't have come at a worse time. McMahon was negotiating to produce a live wrestling program from Turner's for the first time in his career. The televised offering would be presented on the District's DuMont affiliate, WTTG, and feature an hour of grappling a week, from 10 to 11 p.m. every Thursday night. To satisfy TV executives, who didn't like to stage programming from venues with "personal names," McMahon revealed he was renaming Turner's Arena the Capitol Arena on December 24, 1955. Incidentally, his father, Jess, promoted a different Capitol Arena during the 1940s: his venture was in Albany, New York.

Owing to the worries of honchos at DuMont, McMahon had to prove the value of his TV endeavor before he landed a contract. He was forced to invest his own money for the first two weeks of production, which began on January 5, 1956, and successfully demonstrated his professionalism, earning a long-term deal. The next evening, at the Uline Arena, Fabiani debuted his new promotion. With their rivalry in full swing, the unresolved question of whom the NWA was backing needed to be resolved. Muchnick pulled the strings from St. Louis, and Thesz was quickly booked into Washington for McMahon on January 12. It was a much-needed affirmation of support from the Alliance and strengthened his resolve in the war against Fabiani.

With decades in the trenches, Fabiani was a hardened battler and could never be counted out. He pulled a fast one by announcing that former heavyweight boxing champion Joe Louis had been signed to a contract to wrestle for him, and the 41-year-old ex-fighter was going to debut at the Uline in Washington. The story was huge news. Louis, weighing over 240 pounds, was considered out of shape and his health was in doubt. More importantly, he was not a wrestler. He worked out with "Nature Boy" Buddy Rogers, but his fists were undoubtedly his biggest assets. The DC Boxing Commission warned Louis and Fabiani that the Brown Bomber had to wrestle in his local appearance—not box. However, Louis resorted to a right to "Rocky" Don Lee's jaw in his debut performance in March 1956.

Talent entered the Washington wrestling war from two specific locations, New York and Columbus. McMahon was the recipient of workers from the former, importing athletes from the talent pool of Toots Mondt. After his Manhattan Booking Agency was pinned by bankruptcy in 1954, Mondt opened up a new company known as Manhattan Wrestling Enterprises and kept a stranglehold on as many clubs as would tolerate his antics. His NWA membership remained valid, and his influence was impervious to reports of misdeeds.

Fabiani, on the other hand, got his wrestlers from Al Haft in Ohio, another Alliance member, and the likes of Billy Darnell, Bobo Brazil, and Angelo Savoldi added to Rogers's box office punch. But as quickly as Fabiani moved into DC he was gone, and the wrestling war ended without any major casualties.

McMahon, unlike many other promoters, ensured his main event was featured on television, providing viewers at home with the best attraction of the night. That reasoning contradicted the long-standing law of grappling on TV, which was to hold back the popular match to entice people to attend the program live. It was a risky proposition, but McMahon's move worked, and the Capitol Arena was packed with spectators. Once people saw the dramatic main event play out in their living rooms, they were eager and motivated to witness the same excitement in person. The novel formula invigorated fans and changed the way promoters handled their TV interests.

Another aspect of McMahon's promotional methodology pertained to how he booked the wrestlers themselves, and the emphasis he placed on the time-tested philosophy of good versus evil. He wanted his fan favorites to be real heroes in the ring, fighting against a true-blue heel. His rule breakers were over the top and went the extra mile to create chaos and grind the audience's gears. Ironically, the most caustic bad guy in the territory was a wrestler from Michigan portraying a Nazi from Germany. Karl Von Hess, born Frank Faketty, was an expert at manipulating the crowds' emotions, and he was a terrific box office attraction. Among the other successful heels in the District were the Gallagher brothers and Hans Schmidt, while their rivals, fan favorites Antonino Rocca, Red Bastien, and young Dick Steinborn, kept people cheering.

The exceptionality of McMahon's promotion and the TV program he produced inspired a number of conversations among high-ranking DuMont executives. These discussions revolved around the idea of replacing a dullish studio wrestling production from the DuMont Telecenter in Manhattan with a live feed from Washington. Switching to McMahon's enthusiastic broadcast was seen as an immediate way to boost the quality of grappling on Thursday nights on WABD. It was also a cost-cutting measure. Beginning on June 21, 1956, the colorful happenings of the Capitol Arena were televised throughout the New York metropolitan area, and in an instant, McMahon's influence was increased tenfold.

His vibrant product was captivating the wrestling audience in America's most populated city. The wrestlers he featured became hot-ticket attractions at local arenas, and the same successful booking formula in Washington was now a necessity in New York.

Grappling in New York City was administered by a melting pot of personalities, and, of course, Toots Mondt was the crown prince of disorder and mismanagement. Time had minimized his previous failures, and his principal objective remained the draw at Madison Square Garden. Throughout 1955, he chased the ever-elusive sellout, and the numbers were far below expectations in spite of headliner talent. Rocca, Thesz, Gagne, Schmidt, Don Leo Jonathan, Pat O'Connor, and Yukon Eric were unable to recapture the imaginations of fans, and the territory languished in misery.

Charley Johnston, the licensed wrestling promoter for the Garden, had tried to play by Mondt's rules and had given him free rein to work his alleged matchmaking magic. When fewer than 7,000 turned out for an October 1955 program and the show was canceled the following month, Johnston knew the boiling point had been reached. He ran a final event on December 12, 1955, drawing an estimated 8,000 people, then retired the grappling concession at the Garden. It just wasn't a winning proposition anymore, and a real miracle was needed to resurrect the enterprise.

That's where McMahon entered the picture. He delivered a miracle to Johnston and Mondt, and the trio utilized the Thursday night TV program to promote the return to the Garden on November 26, 1956. Over 10,000 spectators were on hand for the homecoming to the nation's foremost grappling center, and the only disappointment of the evening was Gagne's nonappearance in the semifinal against Schmidt. In the main event, Rocca used a backbreaker to defeat Dick the Bruiser, and Schmidt won over his replacement opponent, Dick Steinborn, with a body slam.

Looking at the composition of the Garden program, it was obvious the new promotional team had taken a page out of McMahon's playbook, creating an exceptionally diverse lineup of competitors. Each wrestler brought something unique to the table, whether it was hero magnetism or a fever for rule-breaking, and they were billed as being from all over the globe. Schmidt, who was actually from Canada, was the German heel of the evening, and Mr. Moto represented Japan. The popular Miguel Perez hailed from Puerto Rico and Skull Murphy from Cork, Ireland.

Rocca made his home in New York, but his previous residence in Argentina was commonly acknowledged. Bruiser was billed as being from Reno, Nevada, the "Cowboy" Rocky Lee from Texas, and Kenny Ackles from California.

The variety of entertaining characters was a trademark of McMahon's promotion. He liked to have a standout hero and a top-rated bad guy at the top of the bill, balanced out by a range of colorful secondary players. The preliminary ranks were made up of cowboys, brawlers, pretty boys, highfliers, technicians, and grapplers who used a plethora of gimmicks. Each performer, regardless of how high or low on the card, was expected to fulfill a certain purpose for the evening, and the name of the game was sending the crowd home happy. That usually meant Rocca was winning the main event, and the customary result satisfied fans.

Although there were passable relations behind the scenes in New York City in 1956, some felt McMahon's meteoric rise was unmerited. DuMont officials basically handed him New York on a silver platter. But the core of the situation was that everyone involved in wrestling in New York had their opportunity to be successful, and they ran the ship aground. The territory was quickly dying, the Garden was again off limits, and no one had any real answers about how to turn things around. McMahon, after only one show, already demonstrated he had the guts to lead New York into a new era of prosperity.

The exciting prospects didn't completely repair the tumultuous atmosphere in the territory. Quarreling was commonplace, and fragile egos often got the better of those in charge. Lines were also drawn in the sand. Johnston relied on his nephew Walter Smallshaw and ex-wrestler Kola Kwariani, who had, at times, worked as a matchmaker for the group. (Kwariani had discovered Rocca and had the carpet pulled out from under him by Mondt in the late 1940s.) There was no love lost between the two men despite the close proximity, and tempers flared from time to time.

On the other side, McMahon gravitated toward Mondt because the two needed each other to prosper. McMahon naturally settled into a leadership role, whereas Mondt handled the talent and sort of acted as a layer of defense for McMahon. Another major ally was Willie Gilzenberg of Newark, New Jersey. A promoter since the 1920s, he was the kind of unyielding business partner who was valuable to have: he stood by his friends and his word was his bond. Gilzenberg wasn't interested in gambling, the nightlife, or random shenanigans. He was a family man and a sportsman at heart. Through his years in boxing, he had dealt with many shady figures, but he never compromised his principles to get ahead. He shared that in common with McMahon, and the two clicked almost instantly.

Moving forward, Gilzenberg and Mondt were both going to be instrumental allies in the consolidation of the Northeastern territory. McMahon was in the perfect position to strengthen his role in the industry, and the general sense was that he was destined for great things.

The Department of Justice's inquest into the National Wrestling Alliance ended in 1956, but many questions remained. Internal recommendations from investigators relating to the scope of the prosecution were sent up the ladder, and critical choices were made by those in charge. Their decisions were highly favorable to the NWA. Instead of a criminal action against each specific member, officials chose to file a civil complaint against the Alliance as a whole. Additionally, rather than staging the trial in Los Angeles, where it was expected to receive considerable press coverage, the case was shifted to a federal court in Des Moines, Iowa. The move was seen as a way to limit the public's exposure to revelations about wrestling's inner workings during the course of the trial.

But the NWA's political reach pulled enough strings to avoid a trial altogether. Friends with influential U.S. senators, representatives, and other high-ranking officials, Alliance members successfully gained approval for a consent decree to resolve the entire matter. That meant the organization was going to dodge any embarrassment, and the damage the case posed was greatly diminished. Furthermore, the government was going to allow the NWA to continue operating under the condition it fully conformed to antitrust laws. All members would be compelled to sign the decree, agreeing to the new regulations, and from that point on, the Alliance was back to doing business without the fear of interference.

That is, if the NWA truly amended its practices. Government bureaucrats reserved the right to reopen the case anytime in the future, and if Alliance members failed to halt the threats of black-listing, restraint of trade, or other devious customs, they were going to be prosecuted to the fullest extent. Understanding the possibilities, the NWA, in full transparency, took the steps nec-essary to obey existing laws. The Alliance bylaws were modified, and potential candidates for membership were scrutinized less discriminatorily. However, behind closed doors, the Alliance car-ried on as if the inquest had never happened. The same ritualistic methods continued unabated, and there was a general sense the NWA was above the law.

Considering what Alliance members had gotten away with, it certainly appeared that way. While the organization was dealing with poor financial conditions at the box office and diminishing membership numbers, it still had a death grip on professional wrestling. It seemed the only lesson NWA promoters learned from the entire government investigation was that they needed to better conceal their corrupt behavior. That was the kind of arro-gance everyone working in the industry had to deal with, and it certainly wasn't going to change anytime soon.

(9)

CAPITOL BECOMES CAPITAL

The first half of the 1950s was a record-setting period for wrestling promoters, and it was all thanks to the emergence of television. Network executives found grappling to be a simple way to fill their vacant programming slots, and the sport blossomed into a massive hit.

People in their living rooms, already fascinated by TV, were hooked by the riotous action of the squared circle. It was a perfect mixture of combat, comedy, and athleticism, and matches captivated the attention of men and women, young and old, from all social and economic backgrounds. In fact, wrestling was accepted as a mainstream brand of entertainment, and the stigmas that were attached to grappling in previous years were quickly forgotten.

Television's success turned popular wrestlers into national celebrities and genuine idols. Antonino Rocca was at the top of the list of heroes. He was a household name, a bigger-than-life superstar who bounded from corner to corner in acrobatic fashion and wowed the audience with somersaults and flips.

His ring techniques were awe inspiring, especially when he was compared to his slower contemporaries. Where promoters like Vincent McMahon were accountable for arranging the entire spectacle, guys like Rocca were responsible for putting people in the seats. Fans typically weren't buying tickets because of who the promoter was, but for the attractions on the bill. And they didn't come any bigger than "Argentina" Rocca.

Although born in Italy and having spent most of his early years in Rosario, Argentina, Rocca was adopted by the swelling Puerto Rican population in New York City. Fans saw him as a working-class hero, constantly fighting wrestling's evildoers. Through his never-ending string of victories, he proved invincible, and his unconquerable spirit and determination offered a glimpse of hope to his followers. His entertaining personality and sense of humor were never lost on the crowd, and the regard people had for him was heartfelt. No city in America embraced a wrestler like New York did Rocca.

Rocca remained the surefire number one headliner at Madison Square Garden. McMahon knew his importance, and under his regime, Rocca was booked as the centerpiece of the promotion. His popularly increased, and the attendance numbers of early 1957 demonstrated that the newfangled approach was a gigantic hit. On February 4, 1957, he teamed up with Verne Gagne to topple German instigators Hans Schmidt and Karl Von Hess before over 19,000 and then beat Schmidt in a singles bout the following month with nearly 20,000 in attendance. It was a remarkable turnaround for pro wrestling, and everyone was taking notice.

In March 1957, Rocca allied himself with a new tag-team partner, Miguel Perez, a charismatic 19-year-old grappler from Puerto Rico. In their first Garden showing, on March 30, they captured the world tag team title from Don Stevens and Jackie Fargo. A massive crowd of 20,125 saw the victory, and McMahon and his partners collected a gate of over $60,000. Everything New York promoters touched was turning to gold, and the booking philosophy pushing Rocca first and foremost was paying off. The supporting players, from ballet dancer Ricki Starr to Professor Roy

Shire and Dr. Jerry Graham, provided vibrancy throughout the evening's entertainment, and the variety of performers sparked attendance throughout the Northeast.

Prosperity wasn't universal in professional wrestling, and many regions faced mediocre attendance and lackluster fan support. The cancellation of the influential Saturday night DuMont program from Chicago nearly two years before had been detrimental to many promoters, and the experiment of Lou Thesz and Leo Nomellini as duel champions was a failure for the NWA. After a legitimate injury to his ankle in early 1956, Thesz temporarily gave up his world championship to Toronto's popular superstar, "Whipper" Billy Watson, but he returned and won a rematch on November 9. A majority of the ideas produced by regional members and from the headquarters of the National Wrestling Alliance were uninspiring, including the decision to give Watson, and not Gagne or Buddy Rogers, the heavyweight title. But in 1957, there was a new plot to rekindle attendance, and many of wrestling's leaders were excited by the prospects.

The plan was based on the same model as the Thesz-Nomellini scheme. That was a scary thought considering the substandard results produced in 1955, but NWA officials assumed they were in a better position because Edouard Carpentier, in the Nomellini role, was a better drawing card. The question of whether the public would accept the recognition of two rivaling champions, building into a high-profile unification match, had previously been answered in Los Angeles when Thesz battled "Baron" Michele Leone in 1952. Their matchup, which concluded many months of skilled promotion, set a new national gate record. The situation needed two red-hot performers at the top of their game, and if Carpentier brought the kind of attention Leone did, it was going to be a huge triumph for the entire NWA.

The 30-year-old Carpentier was a distinctive performer, along the lines of Rocca in the way he could navigate the ring. His gymnastics background was a tremendous benefit, and when he wasn't running circles around opponents in an amazing display of athleticism, he was maneuvering out of tight spots with ease. Audiences were impressed, and word quickly got out to promoters that he was the next big thing.

During this same time frame, NWA president Sam Muchnick faced a multi-layered assault from disgruntled members, many of whom were griping about the Department of Justice's consent decree. There was panic in some quarters, and certain promoters were busily writing their congressmen and senators hoping to squash the recent ruling by the government. Other members predicted the collapse of the Alliance and were already planning to branch off and form regional sanctioning bodies with neighboring promoters. Muchnick himself found time to complain about a lack of cooperation in simple matters such as mail-in votes and expressed a desire to shore up avenues of revenue for the NWA outside of the four percent in fees gained from booking Thesz.

There was another concern of note. Behind Muchnick's back, Thesz began preparing an elaborate overseas tour with Los Angeles booker Jules Strongbow. The journey would begin in Australia in late August 1957 and continue into October, and for that period of time, the heavyweight champion would not be making any important appearances for members back home. Muchnick addressed the topic in his bulletin to the NWA on June 26, 1957, acknowledging that "many American promoters have been after Thesz's services unsuccessfully, and feel that he should make commitments here instead of going overseas."

Thesz, according to Muchnick, felt "such a trip would be financially beneficial to him and also to the NWA," and as far he was concerned, it was a foregone conclusion. Muchnick was in no place to quarrel with him and knew if the Alliance wanted to use a champion on their home turf while he was gone, members had to run the old Nomellini ploy. Muchnick went into peacekeeping mode, arranging the puzzle pieces to maintain harmony, and discussed the various options with Carpentier's personal manager, Eddie Quinn, the NWA member in Montreal, Fred Kohler, Jim Barnett of Chicago, and one or two others. Quinn agreed to post a $10,000 forfeit to guarantee that Carpentier would adhere to all scheduled bookings and lose back to Thesz when directed.

As a middleman between the various entities, Barnett was assigned the job of central booker for Carpentier and was responsible for equal distribution of the Frenchman's appearances. After the June 14, 1957, bout in Chicago saw Carpentier beat Thesz by disqualification and claim the championship, all of the parties involved at management level went into full-blown promotional mode to sell the storyline. Articles went out in newspapers and magazines, Muchnick made public comments in the *Montreal Star*, and Carpentier ventured out on the circuit as wrestling's newest heavyweight claimant.

Behind the scenes, Muchnick sent out a letter to members on June 26, 1957, notifying them of the recent happenings in Chicago. He reminded everyone that four years earlier, the organization had voted 25–8 in support of the measure barring champions from losing their belts by DQ. Thus, Thesz remained the rightful NWA world champion. He added, "This does not keep Carpentier from claiming the title and whenever he wrestles for any promoter, that promoter should publicize the result of the Thesz match in Chicago and state that Carpentier is claiming the title."

The resulting confusion of two titleholders was exactly what the NWA wanted. Carpentier went in one direction, Thesz the opposite, and when they crossed paths, or even engaged in a rematch like the one in Montreal on July 24, they both were acknowledged as claimants. Just before Thesz was scheduled to leave for Honolulu en route to Australia, he attended the Alliance convention in St. Louis, beginning on August 23. That evening, he wrestled Pat O'Connor while Carpentier battled Fritz Von Erich in the semifinal. The two matches were exciting but paled in comparison to the ferociousness of the battles at the Claridge Hotel, where the leaders of the NWA gathered to hash out the difficulties of the day.

Quinn, having flown in from Montreal, was one of the 21 members present. He looked forward to the social aspects of the meetings, telling stories, and kidding his friends. His joy left the moment he spotted Jack Pfefer, a nonmember, carousing among his peers. Pfefer's presence, simply enough, was a declaration of war, and Quinn was personally offended. He walked out on the convention, left St. Louis, and quit the NWA.

In a letter to Muchnick dated September 4, 1957, Quinn reminded the NWA president that Carpentier was his "personal property" and threatened legal action if his appearance bond was not returned. But in the aftermath of the explosion at the Alliance convention, Carpentier missed three bookings, including one at St. Louis, and Muchnick asked members whether the money promoters lost on those three occasions could be taken from Quinn's $10,000. A special meeting was held by the NWA board of directors on September 28, and it was decided to return the money in full, easing the overall tensions, but wrestling fans across the spectrum were left scratching their heads, wondering what had taken place. Most of the real excitement occurred behind closed doors and wasn't made public until recently.

Muchnick clarified the status of Carpentier and Thesz in his October 14, 1957, bulletin to the NWA. He stated that Thesz lost to his French rival on June 14 in Chicago by disqualification. Carpentier may have claimed the championship, but "according to our rules, Thesz still retained his title." On July 24, Muchnick continued, Carpentier was disqualified in a rematch with Thesz in Montreal. Whatever claims Carpentier had gained at Chicago by DQ were, in turn, lost in Montreal by DQ. "Lou Thesz is the champion as recognized by the National Wrestling Alliance," Muchnick declared in all caps. There was nothing more to be said about it.

Vincent McMahon, at this point, was on the periphery of NWA political disputes, but Toots Mondt had a front-row seat. He watched the fireworks unfold in St. Louis and waited for the smoke to clear. As far as his territory was concerned, he was reaping the benefits of the NWA scheme, as was McMahon. Almost immediately after Carpentier beat Thesz in June, Mondt began coordinating dates through Barnett and scored the new titleholder for appearances at the Capitol Arena beginning in July. When wrestling returned to Madison Square Garden on September 16, 1957, after a layoff of several months, Carpentier was in the main event against fellow fan-favorite Antonino Rocca. The two tumbled around the ring for 25 minutes in a bout that was called a draw at the 11 p.m. curfew; 19,165 people were in attendance.

Carpentier missed the next Garden show but stormed back to wrestle Killer Kowalski to a curfew draw in the semifinal of the November 2, 1957, program. The 20,675 attendance was believed to be the largest crowd at the Garden in over a decade, and McMahon, Mondt, and their associates scored $63,876.14 at the gate.

A little over two weeks later, Carpentier returned to New York City to team with Rocca against Dick the Bruiser and Dr. Jerry Graham, who subbed for the missing Kowalski. The match was the typical back-and-forth combat, and the heroes prevailed with a DQ victory before nearly 13,000 spectators. However, the brawl took a stunning turn after the final bell when Rocca and Graham continued their bloody warfare. Excitable fans took a cue from the in-ring violence and began a chaotic demonstration of their own. The Garden quickly deteriorated into a riot, leaving many fans injured. Over two dozen officers were called in to calm the violence, and all four wrestlers were fined by the New York State Athletic Commission. State officials were far from pleased, and promoters were warned that if such antics happened again, there was a possibility pro wrestling would be banned altogether.

Losing the New York market would have crippled McMahon's enterprises. He didn't want the shenanigans of unruly patrons at the Garden to jeopardize his biggest moneymaker. If he had to tell Rocca and Graham to tone down their act, hire extra security, or perform other preventive measures, it was all necessary to keep things from completely unraveling. The New York commission was the most stringent in the country, and when they issued warnings, it was imperative to listen. McMahon was paying full attention and understood that it wasn't the time to risk unsettling their momentum.

In recent months, McMahon had gone to great lengths to strengthen his role in the Northeast. One of the first things he did was size up his relationship with Mondt. He knew Toots was no longer the mesmerizing matchmaker he once was. Mondt's focus on harness racing was routinely a distraction, but for every misstep and every disturbance Toots caused, there were ample benefits to having the big guy around. His management deal with Rocca was lucrative, and the way Mondt handled Kola Kwariani and other influential figures on the New York scene took a lot of the pressure off McMahon. But to make up for the loss of Mondt's formerly sharp booking skills, McMahon went into partnership with Johnny Doyle of Los Angeles.

Toots had no problem with the idea. Doyle was a longtime friend, and his presence would lighten his personal responsibilities too, giving him more time to freelance at the track. For Doyle, it was a unique opportunity to regain a position of substance after several years of running as an independent in Southern California. His anti-NWA stance during the Department of Justice investigation was frowned upon by the hierarchy of the Alliance, and his former partners in Los Angeles were anything but accommodating. He was grateful that the circumstances in the East opened up a consequential job for him, and he promptly moved his family to Arlington, Virginia, outside Washington, DC, so he could get to work.

The combination of McMahon, Mondt, and Doyle was formidable. Together, they created a new company known as the Capitol Wrestling Corporation on August 1, 1957, and filed the documentation with the superintendent of corporations of the District of Columbia four days later. Not so surprisingly, Mondt, at the time of incorporation, was short of financial resources and unable to share the heavy investment with his partners. But he wasn't slighted in the least. His shares were temporarily placed in the capable hands of the trusted Philip Zacko, a promotional ally out of Pennsylvania, and later, when Mondt was able to come up with the money, the stock was transferred to his name.

Officially, both McMahon and Mondt would own 42 percent of the company's 1,000 shares, with Doyle holding the other 16. McMahon, in a February 2, 1958, article in the *Washington Post and Times Herald*, clarified Mondt's duties in the corporation, saying he was the "contact man who oversees the entire operation, a sort of manipulator." In other words, Toots was semiretired and aiding the company through his membership in the NWA and valuable connections to promoters and wrestlers. Doyle would be the primary matchmaker, vice president, and treasurer of Capitol, and McMahon was the president, making certain everything ran according to plan.

Capitol Wrestling was fundamentally a booking office and started with a roster of 16 wrestlers under contract, six of whom were headline caliber and the rest enhancement performers. Directly from this pool of competitors, McMahon and Doyle arranged shows in Washington, DC, and the surrounding area, often supplemented by one or two special-attraction grapplers who were booked from an outside agency. For instance, the NWA world champion would have been hired from the Alliance headquarters in St. Louis and Edouard Carpentier through Jim Barnett in Chicago. In the case of the popular showman Ricki Starr, a deal was brokered between Capitol and Starr's manager Jack Pfefer that gave McMahon and Doyle his booking rights for a certain period of time.

Capitol's contracted wrestlers were paid on a scale corresponding to their value as a box office draw. Rocca was at the top of the food chain, although his money was always split with Toots and Kwariani. Preliminary workers received much less. It wasn't long before Doyle and McMahon had two to three dozen grapplers working a 40-club circuit from Virginia to Maine. Using the DuMont telecast, seen in 11 states, they rapidly expanded and earned upward of $120,000 in profits in 1957. At each live event Capitol sponsored, McMahon received 60 percent of the gate and then paid the grapplers who worked the show from that amount. Their payouts were fair, and the morale of wrestlers under the Capitol regime was much better than when Mondt was running things alone.

The bookings at Madison Square Garden were handled a little differently. Since Charley Johnston was essentially the man in charge because of his role as the venue's official promoter, he had the final say in how things were run. He refused to relinquish all matchmaking rights to Capitol and instead relied on his own team of associates. Kwariani, Walter Smallshaw, and Harry Finkelstein, a former wrestler turned agent, arranged as much of the Garden bill as they could but lacked the star-quality talent to pull off a winning event. That's where the compromise with Capitol came in. McMahon was not only able to provide top names but featured them on New York TV prior to the show to spike attendance.

The mood in New York was often touchy, and neither the Johnston nor the McMahon groups were exactly thrilled by the arrangements. The setup was a matter of necessity and would, as most things did, evolve over time.

Meanwhile, the leadership of the National Wrestling Alliance was facing a crisis after discovering that heavyweight champion Lou Thesz wanted to drop the belt at the earliest possible date. It wasn't that Thesz was burned out by the intensity of his schedule, but he was more or less fed up by the collective hotheadedness of NWA members. Their complaints about his fees, accommodations, and his consistent push to have Ed "Strangler" Lewis on the payroll were too much to endure any longer. His relationship with president Sam Muchnick had also soured, mainly because of the two and a half percent cut Muchnick received for every booking Thesz made. Additionally, Muchnick was in a position to appease all sides.

Once again, NWA members were confronted with the possibility of acquiring a heavyweight champion whose magnetism and showmanship could draw record gate numbers across the organization. Thesz was a textbook wrestler and took pride in allowing his legitimate grappling knowledge to shine through. Guys like Buddy Rogers tended to be performers first and wrestlers second. They were flashy, outgoing, loud, and boisterous. Their behavior in the ring and out stimulated intense crowd reactions and inflated attendance. Heroes Verne Gagne and Edouard Carpentier were superstars and, in the past, there had been at least fleeting consideration for Killer Kowalski, Hans Schmidt, and Antonino Rocca as candidates for the title.

The NWA president, board of directors, and heavyweight championship committee would have normally weighed in on the debate, but in this instance, the decision was all up to Thesz. He had already made up his mind that his heir was not going to be a performer, but a real, classically trained wrestler. He wanted the next champion to embody the same aptitude and spirit he had employed during his many years of traveling the Alliance circuit. He'd lose to no one less. Any other standard, he believed, would tarnish all of his distinguished work.

Muchnick was well aware of the growing trend in pro wrestling. He warned members in a bulletin dated November 1, 1957, that attendance was down partly because grapplers had "forgotten all of the fundamentals and [were] doing everything but wrestling when in the ring." He recognized that the untamed style of brawling had an immediate effect on the box office but believed it did damage in the long run. He wanted to remind the athletes that they were "supposed to be wrestlers" and felt the sport would attain greater respect from the public and press if the emphasis returned to matching holds rather than bloody, riot-inducing carnage.

For that reason, he too liked the idea of a straight-laced champion to replace Thesz. The heavyweight titleholder should present a squeaky-clean image and a legitimate background to support his claim to be the top grappler in the world. Thesz and Muchnick concluded that 6', 235-pound Dick Hutton was the perfect solution to the problem, and on November 14, 1957, at Maple Leaf Gardens in Toronto, the ex-Olympian from Tulsa beat Thesz and won the NWA championship.

Shortly thereafter, Muchnick announced the following in a memo to the NWA: "Dick Hutton, unquestionably, is the undisputed World Heavyweight champion, and is recognized as the title holder by the National Wrestling Alliance, an organization of promoters, and the National Wrestling Association, an organization of State Athletic Commissions, affiliated with the National Boxing Association."

The Thesz era of dominance in the NWA had officially ended, and many people, including Thesz himself, were elated.

Hutton was the opposite of Buddy Rogers in terms of in-ring performance. He displayed all the fundamentals, mixing his knowledge of collegiate grappling with an entertaining range of pro maneuvers. His size and strength were intimidating, and he carried himself with confidence and dignity. He looked the part of the world heavyweight champion, but he lacked the color of Rogers, and that lack of charisma failed to boost attendance in the ways Muchnick and other NWA members had hoped. Hutton was more along the lines of Jim Browning, the impressive champion of 1933–34, but his reign was disappointing because he couldn't inspire larger crowds. It was soon feared Hutton's time as champ would end on a similar note.

Following the riot at Madison Square Garden on November 19, 1957, fans were reluctant to return for the next program. On December 9, only 9,200 watched Rocca and Miguel Perez beat Dr. Jerry Graham and Danny McShain. But this tentative support didn't last long. In fact, wrestling was about to experience an enormous revival. Fan favorites Rocca, Perez, and Carpentier were joined by Ricki Starr, an energetic St. Louis native who combined his love of dancing with a career as a wrestler, and New Zealander Pat O'Connor. Both Starr and O'Connor had amateur grappling backgrounds and were compelling in their supporting roles. Another addition was the Sheik of Araby. McMahon promptly shortened his name to the Sheik, but he was really Edward Farhat of Detroit, and he became one of the most talked about heels in the territory in early 1958.

Seven Garden shows were staged between February and August 1958, and for each program, attendance remained over 15,000. The constant variable during the hot streak was the tag team of Rocca and Perez, who were unparalleled attractions and were featured in every main event. Their opponents were villains of all variety, including three sets of brothers, the Toloses, the Hamiltons, and the Grahams. The Fabulous Kangaroos, a dynamic combination composed of Australians Al Costello and Roy Heffernan, also joined the tag team wars and twice drew over 20,000 people against Rocca and Perez in August 1958.

Newcomer Johnny Valentine, a blond tough guy from the Pacific Northwest, stampeded over foes while building a respectable winning streak on Capitol television. Later, he was recognized as the official "TV champion" of the region, claiming to have won a tournament in Chicago, but the title win was fabricated to heighten his importance. Not that he really needed it. Valentine was a remarkable performer, brutal in the ring and confident to the core. His training under the legendary Zbyszko Brothers and vast experience made him stand out regardless of his company.

The financial success at the Garden made some NWA members jealous. It got to the point that a number of individuals complained to Sam Muchnick about Toots Mondt's failure to advertise Dick Hutton as the official world titleholder. They wanted Mondt punished, maybe even banished from the Alliance. Mondt admitted the wrongdoing and claimed there were extenuating factors for his lack of publicity. He managed to rectify the situation in June, and again in September 1958, scheduling the champion for matches in Arlington, Virginia, and at the Capitol Arena in Washington. In the latter showing, due to the NWA kingpin's massively reduced importance in the Northeast, Hutton was not in the show's main event but booked underneath a tag bout featuring Rocca and Chief Big Heart against the Kangaroos.

That kind of stunt would normally have drawn the ire of the by-the-book Muchnick, but the NWA president almost always cut Mondt extra slack. Going back to the early days of the Alliance, Muchnick seemed to look the other way when it came to issues involving Toots, and the fact that Muchnick considered him a mentor likely had something to do with it. He knew Mondt, and McMahon for that matter, adhered to a loose interpretation of the organization's regulations. When pressured to speak out against the so-called infractions, Muchnick did so, but most of the time he extended a certain leeway other members didn't receive.

It was definitely favoritism, but it was acceptable to keep the most valuable territory in the world aligned with the NWA. Muchnick didn't want any problems.

The composition of Capitol Wrestling's office changed in 1958. Johnny Doyle left the company to become Paul Bowser's matchmaker in Boston and was the chief coordinator for a new studio wrestling program on WBZ. He brought in Sam Menacker to handle the announcing and worked closely with Tony Santos and Eddie Quinn of Montreal in rebuilding the entire New England landscape. In early May, the Boston Garden was packed with an estimated 10,000 screaming fans as Killer Kowalski upended Edouard Carpentier and won the latter's claim to the heavyweight championship. Continued strong relations between McMahon and Doyle solidified the easy transfer of wrestlers from New York through the Boston area and all the way up to Montreal.

Doyle was a natural salesman, and he turned his attention back to New York City, where he highlighted the merits of the Boston TV show to network executives. At first it appeared he was helping to arrange a prospective wrestling show televised from the Sunnyside Garden in Queens, but his real focus was on a separate WOR-9 TV presentation of the Boston studio program on Friday nights. On November 7, 1958, the show debuted in New York at 9:15 p.m. and offered local fans a distinctive new brand of shenanigans led by Kowalski.

Sunnyside Garden, incidentally, got its own TV deal, prompted by Rudy Dusek and National Basketball Association pioneer Haskell Cohen. This same duo was responsible for the old DuMont studio show from the Telecenter, which was replaced by McMahon's Washington offering. In conjunction with Sunnyside owner Manny Heicklen and affiliated with Kola Kwariani's booking office, the program debuted in late September 1958 on Tuesday nights on WNEW-TV, formerly WABD, the same channel that featured McMahon's show. McMahon was livid at network executives for the lineup addition, which he believed distracted from all the good he was doing on Thursday nights. TV from

Sunnyside also reduced his power by giving an outlet to Kwariani for the promotion of his own wrestlers prior to Garden events.

Attaining his own TV setup was the one major issue Kwariani needed to level out the playing field. For over two years, his troupe had adjusted to the whims of McMahon and his Washington effort. Finally he had his own local television operation. To support his growing influence, he made arrangements with booking agent Pedro Martinez of Buffalo to import a slew of big-named grapplers into the region. Ilio DiPaolo, Tony Marino, the Gallaghers, and the Brunettis flooded the New York City area with dozens of their compatriots. On October 20, 1958, the Garden drew more than 20,700 people but had 9,000 less viewers at the next show, on November 17. Two weeks later, with Martinez workers appearing up and down the bill, attendance was back up over 20,000.

The changes in the topsy-turvy promotional scene in New York City left 57-year-old Rudy Dusek out in the cold. His stable of wrestlers dwindled to nothing, and whatever clout he once had thinned to the point that he was no longer relevant. Like Al Mayer before him, Dusek became a casualty of the transforming environment, and after nearly three decades of work in New York as a wrestler and matchmaker, he was forced to the sidelines. He retired to his home in Passaic, New Jersey, and passed away in 1971.

As far as the in-ring action was concerned, a high spot for fans of Capitol Wrestling in 1958 was the arrival of Buffalo natives Don Curtis and Mark Lewin. As a tag team, they were among the best in the world, sharp in the ring and appealing to audiences. Curtis and Lewin were the perfect contrast to McMahon's many heel tandems, and by July 1958, they were claiming the United States championship based on a fictional tournament win in Kansas City. The U.S. tag team title would fast become the central prize on Capitol television programs and was the only regional championship to actually change hands with any frequency. The title passed from Curtis and Lewin to the Graham Brothers (Dr. Jerry and Eddie Graham) on September 4, 1958, and then back to the heroes in December.

Losing his TV stranglehold in New York was a significant setback for McMahon, but he used the temporary disadvantage to strengthen his television empire. He added a second wrestling program on WNEW from 8:30 to 10:30 p.m. on Wednesday nights, staged from the Knights of Columbus Hall in Bridgeport, Connecticut, beginning on February 11, 1959. The weekly shows were promoted by Joe Smith, a valued friend of the family going back to the 1910s, when he started out as a boxing manager, working alongside Jess McMahon. He naturally continued his association with Vincent in later years and was acknowledged as the vice president of Capitol Wrestling, Inc. on documents filed in Connecticut. His wife, Bertha, was listed as the corporation's secretary, and the Smiths maintained an office at the Washington Avenue arena.

The contentious game of one-upmanship between McMahon and the Kwariani faction was relentless. It was almost as if McMahon needed the Bridgeport show to reestablish his credibility at the top of the pecking order. In the New York market, appearance was everything. Having two shows, McMahon was above Kwariani and the authority of all things wrestling. That was an important distinction because it gave him a leg up in certain circumstances, especially at Madison Square Garden, where the fight to reign supreme never ended.

The two sides were clear, and while most things between them were black and white, there was a gray zone where both McMahon and Kwariani met. When it came to their individual TV shows, Kwariani only used his Sunnyside Garden effort to promote the wrestlers in his stable, plus the gang flowing out of Buffalo from Martinez. McMahon did the same for his Washington and Bridgeport programs, exclusively featuring the grapplers on his roster. Generally, wrestlers didn't cross over and appear on their rivals' shows, but there were exceptions in the case of Rocca and several others. There was much more of a compromise at arena shows, and both McMahon and Kwariani shared the booking at venues throughout New York City, parts of New Jersey, and, of course, at Madison Square Garden.

Ricki Starr was one of the few who appeared on TV for both McMahon and Kwariani. He was given special considerations because he wasn't "owned" by either promoter, but by Jack Pfefer, who, in 1959, was making a play to return to New York City after many years of traversing the country as a matchmaker-for-hire. He wanted back into the big time and planned to use Starr's drawing power to gain a footing.

Quirky through and through, Pfefer prided himself on the creation of memorable attractions, some of whom imitated the sport's top superstars. His Argentinean highflyer, Amazing Zuma, was a knockoff of Antonino Rocca but impressed audiences with his ring-work. He might have been groomed as a copycat, but he was extraordinary on his own, and Zuma's popularity in New York rose fervently. Between the success of Starr and Zuma, Pfefer was welcomed into the promotional hierarchy, but he was no lightweight. He knew how to play both sides of the fence when needed and was a master manipulator, far more adept than McMahon or Kwariani. That didn't mean he was a better promoter or matchmaker, just that he could get inside the heads of his peers and adversaries like no one else. Once he was back in a position of power in New York, he wasn't about to let it go.

Attendance was booming all over Captiol territory. At the Island Garden Arena in West Hempstead, owner-operator Arnold "Whitey" Carlson drew a record crowd for Long Island on April 11, 1959, when 7,419 paid $18,180.13 to see the Graham Brothers defeat Rocca and Gene Stanlee. McMahon set more records in Washington, DC, at Griffith Stadium on August 24 when 11,200 paid almost $25,000 to see 22 wrestlers compete in a mammoth spectacle. In the main event, Rocca led a contingent of four fan favorites to victory in an eight-man tag bout, and referees Max Baer and "Jersey" Joe Walcott, former boxing champions, were brought in to maintain order.

Fans loved the diversity of talent and the exciting matchups all over the Northeastern territory. In their collective opinion, whatever chaos was happening behind the scenes was secondary to the wrestling in the ring. Going into the future, they didn't care what combination of promoters ruled the roost, as long as the quality bouts and thrilling shows continued. But for McMahon, Pfefer, Mondt, Kwariani, Johnston, and Martinez, the fight for a place at the table was going to be sustained until there was a guaranteed victor. There was too much at risk and too much money on the line.

(10)
UNDER THE SHADOW OF GOVERNMENT INQUEST

Success in professional wrestling was cyclical during the territorial days, and some argue that it remains so today, even as international conglomerates such as the WWE rule the business. But during the 1950s, many territories went through regular cycles of success and failure, and New York City was no exception. In 1958–59, Vincent J. McMahon and others throughout the Northeast were using TV to their advantage, building massive armies of enthusiasts and adding tens of thousands of dollars to their coffers. In Chicago, it was just the opposite. Fred Kohler, who pioneered wrestling on television and had been padding his accounts while New York was suffering earlier in the decade, was nearly bankrupt. The loss of his once-dominant Saturday night DuMont program sent his entire empire into a tailspin that was apparently irreversible. Wrestling was on its last legs in the Windy City.

McMahon was aware of the problems in Chicago and saw an opportunity to intercede with the interests of both Kohler and Capitol Wrestling in mind. He knew that it was a big-time wrestling city and had loyal supporters if the conditions were right. If things could be rebuilt with a heavy eastern influence, Chicago could again become a tremendous moneymaker. For Kohler, it was a chance to regain his equilibrium after an exhausting effort to remain afloat. With Eddie Quinn of Montreal remorselessly invading his territory, he needed whatever help McMahon could offer. If it came in the form of TV and a booking arrangement to present Capitol workers in Chicago, it would be a godsend.

Just like in New York, McMahon used his television program and its reputation to influence executives at Chicago's WNBQ so they would broadcast his weekly show on Saturday nights. This time it wasn't the matches from Washington being transmitted but the newly developed Bridgeport telecast. Smartly, McMahon entered into a partnership with Kohler to act as his primary matchmaker. The deal was highly beneficial to each party, and on September 19, 1959, the program debuted with Kohler buying up advertising time to promote his local events. The hard-hitting East Coast grappling style quickly indoctrinated fans, and it didn't take long for people to embrace McMahon's performers.

The move into Chicago was another brilliant maneuver pulled off at the perfect moment. McMahon had successfully expanded into the "second city" without the appearance of a hostile take-over. Instead, he exploited a dire set of circumstances to not only help a friend but strengthen the reach of his company. Other avenues for enlarging Capitol Wrestling's territory were being studied by company officials as well.

The Antonino Rocca–Miguel Perez tag team continued to dominate the headlines at Madison Square Garden. They were unstoppable against the Grahams, Johnny Valentine and the Sheik, and the Tolos Brothers, and while every show wasn't a guaranteed sellout, the enthusiasm was generally sustained from month to month. By the summer of 1959, Pedro Martinez had retreated from New York City, initially pulling out of the Garden around March and then out of Sunnyside Garden in August. Jack Pfefer's status in the region was prolonged because of the skyrocketing importance of the Mighty Zuma. The success of the Argentinean hotshot, along with Ricki Starr and "Wildman" Jackie Fargo, gave Pfefer incredible power beginning in June and July 1959.

Pfefer skillfully managed to get along with both New York booking factions. His got his men featured on television from Sunnyside Garden, Bridgeport, and also the Capitol Arena in Washington, DC. He walked the tightrope between the Kola Kwariani and Joe "Toots" Mondt entities and initially followed the lead of McMahon and the Charley Johnston group at Madison Square Garden. But where Pfefer could throw his weight around, he did so with reckless abandon, and those members of the wrestling tribe susceptible to his old-school magnetism were bound to eventually follow his orders. His web of influence grew slowly but surely, and Mondt and McMahon were exceptionally weary of his manipulations.

The rise of Zuma as a box office attraction led to the first Garden singles main event in over two years on November 13, 1959, when he was pitted against the original wrestling acrobat from Argentina, Antonino Rocca. The battle between the innovator and the mimic was high drama in New York City, especially in the Latin community, and the large segments of Puerto Rican and South American grappling fans had to choose sides for what was expected to be a close contest. The excitement resulted in 21,890 fans jamming the Garden, paying $64,125 and establishing high marks for attendance and at the gate. In the closing moments of the bout, Rocca heaved his opponent from the ring and won by count out when Zuma was unable to return.

Despite the high numbers, Pfefer was anything but happy. He was so disgruntled by the backstage politics of the Rocca-Zuma matchup that he vowed never to be associated with Rocca again. But with Kwariani and Johnston looking for another huge draw, he broke down and consented to a rematch. In a letter dated December 16, 1959, Willie Gilzenberg warned his longtime friend Pfefer about the dangers. Gilzenberg explained that Zuma needed to be sold to the marketplace as the second coming of Rocca and, without saying the words exactly, cautioned against any unnecessary defeats. Zuma needed to be protected to reap the rewards of being a Garden headliner on a national level. However, Pfefer was short-sighted and went forward with the bout anyway.

The numbers were massive, just as everyone had predicted. Part two of Rocca versus Zuma, on January 2, 1960, drew another set of Garden attendance and gate records, 21,950 and $64,680, respectively. Similar to the last time around, Rocca won by count out and there was talk of a third bout almost immediately. Dan Parker of the *New York Daily Mirror* remarked in his January 8 column that the Zuma-Rocca feud was the "biggest thing in wrestling since Jimmie Londos, the Golden Greek, and Joe Savoldi used to turn them away, 25 years ago."

According to Parker, Pfefer wanted the Garden ring surrounded by chicken wire to ensure all participants remained in the squared circle for the third Rocca-Zuma bout, on January 25, 1960. The madcap request was denied by the virtuous state athletic commission, but the appeal, had it been heeded, might have saved Zuma from being knocked out of the ring by Rocca's ferocious dropkick and again being counted out. It was the third unsatisfactory finish, and although 15,675 paid over $47,000 to attend the show, the rivalry was burned out. In the aftermath of the series, Zuma was bumped from future Garden main events, and his career would never again attain the same success. Rocca continued to reign as the number one hero in New York.

Promotional unrest continued in professional wrestling from Western Pennsylvania to Virginia and across Capitol territory. Rumors about invasions, takeovers, and warfare were rampant, and paranoid promoters were taking precautions. Altogether, there were too many unbelievable power plays going on, and it was hard to take any of them seriously. For instance, gossip sprouted up that Buddy Rogers was working with Al Haft of Columbus to annex Pittsburgh for a growing new syndicate with ties to Eddie Quinn in Montreal. Considering Quinn's battle in Chicago, he had no qualms about fighting for outside territory. Plus, his widespread ties to St. Louis and Boston made him a considerable threat. Rogers was as well, and his status as one of wrestling's biggest draws was unquestionable.

In reaction to the Pittsburgh rumor, McMahon reportedly sent Phil Zacko to shore up the city in advance of a large-scale Capitol operation later in 1960. Aside from that, there was a more significant conversation going on behind the scenes relating to Rogers and a possible role in the company. Rather than letting another promotional syndicate bank off the immense drawing power of the Nature Boy and interfere with McMahon's own expansion plans, he wanted to make the first move and sign Rogers to a long-term deal.

Rogers was a complicated man, probably the most complicated performer in the business. He was an exceptional showman with almost two decades of experience, but in recent years, he was much more than the standard performer, being more or less a partner in every territory he ventured into. It wasn't that he was always cut into the ownership, but he usually assumed a higher responsibility in the backstage politics, working with the promoter in the day-to-day booking. In certain instances, Rogers became the focal point of the entire promotion.

Rogers had incredible business smarts, and in the ring, he did what was necessary to garner larger gates. He'd go over when it was fruitful, but he was also willing to put over an adversary when it made sense in light of the promotion's booking scheme. Gone were the days when he took regular defeats, and he always had a say in the direction of his character. His freedom to write his own ticket often put him on the wrong side of fellow wrestlers in the locker room, and there was a perceived sense of entitlement when it came to Rogers. As his power continued to escalate, so did the animosity among his peers. But for promoters, he was a million-dollar box office attraction, and they were willing to accept his idiosyncrasies to keep the money rolling in.

McMahon saw Rogers as an earner first and foremost. Any baggage that accompanied the blond-haired heel was chalked up to the cost of doing business. Interestingly, Toots Mondt had a broader perspective of Rogers based on his previous dealings with him, and his impression of the wrestler was not entirely positive. Back in 1951, after Rogers had broken from Jack Pfefer's managerial stable, he ended up on the wrong side of Toots when he aligned with Quinn to take hold of a small Pennsylvania promotion Mondt claimed was his. Four years later, their relationship nose-dived again when Rogers, after working a rare Garden date, bickered with Mondt about his payoff.

The funny thing about the strained rapport between Mondt and Rogers is that Toots seemed to be the most logical booker for Rogers in the National Wrestling Alliance. If Mondt could have compromised and given Rogers free rein to do his thing, his gates would have been greatly improved throughout the better part of the 1950s. But Mondt's own lack of discipline and the terrible period of instability that came as a result prevented the kind of atmosphere needed for Rogers to be successful in the Northeast. But McMahon was ready to do what was necessary to get Rogers into the region for a prolonged run. Any bad feelings over previous quarrels had to be forgotten.

Rogers agreed to McMahon's proposal and made his Capitol debut in March 1960. As part of the agreement, Rogers was acknowledged as the United States heavyweight champion, which was a billing isolated to McMahon's territory. Additionally, there were future beneficial considerations, from McMahon petitioning the NWA for a potential reign as world champion to Rogers maybe entering the promotional side of Capitol Wrestling. Nothing was chiseled in stone, but their new association was sure to pay off through increased attendance, particularly at Madison Square Garden.

In spite of the encouraging news surrounding Rogers, there were stunning new concerns that put Capitol in serious jeopardy. The year before, on March 14, 1959, to be exact, McMahon had lost one of his most important promoters when Ed Contos of Baltimore suddenly passed away. Originally from Greece, Contos was a 20-plus-year wrestling veteran, and his death was expected to leave a significant vacancy in McMahon's circuit. But the Contos family decided to continue the business, and things remained unchanged for several months. That summer, after McMahon requested an additional 10 percent of Baltimore gate receipts on top of the 50 percent he already commanded, the Contos family balked and completely severed ties from Capitol Wrestling and McMahon's local operation, the Maryland Wrestling Corporation.

Ed Contos Jr., in charge of the Baltimore promotion for his family, defiantly signed a new booking arrangement with Pedro Martinez of Buffalo, a lifelong enemy of Capitol Wrestling. Martinez's newfound influence in the region was alarming, and pundits wondered if it was just a matter of time before he broke into Washington, DC, and opposed McMahon. Before that could happen, Contos's indispensable TV hookup was canceled, and he saw a massive decrease in attendance. By January 1960, Martinez had lost upward of $30,000 in his Baltimore effort, and he decided to buy out the remainder of his contract with Contos and return to Buffalo.

Desperate to get business cooking again, Contos tried to mend fences with Capitol Wrestling, and although McMahon wasn't averse to working out a deal, he ultimately decided to switch to a new promoter in Baltimore, ex-referee Harry Smythe. The news didn't sit well with the Contos family, and on February 26, 1960, Ed Jr. and his mother, Alta, filed a $300,000 federal lawsuit against McMahon, Toots Mondt, and Capitol Wrestling. Their charge was that Capitol illegally tried to monopolize wrestling in the region and was engaged in a conspiracy involving members of the National Wrestling Alliance. Red flags went up for members of the Department of Justice, and they prepared to examine the Contoses' claims.

With good lawyers supporting Capitol's cause, the Contos lawsuit seemed manageable. But there was yet another issue directly related to antitrust matters involving McMahon's organization that made the Contoses' complaint drastically worse.

The concern originated in Virginia, where former wrestler William Olivas, known as the Elephant Boy during the 1950s, opened up shop as an independent. He was informed by the Maryland Athletic Commission that he didn't qualify for a pro- moter's license in the state because he hadn't been a resident for one year. He was permitted to obtain a booker's license, and he acquired the necessary documentation in June 1959. Motivated and eager to get his new business off the ground, he lined up a vast network of small towns in Virginia—as many as 19 in total. He also skillfully managed an agreement with WTAR-TV in Norfolk for a locally filmed weekly wrestling show.

Naturally, Olivas's autonomous exploits were eye-opening to NWA members Bill Lewis of Richmond, Virginia, and his partner in the Carolinas, Jim Crockett. Even though the 1956 consent decree ordered by the U.S. government explicitly forbade any exclusive territories, the mindset of Alliance promoters never really changed. Olivas was infringing on sacred NWA turf, and over the course of several months in 1959, he received threatening phone calls telling him to get out of Virginia. To make things worse, Leo Voss, a referee for Crockett, menaced Olivas to the point that he actually pulled a knife on him. In January 1960, Crockett offered to send grapplers to Olivas if he'd drop charges against Voss, and Olivas agreed, but Crockett's support of the NWA outsider ended the following month.

The freeze-out of Olivas was relentless. Lewis made phone calls to the wrestlers working for the indy outfit and tried to coax them to either join him or work elsewhere. The anonymous and more threatening calls continued as well. Chief Little Eagle, a popular grappler throughout the East, consented to appear on Olivas's TV show and canceled a date in Capitol territory to do so, telling McMahon he had a personal matter to attend to. Once officials discovered that the Chief had skipped out on them to wrestle in Norfolk, he was effectively banished from working for Capitol again, and it was easy to perceive the so-called punishment as a full-fledged blacklisting.

Olivas didn't sit passively by and accept what was happening to him. The multipronged attack on his enterprises forced him to write a letter about the monopolistic conditions in the state to Virginia governor James Almond. He hired an attorney and spoke out during hearings of the athletic commission, explaining his version of events. Detailed reports were sent to the Antitrust

Division of the Department of Justice and NWA president Sam Muchnick was notified of the situation in early 1960. On February 1, Muchnick visited Washington, DC, and spoke with Justice employees. As he later described in a bulletin to the NWA, Muchnick relayed his anxieties with the consent decree and wanted it altered or even dismissed. He told officers that because of the judgment, membership in the NWA had fallen from 38 to 23 individuals.

Muchnick attributed the happenings in Virginia to "a lot of heresay [sic]," but he wasn't aware of the complete picture. The Department of Justice had more evidence than the NWA realized and pushed, in March 1960, for a further investigation, including a laundry list of interviews with the people involved. Whereas Olivas's gripes might have been unsubstantiated early on, the wheels were in motion to dredge up anything and everything leading toward the government's second case against the National Wrestling Alliance. Worse yet, if the government decided to single out NWA members who'd signed the consent decree and failed to live up to its regulations, there was a major crisis on the horizon. Especially when it came to potential federal contempt of court actions against Bill Lewis, Jim Crockett, and Toots Mondt, each of whom had signed the 1956 decree.

McMahon, incidentally, wasn't out of the woods himself. Investigators were paying close attention to whether McMahon, Phil Zacko, and Rudy Miller knew what was outlined in the consent decree. If it was determined that they were informed of the particulars of the judgment and still violated it, they too could be held liable.

FBI Special Agents Carlton Broden and Robert Reiser were tasked to the offices of Capitol at 1332 I Street NW in Washington, DC, and made an in-depth inquiry between July 12 and July 19, 1960. Mondt was the first interviewed and he tried to downplay his role in the company, explaining that he was in a "semiretired position." Regarding the NWA judgment, in his opinion, none of his coworkers had been enlightened to its terms. McMahon admitted to seeing the judgment but was "not familiar" with all provisions. He confirmed Toots was semiretired and used in an "advisory capacity." He made it clear that "99 per cent of all the business [was] conducted without consulting Mondt."

It was an important distinction. Mondt, after all, was legally bound and couldn't deny knowledge of all stipulations in place since he had signed the consent decree. If it was established that he was dictating policy for Capitol in a monopolistic fashion, the entire company was going to sink. During Mondt's interview, there was another revelation that wasn't overly important to the FBI but was indicative of the current state of affairs for Capitol's overall business. Toots said the company was furnishing talent to Whitey Carlson in West Hempstead and Newport, Long Island, Willie Gilzenberg in Newark, and Harry Smythe in Baltimore. He didn't mention anything about booking wrestlers to Madison Square Garden in New York City.

The reason was because Capitol had broken from what *Long Island Press* sportswriter Jack Edward Lee called the Manhattan Wrestling Alliance around mid-June 1960. The Manhattan Wrestling Alliance may have been misrepresented in name, but the gist was that McMahon was no longer operating in conjunction with the Kola Kwariani–Charley Johnston–Jack Pfefer group at the Garden. Beginning on July 16, 1960, the same week as the FBI interviews, Johnston promoted a seven-match program at the Garden, and the longtime influence of McMahon was absent. It appeared the growth of Capitol, despite its impressive gains into Chicago, was stifled.

Add the Contos case and Department of Justice investigation, and McMahon was facing the worst crisis of his wrestling career. The bad news continued. Dr. Jerry Graham, one of the wrestlers he used to book, spilled his beans to the FBI and William Olivas's attorney, George Little, and all of it was documented in the growing file covering Capitol's nefarious methods. Among his statements was that McMahon was "just a figurehead," and he confirmed officials' suspicions that Toots was the man in charge. Mondt "calls all the shots," Graham declared and was the central "policymaker" for wrestling in the territory.

Investigators were also tipped off to allegations of unreported income by Mondt, and between his high earnings from managing Rocca and his gambling, it was definitely an area to explore. McMahon realized Toots was the lightning rod for government interest and knew he had to detach him from the day-to-day activities of Capitol Wrestling—even if it was in appearance only.

Graham spewed forth a geyser of information, but officials quickly ascertained that his troubling criminal record would thwart his credibility on the stand. He had recently been arrested in New Jersey for carrying a loaded pistol in his car and had been suspended by both the New York and Virginia State Athletic Commissions for missing matches and acts detrimental to wrestling. The National Wrestling Association did likewise. After breaking from McMahon, he worked with Olivas in opposition to Capitol in Washington, DC, and attempted to run Griffith Stadium, but the show was axed at the last minute when the talent they lined up failed to show. He paid a fine in New York and resumed local appearances as a key member of the Kwariani troupe.

Both Graham and sportswriter Dan Parker made unflattering remarks about McMahon's latest find, a popular 24-year-old newcomer to pro wrestling named Bruno Sammartino, who was making a big splash across the region. Sammartino, a strongman from Italy, was discovered by promoter Rudy Miller in Pittsburgh and had debuted the year before. In his newspaper column in the *New York Daily Mirror* on January 18, 1960, Parker stated, "With the Puerto Rican trade about milked dry, the rasslin' brains are now about to woo the Italians, who jilted them about 20 years ago, by building up a burper of ordinary ability named Bruno Samartino [sic] into a 'superman.'"

Graham made his comments privately to the FBI on April 21, 1960. He said Bruno had "very little ability and [was] completely dominated by the promoters." Two weeks before, he had been booked to lose to Sammartino, and Graham claimed he refused. Regardless of the skewed remarks, Sammartino was viewed fondly by the leaders of Capitol Wrestling, and they already had high expectations for the former power lifter. In the midst of the promotional struggle in New York, Sammartino was stolen from Capitol's roster by Kwariani in an underhanded deal that coincided with McMahon's loss of the Garden. It was a tricky play, and, once again, McMahon got the short end of the stick.

Up in Boston, promoters were also at war. The longtime association of Paul Bowser and Eddie Quinn had soured, allegedly because Bowser disliked Quinn's links to mobster and boxing mogul Frankie Carbo. Outgunned as far as talent was concerned, Bowser was drawing far less than his rival at the box office and decided in April 1960 to pay three years of delinquent NWA dues to be reinstated in the Alliance. He figured the solid NWA partnership would aid in his battle, but three months later, Bowser passed away at the age of 74. Things mellowed soon thereafter, with Johnny Doyle, Tony Santos, and Eddie Quinn working in cahoots at the Boston Garden with talent coming in from Montreal and New York.

Out west in Minneapolis, there was a significant happening that would alter the way fans and promoters viewed the wrestling landscape. For 12 years, the National Wrestling Alliance had been the only universally accepted and formal sanctioning organization with the power to recognize, support, and modify champions. It was the standard bearer for promotional cooperation, and professional wrestling experienced a tremendous period of growth with the NWA in charge. But to many affiliates, the consent decree and the continued pressure on the Alliance by the Department of Justice had purged the NWA of its positive attributes. With an ongoing antitrust investigation, it was clear that an obvious reform of wrestling was needed. That meant that instead of there being one sanctioning outfit with all the control, there would be two.

The wheels for this massive change began when Dennis Stecher, son of NWA originator Tony Stecher, retired and sold his interest in the Minneapolis promotion to Wally Karbo and Verne Gagne in early 1960. Sam Muchnick sent out a notice to the Alliance on February 19, 1960, and explained that Karbo would "be given every consideration" if he desired to join the organization. But Karbo and Gagne didn't desire to join the NWA. They instead launched the American Wrestling Alliance, more commonly known as the American Wrestling Association or AWA.

The formation of the AWA was not in spite of the NWA or its problems, but as a way to create competition in the marketplace. To the outside world, the NWA was no longer the singular dominant faction, and common sense said if wrestlers had problems in Muchnick's organization, they could easily travel to Gagne's and find work there. That eliminated the sense there was a far-reaching monopoly in total control of wrestling. Muchnick understood the reasoning but generally disliked the idea. He had fought for a unified NWA with members in every corner of the world.

The AWA diminished the NWA's power and, to Muchnick's chagrin, prompted the recognition of a second "world" heavyweight champion, a champion more on par with the Alliance titleholder than any other claimant in existence. Logically, Gagne was the first AWA champion, and his popularity in the Upper Midwest was remarkable. The cordiality between the hierarchy of the AWA and NWA remained strong, and it wasn't odd to see Gagne or Karbo mingling among Alliance members at the latter's annual convention. Talent was traded as if Minneapolis was still a member of the NWA, and at no time did Muchnick or his compatriots think of bucking the AWA in a fight for their lost territory.

Wrestling in the Midwest was thriving, and Chicago was the finest example. The city was completely resurrected by the influence of McMahon's TV and wrestlers, and promoter Fred Kohler was running things masterfully. Throughout 1960, attendance at the International Amphitheater was consistently in the range of 7,000 to 12,000 people per show. During the summer, Kohler rented Comiskey Park, home of the Chicago White Sox baseball club, and arranged three attractive events with the best talent available. His efforts were handsomely rewarded by the wrestling public as 30,275 attended the first show, on July 29; 17,206 turned out for the second, on August 19; and 26,731 people enjoyed the final, on September 16. The combined gate total for the stadium programs was over $220,000.

Nowhere else was drawing those kinds of numbers, and despite the uncertainty in New York, McMahon was acknowledged by his peers as a premier booking operator for his success in Chicago. For that reason, he was warmly welcomed by the members of the National Wrestling Alliance at its annual convention in Acapulco, Mexico, on August 26–27, 1960. Accompanied by Toots, McMahon joined Muchnick, Kohler, Frank Tunney of Toronto, Leroy McGuirk of Tulsa, Jim Crockett of Charlotte, Roy Welch of Nashville, Karl Sarpolis of Amarillo, and the host of the conclave, Salvador Lutteroth Jr. of Mexico City. Fourteen other members decided not to make the trip and were absent from the proceedings.

The NWA showered esteem on McMahon, unanimously voting to accept his membership into the organization. His entry into the Alliance was slightly irregular in that he didn't follow the usual protocol for new members, which called for prepayment of a $500 initiation fee, $100 yearly dues, and an application form. The membership overlooked these little details to add McMahon to their roster. Muchnick, always a stickler for particulars, sent McMahon several letters and telegrams in the following weeks and called to remind him to submit his dues and paperwork, but he still hadn't received anything by October 11.

At the Acapulco convention, Muchnick withdrew from his position as NWA president after 10 consecutive terms. The organization agreed, from that point forth, to select a different president every year beginning with Tunney. Muchnick would remain in the pivotal role as executive secretary, booker to the heavyweight champion, and treasurer. He was also responsible for all bookkeeping matters. In his diligence, he expressed concern about McMahon's failure to submit his dues and wondered if he had reconsidered joining the NWA. He inquired about the status again in another missive, noting that he had been admitted into the Alliance "because of Toots Mondt, and [his] friendship" with members. He didn't want to be on McMahon's back about things but admitted he had "a job to do."

The delay on the part of McMahon was not because of any

change of heart regarding the Alliance. No, McMahon had grand ideas for his association with the NWA and planned to use his influence to realize his strategies. That was apparent in Mexico, when McMahon convinced the membership to officially declare Buddy Rogers the United States heavyweight champion, widening his recognition beyond Capitol regions to throughout all Alliance territories. At the first opportunity for a publicity snapshot, a photo was taken of Muchnick and Rogers holding the U.S. belt, and it was made known that the Nature Boy would be available to all members for matches in defense of his championship.

In his war against Kwariani and Pfefer, who turned on him after Capitol brought Rogers into the fold, McMahon knew that being attached to the Alliance was a benefit. But a question had to be asked: Why was McMahon's membership approved when Mondt already represented Capitol Wrestling in the NWA? The answer was because Mondt was rotating out of the New York City area for the first time since the 1940s and setting up a new promotion in Pittsburgh, leaving McMahon to command the territory as the central NWA booking agent. This was the solution McMahon found to the Department of Justice's inquiry and the need to create distance between Capitol and Mondt. There was simply too much heat to keep the status quo.

McMahon submitted his application to Muchnick and agreed to "abide by all of the by-laws, rules and regulations" of the NWA on October 17, 1960. One of his first matters of business was seeking dates for world heavyweight champion Pat O'Connor, the New Zealand–born successor to Dick Hutton. O'Connor was a popular grappler, able to blend a style of showmanship with legit abilities, and fans were responding in greater numbers to his bouts than to Hutton's. Muchnick, at the same time, arranged for appearances by Buddy Rogers in St. Louis in November and December 1960. He told McMahon he was "not figuring an O'Connor-Rogers match," stating "that can come later" in a letter dated November 19, 1960.

The rival champions were expected to do big business against each other, but Muchnick knew the time wasn't right. More buildup was needed. In his December 1 bulletin to the NWA, he referenced the vote in Mexico supporting Rogers as the official U.S. champion and said, "at the present time, [Rogers] does not seem to be available to all members, as the World Champion, Pat O'Connor is." He went on to state that Rogers had "met all of the requirements discussed in Mexico, insofar as the St. Louis, Chicago, and Washington promotions are concerned," and he wondered if he should be acknowledged as the United States title-holder "recognized by the NWA" because of "his unavailability to all members." He asked his fellow brethren for advice on the matter, but no one voiced any serious grievances, and Rogers's status was upheld.

The relocation of Mondt to Pittsburgh was coordinated to placate the Department of Justice and the New York State Athletic Commission. Pundits in recent years have linked the move to his intermittently tumultuous relationship with McMahon, but Toots was serving the greater good of Capitol by going west. Now grapplers could venture back and forth between Washington and Chicago and stop in Pittsburgh en route. In the formation of Pennsylvania Wrestling, Inc., which intended to run biweekly at the North Side Grotto and during the summer at Forbes Field, Mondt served as the official NWA matchmaker for the territory and as the secretary-treasurer. McMahon was the company's president and Kohler the vice president. Of the different inter-Alliance factions, this trio was becoming one of the most powerful in the organization's history.

Mondt's removal from the Northeast seemed, on the surface, to lighten tensions, but field investigators were still actively developing the case. On November 22, 1960, a detailed office memorandum was submitted to William D. Kilgore Jr., chief of the Judgment Enforcement Section, and its subject was *Proposed Contempt Petition in United States v. National Wrestling Alliance* (Civ. No. 3-729, S.D. Iowa, Central Division). The respondents, as named in the petition, were Lewis, Crockett, Mondt, and McMahon. Finally, after months of examination, the government was laying out its strongest case in writing, specifically outlining the "facts constituting the contempt" in the 20-page memo. It read:

> The facts fully indicate that there has been a deliberate violation of the [NWA] Judgment by Lewis, Crockett and Mondt with the aid and assistance of McMahon, who admittedly had full knowledge of the Judgment. The case is not a documentary one and may be very difficult. Nevertheless, if presented with a moderate degree of skill, I am confident that a verdict of guilty can be obtained against Lewis and Crockett. The evidence against Mondt and McMahon is somewhat weaker. The industry is not of too great importance or significant, economically it is true, but that very willfulness of the violation makes it significant . . . and one that we ought to bring.

Despite outward confidence, the recommendations were not heeded by superiors in the Antitrust Division, and the contempt action was never brought to trial in Des Moines or anywhere else. The four men whose fate hung in the balance were let off easy, but 1960 was insufferably nerve-racking for each of them. Lewis suffered the most, and his health rapidly deteriorated. He passed away in March of the following year. The other pending antitrust matter, the Contos lawsuit, remained a thorny situation for a few additional years, but eventually a federal judge in Washington, DC, decided that the plaintiffs had failed to prove any intent to monopolize the business by Capitol Wrestling. McMahon was victorious and again avoided any perilous consequences from his ties to Mondt, the consent decree, and the NWA.

The National Wrestling Alliance's weakened nature in 1960 made it easier for a strong leader like McMahon to manipulate it. Using Mondt's intense personality as a battering ram, he powered his way into the confidence of Sam Muchnick and was not only breaking attendance records in Chicago, but he was prepared to retake New York City after a months-long absence. McMahon's vision was clear, but for whatever reason, his peers in the NWA were blind to his grandiose strategy to monopolize the world heavyweight championship. If not blind, they were either ignorant or incapable of stopping the runaway freight train from nearly destroying their entire organization.

(11)
THE NATIONAL WRESTLING ALLIANCE DILEMMA

The quarrelsome conditions of pro wrestling in New York City were a constant during the summer of 1960. Matchmakers Kola Kwariani and Jack Pfefer were in full partnership at Madison Square Garden, but they couldn't achieve the 20,000-person houses of 1959. They pushed heel Pampero Firpo, featured popular Antonino Rocca and Bruno Sammartino as a tag team, and filled out their shows with talent from Pedro Martinez. Nothing worked. A controversial situation in White Plains, New York, on September 24, 1960, resulted in Kwariani being suspended and fined by the athletic commission for "acts detrimental to the best interests of wrestling." What he did wasn't disclosed in public reports, but Sammartino was also chastised for his actions and fined $100.

Kwariani apologized to the commission and promised to never step outside the bounds again. However, he failed to remit payment for his fine and remained on the suspended list maintained by the National Wrestling Association. Thus, his formal role was diminished, and Pfefer was seen as the primary leader at the Garden as attendance fell from 16,000 in August to an estimated 10,000 on October 1. Even a Rocca–Miguel Perez reunion couldn't spike the box office take. On October 24 and November 14, 1960, Rocca wrestled Sammartino in the main event, but only 12,000 individuals paid to see the two Italians battle on each occasion.

Shareholders of the Madison Square Garden Corporation, holders of the license to promote wrestling and boxing at the venue, were anything but content by the way grappling was being run and expected much greater returns. The Pfefer-Kwariani combination exhibited a temporary glimmer, but their inability to improve the numbers forced an overhaul in the booking department. The December 12, 1960, program was canceled and completely rebooked by Vincent J. McMahon, who was rehired as the central matchmaker for the Garden. However, bad weather canceled his replacement offering. Eleven days later, McMahon's return show drew 11,612 fans.

Featuring the Fabulous Kangaroos, Johnny Valentine, Bearcat Wright, NWA United States champion Buddy Rogers, and NWA world heavyweight titleholder Pat O'Connor, McMahon revitalized the arena within two months, drawing over 20,000 on February 27, 1961. Instead of losing venues to rival factions, Capitol was again expanding, and McMahon now had nothing to worry about from Kwariani, Martinez, or Pfefer. The Department of Justice probe was also in the rearview mirror, meaning that McMahon had not only won the wrestling war but survived the government inquest. Holding considerable interest at the Garden and in Chicago, the top-drawing city in all of grappling, McMahon was judged by many observers as the sport's premier booking agent and the closest thing to a "czar" that wrestling had.

Sammartino rejoined Capitol Wrestling when Kwariani went under, but he kept his word and fulfilled a booking the latter had arranged in San Francisco on March 4, 1961. The excursion to California for promoter Roy Shire's initial event at the Cow Palace offered him the opportunity to wrestle before 16,553 enthusiasts and, all in all, was a historic evening. But back home,

McMahon was incensed. He wanted Bruno in Baltimore on the same date, and for the second time, Sammartino had seriously disappointed him. The Maryland Athletic Commission promptly suspended the grappling strongman pending a hearing, and the National Wrestling Association placed a nationwide ban on him in member states.

Only two years into his pro career, Sammartino was fast becoming a mainstream idol. McMahon was all too aware of his potential, but their relationship so far was rocky at best. The suspension led Sammartino away from Capitol territory, and while he appeared for matches around the Great Lakes and Midwest, he personally doubted he had any long-term future in pro wrestling. That is, until McMahon intervened and encouraged the Maryland commission to lift its ban. The National Wrestling Association followed suit on May 23, 1961. Fences were mended, and Bruno returned to Madison Square Garden in August.

The National Wrestling Alliance was on the threshold of change, and McMahon was spearheading the movement. Talks were ongoing about switching the world title from O'Connor to Rogers, initiating a new era in NWA history because, for the first time, the Alliance was going to prop up a showman rather than a shooter as the heavyweight kingpin. The debate was nearly a foregone conclusion, despite the fact that Rogers, as the U.S. champion, was not available for bookings to all members. It was a significant drawback, but top proponents of the switch—McMahon, Fred Kohler, and Sam Muchnick—advanced the cause anyway. They were, at the very least, guaranteed to benefit from the maneuver.

McMahon was a businessman, and in his eyes, getting his man the most prestigious wrestling championship in the industry was a major triumph. Even though titles, per se, were not acknowledged in New York, the fans that lived in the Empire State didn't live in a void. They were exposed to TV from Bridgeport and Washington, DC, read magazines, and knew the significance of the world championship. Kohler and Muchnick were completely satisfied by regular visits from Rogers, who, by this time, was without question wrestling's greatest draw. His availability to other members was going to have to be worked out, Muchnick knew, but the first priority was making the most out of the title change itself, and Chicago was primed for the match of the century.

On June 30, 1961, 38,000 people were attracted by the excitement surrounding the O'Connor-Rogers bout in the Windy City. The show, held at Comiskey Park, a baseball field on the south side of the city, established a new gate record in the United States, $125,000. As anticipated, the participants in the main event delivered an expert performance, and Rogers won the NWA crown in three falls. McMahon's cohort in Newark, Willie Gilzenberg, sent a message to Rogers's former manager Jack Pfefer on July 4, saying, in part, "I just spoke to Vince and they are (Freddie [Kohler], Toots and Vince—also the Fiddler [Ray Fabiani]) still counting the bundles from the last Chicago show. I bet Buddie [sic] Rogers will love strutting around the country as World's Heavyweight Wrestling Champion."

Rogers did love it. So did the fans. Although he was a "rule breaker," Rogers was cheered and jeered at pretty much the same time with half the crowd on each side. But most audiences enjoyed the histrionics, and his eternal confidence and colorful behavior were thoroughly appreciated as part of the wrestling spectacle. Lou Thesz–like Rogers delivered a great show whether he was in small-town New Jersey or at the Garden in New York. Although lacking the impressive repertoire of submissions, he paraded around as if he was wrestling's greatest gift. He was a natural sports entertainer long before the term was in vogue, and his matches were mandatory viewing.

As a worker, Rogers was constantly pushing the right buttons, and he was invaluable to promoters. In both Chicago and New York, he was responsible for drawing more than a million dollars in gate money, and sportswriters bestowed a number of honors on him, including Wrestler of the Year by *Ring Magazine* in 1961 and '62. The Comiskey Park rematch between Rogers and O'Connor on September 1, 1961, scored another $63,326 and figures exploded at the Garden, in Washington, DC, and in Pittsburgh. Capitol Wrestling was experiencing its greatest financial boon in company history, and it was all thanks to McMahon's sly arrangement and Rogers's fine workmanship.

In years past, success by the NWA world champion usually meant the entire organization was in good health. But it was obvious from the start that wasn't going to be the case this time around. The well-being of the Alliance was impaired by upper management's inability to balance the high-demand needs of Rogers in Capitol territory with the rest of the NWA. As a result, nearly every time Rogers left the Northeast on a tour, he appeared for a short list of promoters, covering the essential regions like Chicago, Philadelphia, Houston, and St. Louis. Smaller cities, operated by faithful, dues-paying members, were ignored for one reason or another, but it was generally believed they were second-rate and a waste of time.

After all, Rogers was drawing real money in prospering regions. Why was he going to appear at a high school in the middle of Kansas when he could light things up in a proven venue and make his handlers even richer than they already were? To NWA purists, the answer was simple: It was a matter of fairness. By sending Rogers to the high school in Kansas, the Alliance was acknowledging that Orville Brown's territory was just as important to the organization as Madison Square Garden. It was also upholding the custom of appearing in arenas large and small, ensuring all members got their money's worth, a tradition first established by Thesz.

From the perspective of Rogers and Capitol Wrestling, it was important to group as many matches into as condensed an area as possible, trimming down time and money lost to travel. The Northeastern circuit was crafted with that strategy in mind, allowing Rogers to appear at a different arena nightly. In a given month, he could wrestle all over the territory with few repeat showings, including a shot at the Garden. It was an ideal region for Rogers, especially considering that New Jersey was his home. He had the conditioning to grapple five to six nights a week, and if he was called upon to venture elsewhere, he fulfilled his narrow NWA requirements as outlined by the Alliance and McMahon, his personal manager.

According to the NWA's constitution, the world heavyweight champion did not belong to one man but to the Alliance as a whole. The only true benefit to the entire organization was that its treasury grew each time Rogers wrestled, no matter where he was. Facing a rejuvenated Department of Justice investigation and a potentially damaging civil suit in Des Moines (*Harold C. "Sonny" Myers v. P.L. George and the National Wrestling Alliance*), the NWA needed a significant amount of money for its legal fund. The Alliance likely approved the controversial Rogers title switch based on this motive.

Sam Muchnick lived and breathed the NWA. More than anyone else, he knew McMahon's track record when it came to sharing his champions, but he understood the needs of the NWA and acknowledged that Buddy's box office value was greater than all previous Alliance champions. After years of dismal returns and brewing threats on the horizon, this was their chance to pad their accounts like never before while protecting the union.

Still, observers felt the powerful minority faction made up of Muchnick, McMahon, and Kohler had moved the title to Rogers to satisfy their own personal greed. It looked as if NWA management purposefully ignored the possible dangers because members were transfixed by McMahon's incredible success. Choosing to improve their financial worth over harmony was the real threat to the organization's future.

Overlooking existing complaints, the members of the Alliance were all too willing to cooperate with Capitol Wrestling. They gave up dates they had with Rogers to help McMahon and even rewarded Buddy by boosting his per-appearance payoff amount at the August 1961 convention in Toronto. The share, as a whole, remained the same, 15 percent of each house, but instead of the titleholder receiving a flat 11 percent (the remainder went to the Alliance for administrative fees), Rogers's pay was raised to 11.25 percent. When out of Capitol territory, the local promoter would pay Rogers by cash or check and mail the NWA's cut to Muchnick. Inside Capitol territory, the same system was supposed to be followed, with Rogers being paid and the Alliance fees sent promptly to St. Louis.

As the executive secretary of the Alliance, Muchnick was the middleman between the NWA and Capitol. He was well acquainted with McMahon and Mondt on both a personal and professional level, and he took on much of the burden of keeping them in line when it came to following protocol. For years, he was responsible for booking the heavyweight champion and arranging the title-holder's schedule in a fair manner. He was exceedingly competent at running the NWA, and although he was no longer president, he was still acknowledged as the backbone of the union. In 1961, his concerns regarding Capitol had less to do with where Rogers was or wasn't appearing and more with the timeliness of the checks due the Alliance for all of Buddy's appearances.

The lackluster approach to remitting money owed the Alliance disappointed Muchnick, and he was constantly displaying his anxiety over the accounting delays in letters to McMahon. At one juncture, he noted that Washington, DC, was "the only office [that was] always behind in sending the NWA fees."

The lax payments to the NWA were further evidence that Capitol Wrestling was still playing by its own rules. By mid-August 1961, 12 payments were late. The following month, Muchnick told McMahon to keep Rogers out of places like Poughkeepsie, Sunnyside Garden, and Lodi, New Jersey, because of small gates, saying, "There are so many places that I know that he could do much better." Muchnick, in a letter dated September 28, 1961, also discussed a conversation in which Rogers "protested" about appearing in tag-team bouts. "No champion before has been in tag matches and I must agree that this certainly does not dignify the title," Muchnick said.

But tag-main events were commonplace at the Garden, and Rogers was almost always booked into bouts alongside Bob Orton Sr. or Johnny Barend versus a pair of heroes. Only occasionally did his routine change at the venue. He did have a notable match against Antonino Rocca and a successful series against "Cowboy" Bob Ellis.

This was a perfect example of how the fundamental attitude of wrestling in Capitol territory differed from what Muchnick expected out of the NWA's members. He saw things one way and McMahon another, and their different perspectives on how business should be conducted caused plenty of conflict, though it was manageable. They often saw eye to eye, but rarely did a month go by without some sort of quandary. No matter how hard Muchnick tried to get Capitol to bend to the old-fashioned traditions of the NWA, he (and the Alliance) ended up being the ones to compromise.

Muchnick was tactful in his suggestions to McMahon, and he often prodded his friend to "get after Phil" so he could bring NWA finances up to date. "Phil," in this instance, was McMahon's secretary and right-hand man, Phil Zacko, who handled all of the money relating to Rogers's bookings. Zacko, originally from Pottsville, Pennsylvania, entered the wrestling business around 1948 and spent many years collaborating with Ed Contos in Baltimore. He promoted outlying towns across the region and earned the trust of McMahon and Mondt through his first-rate work ethic. The ever-conscientious Zacko informed Muchnick that he was doing his best to get things in order, but initiating real change in company policy was nearly impossible.

Both Muchnick and McMahon had two separate spheres of responsibility and stress. Muchnick was answering to the rest of the NWA about every little detail relating to the heavyweight champion. He was worried the Alliance was going to collapse under the leadership of new president Fred Kohler, troubled by the financial state of the organization, and anxious over the Department of Justice's inquiry and the Sonny Myers trial in Des Moines. He was also forced to deal with his own sudden health concerns.

The increased Department of Justice oversight was nagging McMahon as well. That and the constant hassle of trying to measure up to Alliance expectations became too much, and on October 24, 1961, McMahon sent Muchnick a surprising telegram announcing his resignation from the NWA "effective immediately." Muchnick responded by letter on October 27, stating that due to a sticky situation involving the membership committee, of which McMahon was a member, and also the Department of Justice, he wasn't comfortable accepting his resignation without further examination. McMahon didn't want to hear that, and a few days later he reiterated his resignation, declaring he'd "severed all relations with the organization." He held no bad feelings toward Muchnick or anyone else. In fact, he wished Muchnick a "speedy recovery" in his health battle by telegram in early November.

Later in the month, Rogers went out of commission with a serious arm injury, and it was believed his impairment stemmed from a November 27, 1961, bout against Bearcat Wright in Washington, DC. But a letter from Muchnick to McMahon dated October 18, 1961, reveals that they verbally agreed Rogers would cease wrestling on November 27 and then undergo an operation two days later. Muchnick predicted he would likely return "sometime after the first of the year." This information confirms Rogers was injured well before November 27 and dutifully wrestled with a bad limb for over a month before succumbing to the need for surgery.

With everything touch and go, McMahon's status in the NWA remained in question, and Muchnick was rightfully concerned. After all, there was plenty on the line, including what was shaping up to be an argument over the rightful ownership of the world champion for future bookings. They communicated regularly, and on December 1, 1961, Muchnick indicated in a letter that he felt McMahon "had a change of heart and [wanted] to stay on as a member of the National Wrestling Alliance." It was true. McMahon had reevaluated his options and had decided to withdraw his resignation on the morning of December 10. The news lessened the overall crisis, but since Rogers was still on the shelf and there were other brewing difficulties growing within the NWA, Muchnick sought a personal meeting with McMahon sometime early in January to talk the issues over.

Rogers was back in the ring before the end of December, and

McMahon and Muchnick met in Columbus, Ohio, on January 3, 1962, to work through all outstanding matters. Solutions were outlined, but they proved temporary, and by January 22 Muchnick was again grumbling about current conditions. He said he had been working "very hard" to oblige McMahon with regard to the champion and reaffirmed that the NWA depended on the income from the titleholder "to exist." Once again, phone calls pacified Muchnick, but he had little choice but to continue badgering McMahon for owed booking fees. He expressed his displeasure with having to do so, but checks were weeks and, in some instances, months late. Pittsburgh, the territory of Toots Mondt, was almost four months behind in a payment for an appearance from October.

By May, nearly 15 checks were late, and Muchnick told McMahon that the NWA's finances were "low," expressing his eagerness for immediate action. He was angry about the lack of urgency and said he didn't want Rogers appearing in certain cities until tardy fees were paid. He said it was the "first time in 13 years" of booking the Alliance champion that promoters were "getting away with not paying" the necessary organizational fees.

The discord seemed to encumber everyone but Rogers, who managed to maintain his intense workload. His success continued, especially in metropolitan areas, and his heel antics generated tons of heat throughout North America. Conversely, in some rural areas he didn't have the same kind of pull, and promoters refused to use him because he didn't draw. This dichotomy—fans in big cities enjoying Rogers versus fans in smaller territories refusing to support his unsportsmanlike conduct—was revealing and said a lot about the mindset at the time. In West Texas, Dory Funk Sr., co-owner of the Amarillo office, knew Buddy's performance was the antithesis of the kind of wrestling fans expected to see. It also wasn't a secret that he disliked Rogers. Therefore, the decision to reject his laurels was easy. He instead propped up former footballer Gene Kiniski as champion in March 1962.

As each month passed, wrestling's contentious atmosphere divided members of the NWA, but McMahon still wasn't being held accountable for the problems. In fact, the Alliance elected him second vice president at its convention in St. Louis on August 26, 1962. Kohler's presidency concluded at the meetings, and Karl Sarpolis of Amarillo was named to the post. Ironically, Sarpolis was Funk's partner and led the mounting coalition of NWA affiliates opposing Rogers's claims.

It was becoming clear that as long as Buddy was on top, there was going to be animosity. Something was going to have to give, and that meant either the Alliance was going to dissolve or Rogers was going to be replaced. McMahon didn't want a turnover in champions anytime soon, but the second half of 1962 was going to be painfully challenging, leaving Rogers, Capitol Wrestling, and the Alliance scrambling for answers. The inevitably dramatic turn was kicked off when Rogers was confronted by two of his peers in the dressing room of the Fairgrounds Coliseum in Columbus on August 31, 1962.

Bill Miller and Karl Gotch, the aggressors, were part of a national booking outfit running independently of the National Wrestling Alliance and headed, in part, by Johnny Doyle. Since leaving the Northeast and his ties to Capitol Wrestling behind, Doyle had partnered with Fred Kohler's old assistant, Jim Barnett, and the two had built a mighty circuit that was the envy of promoters. They formed a powerful roster of popular superstars, invaded Detroit, Denver, and Los Angeles, and invested money in innumerable territories from Kansas City to Atlanta. During their expansion, one of their primary goals was to join the NWA and solidify themselves as partners in the national clique.

Despite the fact that the Antitrust Division of the Department of Justice was being kept in the loop about Doyle and Barnett's membership request, NWA president Kohler named a membership committee of opponents to the idea and initiated a series of stall tactics to prevent their admittance. Among his allies were McMahon and Mondt, Doyle's former cronies. The Kohler-McMahon group, in attempting to shore up the eastern part of the United States, had put money into Detroit and was engaged in a head-to-head battle against Doyle and Barnett. The latter were also fighting for Columbus versus the local NWA member, Al Haft, who was the promoter on record for the Fairgrounds Coliseum show on August 31, 1962, when Rogers was brazenly challenged backstage.

To this day, it is impossible to know whether or not Miller and Gotch sent that message to Kohler and McMahon on behalf of Doyle and Barnett. It is unlikely they were there on a "hit job" and paid off by either man, Jack Pfefer, or any other enemies of the Nature Boy, as per convoluted rumors that have circulated for decades. They *were* there to make a point, maybe even scare Rogers a little bit, and unfortunate words deteriorated into violence. Rogers was outmatched and outgunned, and even an inkling of cockiness could have sparked fisticuffs. In the end, Rogers was bruised and battered and his left arm was nearly broken when his rivals slammed it in the dressing room door.

Whether intentional or not, the message was loud and clear to McMahon: He needed to protect his champion even more, and Columbus was added to a list of Alliance regions to avoid. Shortly after news of the beating got out, speculation developed, promulgated mostly by the anti-Rogers crowd, claiming Buddy was faking his injuries and the "attack" was exaggerated. Muchnick was annoyed and told McMahon that people were saying Buddy was nothing more than a "terrific actor." Nonetheless, he personally wanted to have faith in the champion and took the injury seriously.

The out-of-ring fight in Columbus caused Rogers to cancel engagements in September, and though he made a few restricted appearances, he didn't return full time until the last week of the month. Smartly, he curtailed his ring repertoire to work around his soreness and resumed his hectic schedule. In Montreal on November 21, he was still not 100 percent when he misjudged a jump from the apron to the Forum floor and fractured his right ankle. His opponent, Killer Kowalski, pinned him for the first fall soon thereafter, and officials halted the match because the NWA champion was unfit to continue.

The news was disheartening. Rogers was going back to the sidelines while critics lambasted the injury story, claiming it was all a work. The Alliance had recently decided that Lou Thesz would return and finally strip the world title from Rogers, perhaps as early as December 14 in Houston, during Morris Sigel's annual Christmas show. But plans had to be altered, and again, those who didn't feel the injury was legitimate saw the maneuver as part of a scripted scenario by McMahon to avoid a championship defeat. Instead, both Sigel and Toots Mondt booked Kowalski as a title claimant stemming from the Montreal match, using Killer in place of Rogers, but the NWA refused any formal sanctioning.

Capitol Wrestling was taxed by financial hardship in December 1962, and the temporary loss of Rogers was painful. His value was immense, whereas the proposed title shift to Thesz was practically worthless to the territory and future box office gates. Even at the height of Thesz's run as champion in the 1950s, he was an uninspiring draw in the Northeast, and there was no reason to believe this time would be any different. McMahon was not fond of the idea but understood it was a necessary aspect of the business, particularly because the NWA had a stranglehold on Capitol's $10,000 mandatory performance bond for Rogers, money McMahon wanted back as soon as possible.

The normal politics of the day seemed to intensify, and Muchnick preached about continued fellowship to McMahon in spite of the difficulties. He discussed Capitol's problems with Mondt and found out that the company needed a swift influx of cash to solve a pending crisis. Acknowledging that he was "using very poor business judgment," Muchnick agreed to return half of the performance bond, stating, "Sometimes you use bad business judgment to do friends a favor."

On December 28, 1962, he sent McMahon a check for $5,559.75, which included all interest, and the friendly gesture was made with the confidence that Rogers would do the job to Thesz when directed. No other delays were anticipated.

Back in the ring the day after Christmas, Rogers was kept on a short leash and appeared in many safe towns with very little unexpected drama. His vulnerability was a danger, and Capitol wanted to ensure he was safe, allowing a full recuperation. His responsibility to the NWA was important, but McMahon was eyeing a bigger picture, one that placed more of an emphasis on Buddy than outsiders realized at the time. Taking somewhat of a cue from Verne Gagne's AWA, he was cultivating a strategy to create a new organization for the Northeastern territory, fully independent of the NWA. McMahon knew relying on occasional visits by Thesz was pointless, and since his region could support its own champion without interference from promoters elsewhere, he had to consider that option first and foremost.

Rogers would be pivotal in maintaining the integrity of the heavyweight division and keeping the status quo. And, of course, the money he'd be bringing in would offset any increased expenditures. The design of a new sanctioning body was easier than one might think and didn't necessarily require significant changes to the promotional structure. Basically, Capitol's foundations were going to remain the same. Increased publicity to raise awareness of the changes was necessary, as was a carefully worded explanation in national magazines to clarify details of the situation. Wrestling fans were mindful of little details, and a departure from the well-known and recognized NWA structure was something that needed to be made clear right off the bat.

Additionally, any change was not going to be made with war in mind. McMahon envisioned a sizable territory, but he didn't imagine expanding into the backyards of his NWA brethren. He had many friends throughout the Alliance, and with Muchnick in the center coordinating the relations of all major booking offices, he anticipated continued peace.

Things were far from finalized, but a rough sketch of the transformation was in place by early January 1963. McMahon and his allies were undaunted by the turbulent road ahead and continued to expand, setting up a promising new promotion in Cleveland. The operation was going to be run locally by veteran fight promoter Larry Atkins with Mondt as his booker, and McMahon, as usual, was the syndicate president. The Cleveland venture, incorporated as Buckeye Sports Enterprises, was significant because it marked the first time McMahon shaped an independent governing body for any of his promotions. Named the World Wide Wrestling Association (WWWA), the group was seemingly in place to assist in the transition of grapplers from Chicago through Detroit to Cleveland and Pittsburgh and then into the Northeast.

Those four cities were valuable moneymakers, and McMahon wanted to keep it that way by strengthening his management role and ensuring the quality of talent. He had yet to decide whether the WWWA would be the organization to represent the entire expanse of his territory, but the option was certainly on the table.

With all problems behind them, McMahon and Muchnick agreed on January 24, 1963, for the Rogers-Thesz title switch, and both men were present in Toronto to watch the contest in person. Many contemporary versions of the championship bout depict a scenario in which the NWA was holding a "$25,000" performance bond over the head of a reluctant Rogers to actually go through with the match. And Thesz himself had to warn Buddy in the ring that there were two ways things could go, easy or hard. These reports added a lot of sensation to the story but stretched the truth.

The belt deposit only amounted to $10,000, and by the time of the match, McMahon had already received half. The other half wasn't small bills placed in a suspicious black bag, only to be delivered to the dressing room after Thesz won, but sent from Muchnick to McMahon four days after the bout occurred. There were no concerns Rogers would refuse to play ball and everything went according to plan. After 14 minutes and 54 seconds of cooperative wrestling, Thesz beat Rogers to capture the NWA world heavyweight title. Two weeks later, Thesz won a rematch, taking two of three falls before 11,000 exhilarated spectators at Maple Leaf Gardens.

In the Northeastern territory, and in spite of the losses, Rogers remained champion. The explanation given to the public by Capitol Wrestling was that the January 24 bout was only one fall and the world title could not change hands in such fashion. The three-fall rematch was purposely concealed, and without the

Internet or dirt sheets to inform fans, people were oblivious to the fact that a second bout had been staged. Capitol continued booking Rogers in their arenas as the top heavyweight, and the difference between McMahon's promotion and the NWA was now abundantly clear.

McMahon was using the Alliance as the springboard for his new organization, just as the AWA had done in 1960. According to press reports at the time, Minneapolis promoters gave NWA champion Pat O'Connor 60 days to defend his belt against the number one contender, Verne Gagne. When time elapsed, Gagne was proclaimed world titleholder. It wasn't that O'Connor shirked his duties as a defending champion, but it was part of the rationale of Gagne himself, who owned the territory and was supporting the AWA's formation. The story legitimized branching off from the NWA and recognizing another claimant to the heavyweight throne. And in three years, the AWA had become respectable because of Gagne's hard work.

Fans in Minneapolis were inspired by the recognition and availability of a champion who was always headlining in the territory—not on the road for weeks at a time. McMahon wanted the same thing for his region. But the underlying logic needed to make sense to the public, regardless of the truth. The significance of a single titleholder working the entire wrestling circuit was ancient history.

The era of Buddy Rogers and the National Wrestling Alliance concluded, but Muchnick was still in the mud, trying to obtain the outstanding debts owed by Capitol. In a letter to McMahon on January 28, 1963, he said he hadn't received "one cent" for Buddy since he'd returned to wrestling a month before. He explained that he had "kept [his] end of the bargain" and wanted McMahon to reciprocate. In addition to his request, he stated their relationship was not coming to a conclusion and he hoped to "continue to do business, if [McMahon desired], for many years to come."

McMahon wasn't burning any bridges. He was perfectly content with maintaining friendly ties to fellow promoters, but things were moving fast and a lot remained unclear. Specifically, a formal announcement of McMahon's new organization had yet to be made. Wrestling writers clued into recent happenings were confused by Rogers's continued billing as champion in spite of his defeat by Thesz. The latter was already touring at a fast clip, working to rebuild the trust of NWA members and trying to mend the damage created by Buddy's reign. The acknowledgement of Rogers as a titleholder was acceptable, but not everyone knew what McMahon had in store for his champion and territory.

Despite reports to the contrary, Capitol Wrestling did not organize and announce the establishment of its new sanctioning organization on any specific day. Claims that such actions occurred in January are unfounded. On April 18, 1963, Ray Morgan reportedly elaborated about the maneuver on Washington TV and printed material surfaced in May. McMahon's decision to launch the World Wide Wrestling Federation was a compelling and bold act, and although no one would have recognized it in April 1963, the commencement of the WWWF was a game changer for pro wrestling.

(12)
PROMOTIONAL
INDEPENDENCE

The first half of 1963 was shaping up to be a significant period of transition for the wrestling industry. The National Wrestling Alliance was aiming to restructure and strengthen on the back of new heavyweight champion Lou Thesz. But as much as they planned to gain, they were going to lose because of the difficulties instigated by promoters in the rich Northeastern territory. Vincent McMahon, Toots Mondt, and Willie Gilzenberg were at the helm of a radical notion that relied less on what the NWA wanted and more on their own abilities to organize and maintain an expansive independent organization. Their combined experience spoke volumes, and while the various ideas at times appeared scattered, things were expected to settle and make more sense to observant fans as the year dragged on.

McMahon was not following an established playbook when he started figuring out his course of action. In contrast, the AWA, acknowledging its similar path in 1960, was a different beast. That left McMahon searching for answers and working to satisfy all corners of his million-dollar territory. Appeasing the various athletic commissions, particularly the stringent New York, Pennsylvania, and Maryland bodies, was a full-time job in itself. He was also coordinating a vast booking office, sending wrestlers across a multi-state area from Illinois to Virginia, and responsible for the influential TV programs that prompted better house show gates. The innumerable moving parts of the promotion affected so many livelihoods and, ultimately, the entertainment value of an untold number of fans.

Regardless of the belief that Mondt was the "big man" behind the scenes or that Gilzenberg was the "president" of whatever organization, all of the final decisions fell onto the shoulders of McMahon and McMahon alone. He masterminded the shift, and, long term, the ramifications were going to spell doom or prosperity for his business. But things were moving at a fast clip, and he was adapting in the moment. One thing was guaranteed, and that was the importance of Buddy Rogers as the heavyweight champion and central box office draw. Rogers was essential to the entire configuration, and the money he was bringing in throughout the territory was vital.

The publicity surrounding Rogers differed from city to city in the aftermath of his defeat by Thesz, which demonstrated how tricky it was for McMahon to spread a single message to clarify Rogers's status. In some areas, he was billed either as a claimant or as an ex-champion, and in others his title was ignored completely. By March and going into April, there was a surprising shift in focus off Rogers as the one and only champion in two of McMahon's Western cities. In Cleveland, Buddy was dethroned from his World Wide Wrestling Association championship on March 28 by popular Jamaican star Dory Dixon. Around the same time, Fred Kohler in Chicago was advertising massive Moose Cholak as another heavyweight claimant while billing Rogers as a former titleholder. Nevertheless, Rogers remained the top headliner in both towns.

The complexities of growing his independent empire were harrowing, but McMahon was known for his attention to detail. In pro wrestling, some things simply could not be managed, but for McMahon to be caught off guard by the realization of three different heavyweight title claimants running simultaneously across his booking jurisdiction is too far-fetched to believe. That leads to the assumption that Rogers, Dixon, and Cholak were potentially part of a bigger scheme, perhaps even an elimination-type tournament to crown a single, legitimate champion for what was to be known as the World Wide Wrestling Federation. If that was the case, a number of things had to develop exactly according to plan, but the opposite was about to take place.

Rogers had long been burning the candle at both ends, and he fell off a cliff around Sunday, April 21, 1963. Reports that he suffered a heart attack surfaced, but the details remained fuzzy, and promotional representatives of Capitol Wrestling wanted the news suppressed until a more complete diagnosis could be made. Once word got out to the various state athletic commissions, as well as the National Wrestling Association, Rogers was slated to be suspended for medical reasons and declared ineligible to appear anywhere the organization governed. He would thereby be prevented from passing the championship to another grappler prior to being forcibly retired.

The heart ailment that sidelined Rogers had been building for weeks, if not months, and his departure from the everyday ranks of Capitol was crippling, especially because it occurred when McMahon needed him the most. As expected, his critics again discounted his illness as mere rumors. McMahon was a realist and dealing with an ever-changing situation that threatened the stability of his business. Without Rogers, he was handicapped. But there was a second option. Italian strongman Bruno Sammartino had been a prodigy since 1959 and had vastly improved. He had displayed his star power in main events all over the Northeastern region, demonstrating his worth everywhere from Toronto to Madison Square Garden.

The need for Sammartino to swiftly step in wasn't yet certain. Buddy's condition was still up in the air, and there were hopes he'd return. Less than two weeks after his illness, he was back in the ring and participating in short bouts that scarcely put him in danger. Protected by opponents, he did what was asked of him, and in the meantime, McMahon worked on the Sammartino contingency, etching out a Garden event that would shape the future of his promotion. His publicity team circulated a fictional backstory for the World Wide Wrestling Federation, claiming that Rogers traveled to Rio de Janeiro, Brazil, and won a tournament composed of international competition, creatively explaining how he had become the WWWF champion.

The escalation of the WWWF into a genuine outfit came without fanfare. It was more of a subtle move and gained traction in May 1963, with McMahon's agents in various cities promoting Rogers's title claim. Newspapers in Pittsburgh and Cleveland, even after the briefs specifying the WWWF as the principal organization, were apparently so comfortable using the World Wide Wrestling Association name that they continued to do so until corrected. The similar names were easily confused. One of the sport's great unanswered questions is whether the WWWA was the intended label of McMahon's enterprises. The uncomplicated flip of words from "Association" to "Federation" was a pivotal decision that, once made, was set in stone. The WWWF was established and entrenched for the long haul.

A little more than seven weeks went by before Capitol Wrestling returned to Madison Square Garden, on May 17, 1963. Almost up to the last minute, arrangements were being made, but the final call of who'd walk out of the main event as WWWF champion was seemingly settled. There was no choice in the matter: Rogers's heart was in bad shape, and asking him to risk his life to continue wrestling full time was unthinkable. His contribution to the organization would be a concluding masterpiece, putting Sammartino over in the most significant way possible. The match would last less than a minute—a complete squash—and the new titleholder would garner international recognition for demolishing the unbeatable blond heel in record time. Sammartino's reputation and popularity were going to soar, it was predicted, and Rogers would later settle in as a promoter on the WWWF circuit.

The Garden was jammed with 19,648 spectators on May 17 to watch the end of one era and the launch of the Sammartino dynasty. It took the Pittsburgh Italian just 48 seconds to drive Buddy out of the championship picture and become a legend across the Northeastern territory. In a business sense, Rogers's exit was far too premature, and the loss of revenue from outdoor matches during the summer was depressing. But with Sammartino in the driver's seat, Capitol was going in an entirely new direction. McMahon saw the possibilities and, despite their rocky history, was content with giving Bruno the belt of his organization and a push that few wrestlers have ever experienced.

In June 1963, a dire situation exploded in Chicago, but it perhaps wasn't unexpected for McMahon. Fred Kohler, the veteran impresario and McMahon's local partner, was going through a period of turmoil and had instigated a number of feuds that caused a fervor. He pushed to keep Jim Barnett and Johnny Doyle out of the NWA, proposed that the Alliance disband, and shirked remitting fees to Sam Muchnick for appearances by Rogers. As McMahon sought to form his own organization, Kohler did likewise, initiating the International Wrestling Alliance (IWA) and crowning Moose Cholak his top heavyweight. But things rapidly fell apart between Kohler and the Eastern syndicate, and McMahon stopped booking into Chicago.

Kohler, facing a loss of his crucial television setup and the standard appearances of big-name superstars, hired divisive Jack Pfefer as his matchmaker. Kohler successfully landed Johnny Valentine and wanted to build his promotion around him, giving the grappler a win over Cholak for the IWA championship. But soon after, Valentine was convinced to bail on the indie operation, leaving Kohler high and dry. Without friendly ties to the NWA or McMahon to supply talent, Chicago was running flat, and it was hard to believe that the town had been the hottest spot on the wrestling map just a few years before.

Losing Chicago caused McMahon to rethink his promotional strategy. The exorbitant money brought in by Kohler to see Capitol talent was the reason the company had included a Western circuit.

Grapplers were routinely traveling to Chicago, and return stops in Cleveland and Detroit made sense as they toured their way back toward Pittsburgh and across Pennsylvania. But the absence of a first-rate city on par with Chicago hurt the entire operation, and McMahon, in turn, decided to reduce his territory. He wanted a more compact circuit that was even smaller than what he had envisioned for Rogers. Sammartino would travel less and always be available locally for title defenses.

McMahon advised his promoters that the WWWF was the new regional sanctioning body and that Sammartino was the organization's exclusive champion. All information to the contrary was false. He affirmed his business plan during a phone discussion with Muchnick in May, and the latter sent a follow-up letter a short time later. Predictably, Muchnick endorsed the single champion theory, stating that the esteem of pro wrestling would be greater if only one man was recognized as the world titleholder. He strongly supported that concept, even if it meant promoters would only receive bookings of the champion "once or twice a year," as a result of all the traveling the titleholder would do.

The two men disagreed more about this topic than anything else. McMahon felt he needed a permanent champion in his territory, and with Sammartino in place, there was no changing his mind. Still an officer in the NWA, McMahon was unmistakably breaking the union's number one rule when it came to championship recognition. That didn't matter, as most narratives about the formation of the WWWF claim that McMahon severed his NWA ties the moment he created his own organization. But that isn't true. McMahon didn't resign from the NWA in 1963. His membership continued in spite of the WWWF's development, and other than acknowledging a champion other than Lou Thesz, there wasn't a defining moment that formally divided Capitol Wrestling from the rest of the Alliance.

Notably, McMahon missed the annual convention in St. Louis because he was attending to a Garden sellout on August 23, 1963, but he sent his "best wishes" to all members by telegram. With him absent, and as expected, the Alliance discussed McMahon's rebelliousness, and a unanimous vote agreed to give him a probationary period of 60 days to adhere to NWA regulations. Muchnick informed McMahon by letter that if he didn't advertise Thesz as the undisputed titleholder within that time, he'd be suspended for one year.

When the deadline passed, McMahon and Toots Mondt were promptly suspended by the Alliance. They weren't the only ones to be punished by the NWA for that infraction. Kohler was banned for his recognition of an IWA champion in Chicago, and "Doc" Karl Sarpolis, in the Amarillo territory, was similarly suspended for his push of 22-year-old wrestling sensation Dory Funk Jr. Months later, Muchnick classified the Amarillo matter as being a "series of misunderstandings" and recommended that Sarpolis return to the fold. The other three men were a different story.

In WWWF rings, Sammartino was an energetic and popular champion, vindicating his backers by winning over the audience in record time. His strongman performance in matches against heel behemoths became standard operating procedure in the Northeast, and McMahon constantly sought larger and more threatening opponents for Bruno. Beginning in mid-1963 with Killer Kowalski and European titleholder the Great Mortier, who was also noted for his incredible strength, Sammartino faced challenging rivals and knocked them back. With the Shadow, Buddy Austin, Skull Murphy, and others appearing on WWWF shows, there was never a lack of contenders for Sammartino, but fans were well aware that some opponents were significantly more of a threat than others.

The arrival of 300-plus-pound Gorilla Monsoon caused much panic for Bruno's faithful in the summer of 1963, and he was booked as an unstoppable monster. Billed as being from Manchuria and under the tutelage of "Wild" Red Berry, Monsoon was a credible grappler from Upstate New York and competed in international tournaments as an amateur. Announcers played up his menacing size as he demolished opponents two at a time, on occasion, and fans were drawn to arenas to see if Sammartino's days were numbered. Serious contenders of Monsoon's ilk were booked into tag-team victories over Bruno, disqualification wins, and draw situations to develop the storyline.

The specific scenario and the frame-by-frame presentation of the contests changed with the varying performers, but the WWWF strategy for its heavyweight division was basically the same. In the case of Sammartino and Monsoon, the drama intensified prior to matches at Roosevelt Stadium in Jersey City, New Jersey, and at Madison Square Garden, where 19,706 paid over $59,000 to see the champion retain his title by count out on November 18, 1963. Six months later, their feud resumed at the Garden, and another 33,000 spectators were present over the course of two events to witness their feud culminate with a Sammartino victory. Usually wrap-up matches occurred throughout the territory to close the door on one rivalry just as another one was about to begin.

The WWWF operated like clockwork in that way, and McMahon implemented subtle changes to keep things lively. Roster modifications were routine, but the sudden disappearance of Antonino Rocca in 1963 was noteworthy for many reasons. For one, he remained impressively popular and a quiet exit from the spotlight did not reflect the worth of his tremendous contributions to pro wrestling in the area. But things between Rocca and Capitol Wrestling had been on edge for months leading up to his unceremonious departure. Under the reign of Buddy Rogers, Rocca was forced to share the top spot, and in many instances, was ushered aside so the Nature Boy could dominate the headlines. While he was still a favorite, there was no room for Rocca as the principal star of McMahon's promotion. He was expected to languish as part of the supporting cast.

In late 1962, Rocca was hospitalized and pulled out of several key appearances. Around that same time, his schedule in Capitol cities tapered off, and after missing a showing in Cleveland, he was briefly suspended by the National Wrestling Association. McMahon didn't miss a beat in pushing Vittorio "Argentina" Apollo as his South America ambassador in the ring, safeguarding the important Latino segment of the ticket-buying audience. Apollo was not the charismatic superstar Rocca was, but he was a fitting replacement, particularly since he had worked as Rocca's tag-team partner and learned many things from the original Argentinean highflier. Rocca wasn't at all pleased with his former bosses and wanted to personally reclaim a piece of the New York wrestling market.

That typically indicated a wrestling war was imminent. And it was. Rocca cunningly reached an agreement with Jim Crockett, the NWA member in charge of the Carolinas and Virginia, and formed an independent booking office known as the World Booking Agency. His new outfit—using a weekly TV program from Sunnyside Garden in Queens, hosted by well-known DJ Franklin "Lonny" Starr—planned to line up a gaggle of small-time promoters around the region to oppose Capitol Wrestling. The stability of the operation relied on recognizable talent from Crockett, and the Charlotte-based promoter lived up to his end of the bargain until pressure from backstage channels cooled his interest in the New York expansion.

Rocca's talent pool suffered, and instead of presenting a class of must-see workers, he offered rookies, journeymen, and a scattering of established grapplers. It was no competition for McMahon's powerful lineup, and in January 1964, Rocca's program on WOR-TV was canceled. He also lost the Sunnyside Garden and was forced to move to the Bay Ridge Sports Center in Brooklyn. Despite the heavy downturn, Rocca kept fighting to remain afloat, branching out to Poughkeepsie, Kingston, and other towns, headlining most, if not all, of his promotion's shows. But by August 1964, as McMahon continued to pack the Garden and rule the territory with ease, Rocca accepted his fate and shuttered his business.

The extraordinary quality of wrestlers gave the WWWF a monumental advantage over outside promoters. Sammartino's ring wars with dastardly Dr. Jerry Graham and Gorilla Monsoon gave way to a much-hyped rivalry against 46-year-old Fred Blassie. A pro since 1942, Blassie was a four-time WWA champion in Los Angeles and entered the WWWF as a claimant to the Pacific Coast Wrestling Alliance title. He made a number of TV appearances to set up massively promoted events against Sammartino at Roosevelt Stadium on June 26 and Madison Square Garden on July 11 and August 1, 1964. Blassie, a crafty and sophisticated heel, took several victories from Bruno around the circuit, including matches that were ended by a referee's stoppage and a disqualification. According to the usual script, Sammartino won the closer at the Garden on August 1 after nearly a half hour of battle.

Toronto's Walter Sieber, known in the ring as Nazi sympathizer Waldo Von Erich, engaged in a three-match series at the Garden with Sammartino between August and October 1964. Von Erich's fortune was no better than Blassie or his predecessors, and he was defeated. Gene Kiniski of Edmonton, Alberta, was next on the contender's list, and at 6'3" and 275 pounds, he was a challenger to be reckoned with. In fact, he'd held the AWA world championship in Minneapolis and lesser claims in Montreal and Amarillo. Unfortunately for officials, there was a dip in ticket sales from 16,000 to 11,000 between the first and second Garden bouts in late 1964, and the Sammartino-Kiniski feud ended on December 14 with another big win for the champion.

McMahon closely watched fans' reactions to Sammartino's opponents, and if there was an opportunity to cash in with a longer series of contests, he'd take advantage of the situation. If the challengers didn't strike the fancy of enthusiasts, the warfare would quickly cease to allow the next rival to garner attention. Outside of Bruno's Herculean effort as titleholder, the WWWF payroll consisted of many box office draws, and the tag-team division was perpetually strong. Following the high standards set by Rocca and Miguel Perez and the Fabulous Kangaroos were Skull Murphy and Brute Bernard, Monsoon and Kowalski, and the combination of "brothers" Jerry and Luke Graham.

There were two other primary fan favorites responsible for the Federation's extended success: Bobo Brazil and Haystacks Calhoun. Both men were from the South Central United States, Brazil from Arkansas and Calhoun from Texas. Brazil made his wrestling debut first, in 1949, as the protégé of Joe Savoldi in Michigan. As an African American grappler, he overcame much adversity during a time of racial divide, but smart promoters, including McMahon, knew Bobo was a stellar attraction and wanted him at the top of their cards. McMahon billed Brazil as the WWWF United States champion. Calhoun was known for his humongous size, weighing more than 600 pounds, but his affable personality and charm turned awestruck spectators into diehard fans. He wore trademark overalls and a lucky horseshoe, and his massive presence was a big lure for audiences.

Although attendance numbers were favorable, Capitol Wrestling did experience the regular ups and downs. In September 1963, robbers broke into the Capitol Arena in Washington, DC, and stole $2,000 in cash. Four months later, McMahon's lease at the venue ended, but because of his long affiliation with the owners, he was given special considerations, including a one-year extension, which allowed him to search for a suitable replacement arena. McMahon settled on the National Roller Skating Rink (also known as the National Arena) on 17th Street and Kalorama Road NW and launched weekly shows on July 1, 1965.

William Gildea of the *Washington Post* wrote a commemorative article about the soon-to-be razed Capitol Arena on June 27, 1965, and mentioned the Comiskey Park panorama from the night Buddy Rogers won the NWA title, which hung over McMahon's desk, and appropriately alluded to the latter's great success. McMahon responded sentimentally by saying, "All of this grew out of the little garage on W Street. We're going to miss the old place."

For years, the Thursday night spectacles at the Capitol Arena entertained live audiences and home viewers. Even politicians in Washington, DC, were transfixed by the blend of athleticism and drama. Senators Estes Kefauver, Tom Connally, and John McClellan were notable proponents of the mat game, as were General Douglas MacArthur and J. Edgar Hoover. And for those in the 1950s who thought wrestling was barbaric and only for men, First Lady Bess Truman shattered that myth by going on record as a regular fan.

There were always critics of the sport, who lambasted pro

wrestling as lowbrow and detrimental to children. Letters of con-demnation were sent to the White House, and regulators were encouraged to sterilize the airwaves of the unnecessary violence. But wrestling endured, and McMahon's answer was very simple: "There is a knob on each TV set for changing channels. If the show doesn't appeal to you, all you have to do is flip the knob and watch something else."

On October 8, 1964, New York's WNEW, formerly known as WABD and part of the defunct DuMont Network, canceled the local broadcast of McMahon's Washington program. On the air since 1956, the show was a prominent weapon in Capitol Wrestling's arsenal, and it not only promoted Madison Square Garden events but furthered storylines and highlighted the com-pany's most valuable assets. The loss left McMahon with only his Bridgeport telecast to influence the New York market into attending his live presentations. It said a lot about McMahon's ability as a businessman that he had two TV outlets for so many years. After losing one, he had a backup already in place to keep his business thriving.

The WWWF's relationship with the NWA remained amicable. Sam Muchnick returned to the helm of the Alliance in 1963, and in July of the following year he notified McMahon of the coming annual meeting in St. Louis. Invoking a little wishful thinking, he explained that if McMahon wanted to "ask for re-instatement" into the NWA, he should attend the convention. It was obvious Muchnick wanted him back in the union. Less than a month later, he followed up with another letter, further explaining the schedule of conferences on August 28–29, 1964. Neither McMahon nor Toots Mondt made the trip west, but they sent a telegram stating that they believed the NWA was a "great organization for the bet-terment of wrestling."

Members appreciated the kind words, and Muchnick, in a letter back to McMahon and Mondt on August 31, expressed his personal thanks. He acknowledged Mondt as his "advisor and counselor" through the years, and it seemed the only thing that separated the two sides was a difference in promotional philosophy. Muchnick was still adamant about the single world champion concept and pledged not to book Lou Thesz into the Northeast unless he was billed as the solitary titleholder. The NWA was collectively relieved by the Department of Justice's waning interest in pro wrestling, but they did confer about the Bureau of Immigration and Naturalization's recent restrictions surrounding the importation of overseas talent. Promoters were finding it much harder to secure foreign grapplers, and Muchnick arranged for a member of the immigration agency to speak before the Alliance to assist in clearing up the confusion.

At some point in 1965, Muchnick and McMahon opened up a conversation regarding a possible unification bout between Thesz and Sammartino. Much of the exchange was preliminary, but there was a serious underlying intention of reuniting the NWA and Capitol Wrestling. The early discussion produced a basic outline for one of the two champs to win the unified belt, reign for a period of time, and then lose the championship to the other in a rematch. It was to be a trade-off of sorts, deliberately arranged to benefit both the Alliance and the WWWF. There were two major hitches.

For one, Thesz was harboring a lifelong grudge against Mondt stemming from his first tour of Southern California in 1936. Toots was notoriously tightfisted with payoffs and nearly starved young Thesz, leaving a measure of resentment that would never disappear. Thesz trusted McMahon only slightly more. As far as he was concerned, there was no good reason to go into business with Capitol other than for the money, and he demanded upward of $100,000 for the deal.

The second reason pertained to Sammartino. Since winning the WWWF title in 1963, he had enjoyed the limited travel schedule of the Northeast and being close to his family in suburban Pittsburgh. Being thrust onto a national touring circuit and responsible for pacifying the entire NWA was a much bigger obligation. The schedules of the WWWF champion versus the Alliance champion were night and day, and there were concerns over whether Sammartino would fulfill those demands.

The complexities of the unification derailed it, and the two organizations remained separate. By the August 1965 convention, surprisingly, Muchnick's perspective on the single champion policy changed. He elaborated on his thoughts during his annual speech to the membership, asserting that he wanted to eradicate the policy that forced all affiliates to recognize only one titleholder. His unbending stance had gotten him nowhere, and without any leverage to persuade the WWWF and AWA to fall into line, Muchnick had to develop a new line of thought. He believed the Alliance would, consequently, at least regain the membership of the valuable territories they had lost.

The NWA didn't wholeheartedly embrace the concept, and the WWWF and AWA maintained their independent status. Business in each of the three different spheres of influence fluctuated as years passed, and Muchnick continued to wrangle the different personalities and hoped to one day bring everyone back to the same table.

Back in New York, Capitol Wrestling was making a real effort to spotlight legitimate athletes from other sports and the amateur ranks, diversifying its talent pool. Ernie Ladd and Chief Wahoo McDaniel, who were veterans of the American Football League, and Dr. Bill Miller, a 6'5" ex-Big Ten wrestling champion, were colorful additions to the promotion. But prior to Miller's three-match series against Sammartino at the Garden, Bruno faced down the challenge of his former tag-team partner, Bill Watts of Tulsa, Oklahoma. The popular Watts also had a collegiate and pro football background and, standing 6'3" and weighing 275 pounds, fit McMahon's mold for a standout title contender. He turned on Sammartino and took the champion to the wire during their trio of Garden bouts between February and May 1965, drawing sell-outs twice.

A gate of $44,425 was paid by 13,779 spectators at the Garden on September 27, 1965, to see Sammartino beat Tarzan Tyler with his backbreaker. Later that night, the champion dined near the Biltmore Theater, where his car was robbed. Among the items stolen were his wrestling gear, a coat, and his cherished $10,000 championship belt, representative of the WWWF's top prize.

Police and federal investigators sought the culprit and the strap, but a thorough search ended disappointingly. The belt was not found. In recent years some have claimed to have located the stolen belt, but reports have been inconclusive about whether it is the genuine strap.

Over in the NWA, Gene Kiniski, one of Sammartino's conquered opponents, rose to the pinnacle of the organization when he beat Thesz and won the world heavyweight crown on January 7, 1966. Considering Kiniski's recent feud with Sammartino and the way it ended, pundits were quick to compare the two kings. *The Ring Wrestling* followed suit, including an article by Sammartino as told to correspondent Sam Cohen in its January 1967 issue. In the piece, he addressed the talk about a matchup between the two champions and asserted that he'd beaten Kiniski "five times," counting four singles bouts and a tag match in late 1964 and into '65. Needless to say, fans were adept at choosing who was the "real" world champion on their own.

In the ring, the fundamental styles of the WWWF and most NWA offices couldn't have been more different. It started at the heavyweight championship level, where Sammartino was routinely booked against large heel opponents in brawling-style matches. Kiniski, conversely, traversed the Alliance circuit facing heels and fan favorites of all sizes. He was called upon to either brawl or wrestle scientifically, adjusting to the circumstances. Additionally, fans in NWA regions were regularly exposed to a hodgepodge of performers, from technical marvels to clever, high-flying junior heavyweights.

The methodology of the WWWF didn't change much, and enthusiasts in the Northeast supported the organization's customary booking philosophies. Faithful viewers in the New York market followed Capitol's Bridgeport programming as ambivalent network executives shifted it from time slot to time slot. Finally, WNEW moved to cancel the program, and the show went off the air following the April 30, 1966, presentation. McMahon then found himself in an unfamiliar situation. For a decade, his TV shows had influenced the draw at area houses, especially at Madison Square Garden, and had given him the advantage he needed in the promotional war for the territory. Now he was without even one outlet to feature his wrestlers and hype upcoming live shows.

The loss of Bridgeport appeared to be just another blow to the slowly crumbling Capitol Wrestling empire. McMahon pulled the plug on any matches scheduled for the Garden as a result of the TV deficiency and hunted for a new outlet. His diligence paid off. WOR-9 inked a deal to feature Washington tapes on Saturday afternoons starting on August 20, 1966. The following November 7, the WWWF returned to the Garden for the first time since March and drew over 14,000 spectators. McMahon hoped to reverse any sentiment that his promotion was faltering and launched a campaign to rekindle the audience. The kind of publicity George Girsch in *Ring Wrestling* magazine provided didn't hurt. In the May 1967 issue, he wrote that New York was "once again" the "world capital of wrestling."

Through the end of 1966, total fan support was off previous highs, but part of the problem was the fact that Sammartino was booked against lesser-caliber rivals like Tank Morgan and El Toro Ortega. Resorting to an old favorite, McMahon rebooked the Sammartino–Gorilla Monsoon feud, and in March 1967, the Garden drew its largest wrestling attendance in two years. The following month, WOR officials moved the Washington TV program to 12:30 a.m. Sunday mornings. They canceled the show altogether on August 13, once again handicapping the WWWF in New York.

As expected, the ticket sales at the Garden sank to under 10,000 in September and under 7,000 in October. The 6,600 attendance for the October 23, 1967, program was McMahon's smallest audience since 1960. The absence of an innovative TV show was blamed, but others felt Sammartino was overexposed. Facing innumerable challenges, McMahon had to weigh the value of having the same wrestler on top of nearly every major main event in his territory for going on five years. After all, Sammartino was only human and bound to face periods of mediocre gate receipts.

McMahon had to consider the future of wrestling in New York City and make the tough decision about ending Sammartino's reign as world heavyweight champion.

(13)
THE MOST VALUABLE TERRITORY

The time-honored territorial system remained stable going into the late 1960s. The NWA's members and promoters evolved, and in many cities, active wrestlers were crossing through the proverbial curtain and becoming part of management. Fred Kohler, in Chicago, exited the business with a whimper in 1965, selling his local interests to well-known grapplers Dick the Bruiser and Wilbur Snyder, a tandem who shared an entrepreneurial spirit. In Tampa, Florida, Eddie Graham, one half of the famed Graham Brothers tag team, joined his mentor Cowboy Luttrall on the promotional end, as did Fritz Von Erich in Dallas alongside Ed McLemore. The Sheik acquired the Detroit territory from Jim Barnett and Johnny Doyle, and the latter duo ventured to Australia, where they were highly successful.

Former theatrical agent Abe Ford became Capitol Wrestling's point man in Boston beginning in 1963 and ran the Garden in opposition to Tony Santos's enterprises at the Arena. His first show on April 20 turned into a living nightmare when half of his lineup failed to show, including champion Buddy Rogers. Up against claims of "false advertising," Ford tried to jump-start the promotion the following month, but despite heavy publicity, attendance was startlingly poor. He soon ceased operations.

Around the same time, Santos and the 68-year-old Jack Pfefer were proactive, booking a journeyman as "Bruno Sanmartino," a creative knockoff on Capitol's star Bruno Sammartino. Unobservant fans were duped into thinking they were going to see the Italian strongman.

Santos and Pfefer occasionally got Boston press reports to actually spell the name "Sammartino," continuing the confusion. They added wrestlers "Hobo Brazil" (Bobo Brazil) and Pierre Carpentier (Edouard Carpentier), keeping with Pfefer's tradition of mimicking rival superstars, and through the first part of 1965 they held a monopoly over the territory. But Ford hadn't yet given up and stormed back with more aid from Vincent McMahon and Capitol Wrestling. Supported by TV on WIHS, UHF channel 38, Ford placed special advertisements in newspapers explicitly stating that the Bruno Sammartino scheduled to appear at the Boston Garden was the "original" and that there was "only one" true world champion.

Ford's World Championship Wrestling held firm from July to October 1965, but once again, attandence was low. He bowed out of the business a second time, to refocus on other interests, but he returned in April 1967, with better television coverage throughout New England. Four channels covered WWWF-based wrestling, and Ford launched monthly programs at the Garden with Sammartino as his regular headliner. Attendance improved to close to 10,000 people per show by the end of the year. A high spot was the feud between Bruno and Hawaiian powerhouse Professor Toru Tanaka, which included a stunner on September 30, when Tanaka pinned the champion with his feet on the ropes for leverage.

According to the storyline, the WWWF "board of directors" reviewed motion picture footage of the match and determined that Sammartino retained his championship because of Tanaka's illegal actions. Fans were charged up by the feud, and rematches were staged on November 4 and December 9, 1967, with 9,300 and 9,700 in attendance, respectively. For Ford, there was no turning back in fighting Santos for the territory, and his success meant he was in town to stay. People enthusiastically embraced the WWWF, and Boston became one of the most important cities on McMahon's circuit.

Philadelphia was even more essential to the WWWF. Ray Fabiani was the local promoter of record, and he had boldly challenged McMahon for the rights to Washington, DC, in 1956. After McMahon won their brief conflict, the two men became affiliated, and talent was coordinated out of the office of Capitol Wrestling to Fabiani's main venue, the Philadelphia Arena on Market Street. The arena developed into a principal production outlet for original WWWF programming. In fact, it got to the point that McMahon was staging between three to six live events a month in the city, including massive 10-plus-match TV tapings. Footage was specifically tailored to towns around the horn, all working to build up house show attendance.

After upward of 40 years in the wrestling industry, Fabiani provided McMahon with a valuable colleague in a crucial location, strengthening the resolve of the WWWF during its early years. When not focused on wrestling, he spent half his time as the general manager of the Philadelphia Lyric Opera Company and the other half as the American manager of Italian tenor Franco Corelli. In the late 1960s, Fabiani quietly retired. All promotional rights to the City of Brotherly Love were inherited by Capitol's secretary-treasurer, Phil Zacko, and the Keystone Wrestling Club, and the popular TV program *Wrestling from Philadelphia* continued uninterrupted.

For nearly three months, New York City had been dark to televised wrestling, following the cancellation by WOR-9 in August 1967. In the interim, McMahon and his allies had reached out to contacts and persistently pursued a new network opportunity. But executives at the major stations had seemingly washed their hands of pro wrestling, deeming it no longer "hip." However, over in Newark, program director Fred Sayles felt differently. He'd worked as a grappling broadcaster years earlier and knew the benefits of having an expertly managed wrestling program on the weekly schedule. He coordinated efforts through his friend Willie Gilzenberg, who served as the WWWF president, and arranged to feature the promotion's Washington telecast on WNJU (UHF channel 47) starting on November 11, 1967.

The Newark presentation was instrumental in boosting the draw at Madison Square Garden back over the 14,000 mark on January 29, 1968, but the affair was also well attended for another reason. It marked the final wrestling spectacle at the Garden before demolition, capping a 42-year existence conceptualized by the illustrious Tex Rickard. An estimated 250 million people attended over 140 different events at the venue, including political rallies, variety shows, and all types of athletics. Wrestling legends Ed "Strangler" Lewis, Joe Stecher, and Jim Londos captivated audiences there, and in the modern era, Antonino Rocca, Buddy Rogers, and Bruno Sammartino were idols. For Vincent McMahon, the arena was special on a personal level and meant a great deal to him.

His father, Jess, had been the facility's first boxing matchmaker, and he vividly remembered many experiences, both on the main stage in front of spectators and behind the scenes. Vincent told the *Washington Post* in an article on February 11, 1968, that he "was just about the last person in the place" after his final show at the arena wrapped up on the evening of January 29. "It felt eerie," he explained, "thinking about the things that I saw there in the 42 years since my dad opened it."

The new $150-million Madison Square Garden complex at Penn Station on Eighth Avenue and 33rd Street opened shortly thereafter. McMahon christened it for professional wrestling on February 19, 1968, and only 12,989 witnessed the eight-bout program, well below expectations. In the main event, Sammartino throttled challenger Bull Ramos in 12 minutes and maintained his standing as the WWWF's top superstar. Prior to the card, McMahon had extolled Bruno's prized qualities, proclaiming him the "strongest man in the world," and the *Washington Post* reported that he had headlined the Garden 55 times in the last five years. McMahon was thrilled by Sammartino's stellar work and was making no secret arrangements to change his heavyweight champion. As far as he was concerned, the downturn in attendance had nothing to do with Bruno.

Throughout Sammartino's reign, naysayers criticized his restricted traveling schedule. He was known to stay within the Northeastern territory with one-night jaunts to Toronto every now and then. The fact that he didn't journey to other regions became a sound condemnation of Sammartino as a champion and as a peer of the NWA titleholder. McMahon, beginning in December 1964, when he approved a Christmas night booking in Miami, began authorizing visits to other parts of the wrestling world. Between 1965 and '68, Sammartino went to Puerto Rico, Calgary, Buffalo, Nashville, and Memphis, and he made two trips to Australia and Japan. The touring added to Sammartino's mystique and gave the WWWF a great deal of added exposure.

Back home in the WWWF, there was a steady rotation of old and new faces on the circuit. Perennial favorites Edouard Carpentier and Bobo Brazil made appearances, while Italians Antonio Pugliese and Dominic DeNucci joined Sammartino in various feuds. Tony Altimore and Lou Albano made up the Sicilians tag team and dished out many beatings to organization heroes. The rule-breaking pair of Professor Toru Tanaka and Mitsu Arakawa rose to prominence in 1969, claiming the WWWF international tag team championship. Additionally, heels Ernie Ladd, Gorilla Monsoon, and Hans Mortier were joined by Bull Ramos, Luke Graham, and Virgil the Kentucky Butcher as challengers to Sammartino. In 1969, Sammartino's ring problems were compounded by the addition of Killer Kowalski and Waldo Von Erich to the mix.

Another significant threat to Sammartino came from Michigan State University alumni Jim Myers. Myers was trained by Bert Rubi and Gino Brito in Detroit and wrestled as the masked Student early in his career. He adopted the name George Steele and was quickly ushered into a rivalry with the champion upon arriving in the WWWF. On April 14, 1967, in Pittsburgh, 6,304 spectators at the Civic Arena were surprised when Steele beat Sammartino by count out after a wild brawl. The highly anticipated rematch on May 5 drew nearly 8,000 fans, and Bruno was victorious when Steele was unable to continue. McMahon saw the effectiveness of the conflict and continued the feud at Madison Square Garden and in both Boston and Philadelphia in 1968.

Always unpredictable, the Sheik returned in October 1968 and was immediately thrust into the championship picture. Like Steele, he beat Sammartino by count out on October 21 at the Garden, setting up a rematch on November 18, which Bruno won by DQ. The New York State Athletic Commission didn't have much of a sense of a humor when it came to the reckless antics of the Sheik, and undoubtedly he was warned to stay within the guidelines during a match. That was nearly impossible for the rowdy from Detroit. His disorderly style made him internationally renowned, and scaling back was counter to his main objective: riling up audiences. In the finale of their series, on December 9, Bruno was victorious, knocking the Sheik out of commission. The following month, the Sheik inspired a chaotic situation at the Garden after a match with Haystack Calhoun, and the commission banned him for 60 days.

Offering a blend of shows in English and Spanish, WNJU (channel 47) out of Newark was as diverse as they came. Prior to assuming broadcast rights to the Washington telecast in 1967, it featured occasional studio programs produced on the WNJU set. Sammartino, Johnny Valentine, Bill Miller, and Dr. Jerry Graham were among those exhibited on the channel, and WWWF wrestling seemed to be a natural fit for WNJU. Considering the fact that the Spanish-language audience of UHF television in the New York area was 1.6 million, the station was crucial to McMahon's empire. He nonetheless was disheartened when station managers shifted *Wrestling from Washington* from its Saturday night slot at 10:30 p.m. to Wednesdays at 5:10 p.m., directly following *News in Spanish*, on June 4, 1969.

The adjustment dramatically affected ticket sales at the Garden. A few weeks later, on June 30, attendance fell to 5,527 for a Sammartino-Steele program, marking the lowest point in McMahon's management history at the venue. An event scheduled for July was canceled altogether because of a lack of interest. But there was a silver lining. Executives at WNJU offered McMahon an even better option to showcase his brand of wrestling: They premiered *Wrestling from Philadelphia* on Saturday nights at 8 p.m. on August 30, 1969. The program was broadcast in color and was a much-improved visual experience compared to the Washington telecast. McMahon was encouraged by the TV revitalization and resumed Garden shows in October with attendance back over 10,000 fans.

The structure of Capitol Wrestling was solid through 1969, when Joe "Toots" Mondt sold his stock in the company and retired. Since 1961, he had served as Capitol's vice president and was a member of the board of directors, providing McMahon with an unequaled advisor. From 1961 to '66, he ran the Pittsburgh promotion, but as years passed, he was less and less responsible for the everyday operations of the business. By 1969, at the age of 75, he was ready to call it quits and settle far from the base operations of the WWWF. With his wife, Alda, he retired to St. Louis and moved into the Lewis and Clark Towers at 9953 Lewis and Clark Boulevard. His mind still sharp, he never passed up an opportunity to discuss wrestling and often joined local promoter Sam Muchnick for lunch.

Mondt owned 50 percent of Capitol Wrestling at the time of his retirement, amounting to 500 shares of common stock worth $50,000. On September 18, 1969, he agreed to sell 250 shares to Phil Zacko for $24,400. According to the agreement, the shares would immediately be transferred to Zacko, and the latter was to pay $203.33 a month starting on October 15 until the debt was paid off. Zacko signed a promissory note and the deal was finalized. The other 250 shares were sold to Robert J. Marella, better known to wrestling fans as Gorilla Monsoon, for the same amount and monthly arrangement. Both promissory notes were paid and satisfied on June 29, 1979. Notably, Marella replaced Toots as Capitol's vice president.

One of Mondt's associates in Pittsburgh was Rudy Miller, a veteran of the wrestling world going back to 1927. He had joined the staff of Capitol Wrestling when the corporation was founded in 1957 and worked around the office, handling paperwork and answering phones. Miller also served as a road agent. When Mondt relocated to Pittsburgh, Miller was a logical choice to join Toots, given their extensive history. Along with Hungarian Ace Freeman, a well-known local grappler, Miller performed many of the same duties he executed in Washington, DC, and continued in that role after Mondt sold his territorial interests in Pittsburgh to Bruno Sammartino in 1966.

There was another significant change to the Northeastern wrestling territory. On September 16, 1969, Charles Johnston died. Long the wrestling promoter of record at Madison Square Garden, he was the last of four brothers involved in ring sports in New York City and was considered a promotional legend. His death opened the door for McMahon to be named the Garden promoter and gave him total control over the region. After more than a decade of combat, he had survived his rivals and was finally the one and only wrestling maestro in the sport's most valuable city.

Over in the National Wrestling Alliance, second-generation grappler Dory Funk Jr. ended the three-year reign of world heavyweight champion Gene Kiniski on February 11, 1969. Sam Muchnick was reelected president at its annual convention in August, with Atlanta promoter Paul Jones serving as first vice president and Junzo Hasegawa of the Japan Pro Wrestling Alliance (JWA) as second vice president. The membership also unanimously voted to admit Jim Barnett to the Alliance. Ironically, on that same day, Barnett's mentor Fred Kohler, who once worked to keep Barnett from the union, passed away of a heart attack in Arizona. Once Muchnick heard of his death, he called for a moment of silence, and the NWA membership obliged.

Within the structure of the Alliance, there were several particularly strong territories that stood out during the late 1960s. Florida was first and foremost. Run primarily by Eddie Graham, the region included the entire state minus the Panhandle, which was considered part of the Gulf Coast territory. Using an awesome combination of athleticism and creativity, plus an ever-prevalent serving of violence, cities like Tampa, Miami, and Orlando thrived. The mid-Atlantic states of North and South Carolina and Virginia were flourishing as well. Charlotte's Jim Crockett, a kind-hearted gentleman who had been in the business since 1934, formed a popular network of towns that supported his brand of wrestling mayhem. Ex-wrestlers turned promoters Bob Geigel in Kansas City and Paul Boesch in Houston were similarly successful.

The WWWF did splendidly at Madison Square Garden in 1970, completely reversing the struggles of the year before. Sammartino and Ivan Koloff drew the largest audience in over two years on January 19, 1970, when 16,858 saw the champion eke out a victory. Six months later, on June 15, Sammartino and "Crusher" Verdu attained the most impressive Garden wrestling crowd since Antonino Rocca's heyday more than a decade earlier when 20,819 fans jammed the arena to see an upset. The referee, at the 22:43 mark, halted action due to a cut over Sammartino's eye and declared Verdu the victor. Because the bout didn't end in a pin or submission, the title didn't change hands. However, the size of the crowd was notably larger than anything Bruno had been able to pull in previously. It was also bigger than anything Buddy Rogers had been able to accomplish and was the most sensational audience for grappling in the new Garden.

An even larger crowd (20,982) attended the Sammartino-Verdu rematch on July 10, 1970, and this time around, Bruno won in 15 minutes and 11 seconds. The WWWF roster featured an assortment of colorful characters, and among them were two prominent heroes, Victor Rivera and Chief Jay Strongbow. Rivera was originally from Puerto Rico and debuted in the promotion in 1964 at the age of 20. In the years following, he toured a variety of territories and made a real name for himself in Southern California. Hugely popular, he returned to the WWWF in late 1967 and reestablished himself as the leading heavyweight, and his fan support was second only to Sammartino. Strongbow was a close third. He debuted in 1970 after competing for years under his real name, Joe Scarpa, and earned a following as the organization's principal Native American grappler. His war dance and tomahawk chop were always fan favorites.

McMahon welcomed a revival of wrestling's popularity on a grand scale, and the sport at the Garden was once again the hottest ticket in town. Sammartino feuded with Bepo Mongol in September and October 1970, drawing near matching 17,000 houses, and then went over Bulldog Brower to close up the building for the year on November 16. Television coverage stimulated ticket sales and was expanded with the arrival of *Lucha Libre* on WXTV (UHF channel 41) out of Paterson, New Jersey. The station was affiliated with the Spanish International Network and aired footage from the Olympic Auditorium in Los Angeles beginning on Saturday, September 19, 1970. A color broadcast of *Lucha Libre* also premiered on WNJU (UHF channel 47) on Sunday, February 14, 1971.

Well aware that the Spanish interest in pro wrestling was magnified by the two additional programs, McMahon was contemplating a major change. The considerations were spawned by Sammartino's desire to step away from the demands of champion. If a transition was to be made, McMahon had to ensure Bruno's successor was a popular commodity and valuable across WWWF territory. Additionally, he had to bear in mind the demographics of his supporters, especially the growing Spanish-language audience. They were a huge part of wrestling's resurgence, and McMahon had to replace Sammartino with the proper attraction to keep fans motivated to attend live shows.

However, when Ivan Koloff, a Canadian portraying a Russian heel, dealt a top rope kneedrop and pinned Sammartino on January 18, 1971, the title changed hands, but the result did not appeal to spectators. The Garden audience of 21,166 was bewildered by the result, and after nearly eight years of reigning supreme, Sammartino was defeated in the middle of the ring. In that time, Bruno had headlined 75 straight Garden programs, and enthusiasts had expected him to retain his championship. But this occasion was different, and Koloff pulled off the upset of the century. His victory crushed the emotions of faithful viewers and there was a genuine sadness surrounding wrestling in the Northeast. Fans didn't realize that it was all part of McMahon's grand scheme. He deliberately arranged things to unfold in such a manner because he was looking at the big picture and working in the best interests of his business.

Koloff was a clever terror in the ring. Originally from Ontario, he made his debut in 1965 and became a serious challenger to Sammartino in September 1969 in Pittsburgh. Three months later, Ivan beat Bruno at Madison Square Garden when the referee halted the bout due to the champ's blood loss, but he didn't win the belt. The rematch sold superbly, and McMahon knew he had an ace in the hole when it came to Koloff. But a rule-breaking champion was an unfavorable concept in 1971. McMahon wanted someone who could fascinate people across ethnic and economic boundaries. His choice was the always-smiling 30-year-old Pedro Morales of Puerto Rico.

Energetic to the core, Morales was the right man for the job. He was discovered in a New York area gym as a teenager by Kola Kwariani in the late 1950s and wrestled for McMahon early in his career. Over the previous year, he had appeared in Hawaii and Southern California and had returned to the WWWF during the last week of December 1970. He was by then more experienced, and crowds immediately appreciated his vibrant approach to the ring, exactly as McMahon hoped. Billed as the U.S. champion, known as the precursor to the world heavyweight crown, Morales was booked into a bout against Koloff for the latter title on February 8, 1971, at the Garden. After 10 minutes and 41 seconds, he scored a pinfall and became the WWWF king.

The changeover from Sammartino to Morales was effectively handled, and Koloff served his purpose as an interim champion. Whether Morales could sustain the heightened popularity remained to be seen, but McMahon had pulled the trigger and replaced Bruno the best way he could. Fans responded positively: 21,812 paid $86,885 to see Morales beat Koloff for the world title, and another gate record ($88,865) was set during Pedro's first championship defense, against Blackjack Mulligan on March 15, 1971. Going into the summer, he dispatched Tarzan Tyler and Luke Graham at the Garden, and his popularity was extraordinary. Puerto Rican supporters turned out in droves, and Capitol Wrestling was making astronomical amounts of money.

But there were still plenty of adjustments to be made. In September 1970, WDCA-TV (channel 20) in Washington, DC, canceled the live weekly two-hour broadcast of McMahon's National Arena show. The station had featured the telecast since 1966, and commentator Ray Morgan was a local institution. McMahon negotiated with executives and secured a Sunday timeslot for an abbreviated showing on tape. The program shifted from 9:30 in the morning to 3:30 in the afternoon until being silenced completely in September 1971. McMahon himself chose to end the show, as the National Arena events were failing to make any money. It was believed people were afraid to travel to the venue, and its neighborhood, at night. Thus, McMahon ended 43 years of weekly grappling entertainment, according to the *Washington Post*.

McMahon wasn't giving up on Washington completely. He scheduled monthly shows at the Coliseum and maintained Capitol's offices in the District. But without the National Arena, he urgently needed a suitable replacement venue to shoot original TV programs. He had Philadelphia still going strong, but he wanted a cheaper facility within a short driving distance. Hamburg, Pennsylvania, was 79 miles from Philadelphia and 162 miles from Washington, and there was a picturesque location within the city limits. The Hamburg Field House on Pine Street, operated by the Union Fire Company, was a perfect venue for wrestling. It was easily configurable for TV cameras and available a couple times a month. Seating between 1,500 and 2,000 people, it was imposing enough on camera and a comfortable all-around setting for matches, interviews, and the unrestrained WWWF chaos.

Beginning on September 29, 1971, fans in Hamburg paid $2 and $3 for seats at the Field House and witnessed more than a dozen bouts at any given TV taping. The program itself, known as *All Star Wrestling*, featured all the promotion's stars, from undercard performers to the heavyweight champion, and squash matches filled the lineup. That meant the name wrestlers went into the ring against preliminary-type workers and typically pummeled them into defeat in minutes. The bouts were to high-light the stellar abilities and moves of the wrestler of note and push their particular agenda in whatever feud they were engaged in. Promotional interviews demonstrated the quirkiness of the performers and built up future matches along the circuit.

The television host performing commentary and usually interviews was a vital part of the action. He described the var-ious holds, sold the drama, and cowered in the face of intimi-dating heels, putting over the talent like nobody's business. Ray Morgan, a longtime radio and television guy, was the consummate professional and was the voice of Capitol Wrestling. He gave the Washington telecast a polished quality that ranked among the best in the sport. Shortly after the shift to Hamburg, Morgan requested a pay increase, perhaps to coincide with the additional travel time needed to get from his Washington-area home to the venue.

According to arbitration documents from an unconnected case involving Capitol Wrestling, Morgan's request occurred as late as 1972, and McMahon, along with Zacko, communicated with a rep-resentative of the American Federation of Television and Radio Artists (AFTRA) to figure out a better pay schedule. It was deter-mined that the commentator would receive $230 an hour and $1,380 for two days of announcing work. However, Morgan wouldn't be the one getting the improved amount. McMahon instead chose to put his 27-year-old son Vincent K. McMahon into the position, unceremoniously ending the Morgan era on WWWF TV.

Having grown up in North Carolina, Vincent Kennedy McMahon didn't meet his birth father until he was 12 years of age, in 1957. But by the time he was a teenager, he was already following in his father's footsteps, attending the Fishburne Military School in Waynesboro, Virginia. Years earlier, Vincent James had gained discipline and knowledge at a military academy on Long Island, and the similar schooling was no doubt also recommended for his young son. Upon graduation in 1964, the younger McMahon advanced to East Carolina University, and he married Linda Edwards in August 1966. By 1971, he had a son of his own, named Shane, and was already engaged in the promotion of matches for Capitol Wrestling in Maine. He was an instinctual businessman and absorbed all facets of the wrestling business as the keen protégé of one of the sport's most enterprising minds. He was full of promise.

Before the end of 1971, there were two other significant happenings related to the WWWF. First, Zacko pushed for the organization's return to Baltimore after an extended absence. The loss of TV and painfully high taxes purged the city of big-time grappling at the Civic Center, but things improved during the summer of 1971, with McMahon's Philadelphia syndicated show paving the way. The second noteworthy occurrence involved the National Wrestling Alliance and the possibility of McMahon rejoining the promotional coalition. Members gathered in Mexico City during the first part of August for the annual convention and went through the normal routine. Ten days later, NWA president Sam Muchnick sent a letter to Jim Barnett in Australia, updating him on current events. He mentioned McMahon's potential return but explained that there were "things to iron out."

Muchnick felt the move would benefit both McMahon and the Alliance. For the first time in eight years, McMahon seemed to agree. He spoke with Muchnick by phone on November 4, 1971, and made arrangements to attend a special meeting of the NWA board of directors in St. Louis on November 21. At that conference, held at the Chase-Park Plaza Hotel, McMahon was readmitted to the organization. He agreed to downgrade the status of the WWWF championship from a "world" title to a regional honor and fully recognized NWA world champion Dory Funk Jr. as the sport's leading heavyweight. Muchnick was thrilled by the reunion and quickly sent out a bulletin to the membership, informing everyone of the breaking news. He also contributed a brief letter to *The Ring Wrestling* magazine (July 1972) and announced McMahon's return to the NWA under the headline

"Peace on Earth." He said, in his opinion, McMahon would "add to the prestige of the organization."

Paying his $100 dues, McMahon was back in the good graces of the NWA's global promotional cooperative and was able to reap the same rewards as fellow members. There was still the occasional complaint of regional and national mat monopolies, including in the Northeast. In response, a defiant McMahon told the *Washington Post, Times Herald* on June 21, 1970: "I haven't got a monopoly by any means." He explained how he warded off rivals in his territory and simply said it was because of his widespread "friendship" with commissioners, the media, and the wrestlers themselves. It was true. He created a barrier around the WWWF by extending his acquaintance to state regulators and sports-writers. He earned the loyalty of grapplers by treating them with respect. He was fair in his payoffs, and when he said he was going to do something, he did it. The behavior of many of his peers was just the opposite.

Attaining high-quality talent was one of the central benefits of being affiliated with the Alliance. McMahon had certainly used the goodwill of friends to obtain wrestlers in years past, but now that he was again a card-carrying member, any obstruc-tions were gone. In 1971, even before he rejoined the NWA, Eddie Graham of the Tampa affiliate and Dory Funk Sr. of West Texas had appeared at Madison Square Garden, indicating the strength-ening relations. The following year, Graham was joined by his son Mike, and Dory brought in his son Terry to appear on the under-card of Garden programs. Jack and Jerry Brisco, Paul Jones, Black Gordman, and Great Goliath were among the other imports.

The WWWF was using a new strategy by integrating a slew of recognizable wrestlers who were well known for their work in other territories. Most were publicized in great detail in national magazines, and McMahon saw the opportunity to widen his roster, especially at the Garden, by bringing them to town. Fans in New York had long wanted to see the caliber of the Funks and Briscos, Karl Gotch, Jimmy Valiant, and the return of Al Costello, Fred Blassie, and Ernie Ladd. Old taboos were apparently gone as the promotion outwardly acknowledged both the NWA and the AWA and even published photos of champions Dory Funk Jr. and Verne Gagne on the cover of the Garden program in July 1972. Morales, incidentally, was billed as the WWWF champion, and although it wasn't specified as a "world" title, it remained on a par with the NWA and AWA crowns in terms of respectability.

During this noteworthy period of the WWWF's evolution, women's wrestling made its debut at the Garden after a lengthy ban. The Fabulous Moolah was the reigning champion and had been since 1956, when she overcame eight competitors in a tournament to win the world title in Baltimore. Always a colorful character, she was a longtime friend of McMahon and had worked for Capitol Wrestling elsewhere on the circuit. Her showing at the Garden on July 1, 1972, upon the New York Athletic Commission's lifting of the rule suspending women's grappling in the state, was a landmark, and Moolah established her dominance over Vicki Williams and against Susan Green later in the month. In the ring, she was as unorthodox as they come, and fans were repelled by her antics. Just one time, they hoped, to see her beaten.

Morales was a stunning draw, and his Puerto Rican fan base was demonstrably faithful. They were dependable, turning out to see their hero battle challengers Gorilla Monsoon, Stan Stasiak, Toru Tanaka, Pampero Firpo, and the Spoiler time and again. Attendances over 22,000 were commonplace, and the gate at the Garden surmounted the $100,000 mark. Comparisons to Bruno Sammartino were, of course, made, but since they were both fan favorites, the chances of them ever facing off in the squared circle were slim.

The WWWF was in the midst of a terrifically potent movement. McMahon saw the tremendous possibilities and pushed for what was billed as the "Wrestling Match of the Century": Morales versus Sammartino for the WWWF belt.

Unfortunately for McMahon, bad weather hindered what was expected to be a record crowd, and it rained throughout the show on September 30, 1972. Shea Stadium in Queens, New York, the location of the massive event, still accommodated an enthusiastic audience of 22,508, paying $140,923 to witness the one-of-a-kind spectacle. It was 47°F at match time, and Morales and Sammartino battled in a uniquely clean fashion, divorcing themselves from the promotion's regular brawls. They competed for just over an hour, while press reports claimed it was 75 minutes, and the contest was stopped at the 11 p.m. curfew. The competitors embraced in the post-match celebration, despite the protests of some fans, who wanted to see a finish, and there were no lingering hard feelings.

Verne Gagne, for the first time since the 1950s, made an appearance in New York City on November 27, 1972, and wrestled at the Garden in the semifinal beneath Morales's defense against Ray Stevens. Never before had the WWWF champion shared billing with another world titleholder, and the increased cooperation continued. At one point, there was hope that Gagne and his AWA would join the NWA and streamline all territories like the old days. Rumors floated around during the 1970s, particularly after the WWWF rejoined the Alliance, but it was not to be.

The legendary Mil Mascaras, a masked hero across the United States and Mexico, debuted at the Garden on December 18, 1972, and his appearance was remarkable because the New York State Athletic Commission gave him permission to wrestle with his famed hood. Others in the same position, including his opponent, the Spoiler, were forced to unmask before competing in the New York metropolitan area. The show drew a huge crowd of 22,906 fans, and the Northeastern wrestling scene, like many regions, was experiencing an unmatched period of success. McMahon was pulling all the right strings, bringing in the most talked about opponents for Morales and filling out his cards with a diverse collection of wrestlers. On the not-so-distant horizon was, perhaps, his greatest talent import and a man who'd transcend the wrestling business. Years before Hulk Hogan, the Rock, and Steve Austin, there was Andre Rene Roussimoff, known in France as Jean Ferre and soon to be called by the name that made him internationally famous: Andre the Giant.

(14)
THE DESTINY
OF THE
MCMAHON
DYNASTY

Six years before his Madison Square Garden debut, 21-year-old Frenchman Andre Roussimoff was regularly appearing for the FILC promotion in Paris. He was still an understudy of veteran Frank Valois of Montreal, but audiences at the Cirque d'Hiver were impressed by the agility of the 6'10", 300-pound gladiator. Known to fans as Jean Ferre, he displayed extraordinary strength and was well on his way to establishing himself as the biggest drawing card in Europe. By 1968, he was acknowledged as the French champion, and magazines made fleeting mentions about a possible journey to North America. In 1971, along with Valois, he ventured to Canada and then joined Verne Gagne's AWA circuit, leaving fans wherever he wrestled awestruck by his size.

Vincent J. McMahon was equally fascinated. He'd met an untold number of grapplers during his career, but no one approached the physical dimensions and appearance of Roussimoff. He didn't waste any time signing Andre to an exclusive Capitol Wrestling booking agreement, and McMahon instinctively knew he had a once-in-a-lifetime phenomenon on his hands. Dubbed Andre the Giant, he was repackaged and sold to the public as the "Eighth Wonder of the World," standing 7'4" and weighing 424 pounds. A caricature of his likeness towering over the Manhattan skyline appeared in WWWF arena programs, and there was no question he was the most talked about professional wrestler in years. He made his initial showing at the Garden in New York on March 26, 1973, and defeated Buddy Wolfe.

Subscriber-based pay-cable television was in its infancy in 1972–73, and two stations served the New York City market: Sterling Communications and Teleprompter Manhattan Cable. In 1972, Sterling, which served the lower half of the city, forged an agreement with Madison Square Garden officials to provide live content to more than 200 events from the venue, to include hockey games and dog shows. Home Box Office (HBO) had a similar deal in parts of Pennsylvania and Upstate New York and broadcast WWWF Garden events between 1973 and '77. McMahon's *Championship Wrestling* program from Philadelphia was featured weekly on Teleprompter Manhattan, and the organization was already capitalizing on the technological advances being made.

The in-ring strategy of the promotion was given a boost by the antagonistic managers in the vein of Bobby Davis, who had masterfully supervised the career of Buddy Rogers years before. At the forefront of the movement were "Captain" Lou Albano, a stylish ex-wrestler from suburban New York, and the 47-year-old Grand Wizard from Ohio. Albano's dastardly leadership was demonstrated when his charge, Ivan Koloff, dethroned champion Bruno Sammartino, dramatically raising the ire of fans. Once Pedro Morales got the belt, Albano sent Fred Blassie, the Spoiler, Moondog Mayne, and King Curtis after the titleholder, hoping to repeat his luck, but Morales turned each away.

Wizard was motivated in much the same way. Standing 5'7", he was called a "master of psychology" and unleashed Ray Stevens and Don Leo Jonathan against Morales, albeit ineffectively. He also managed Professor Toru Tanaka and Mr. Fuji to the WWWF tag team title on two occasions, in 1972 and '73. Unsurprisingly, the tag division remained an important component of McMahon's TV shows, and at least one tag bout, occasionally more, was usually booked at the Garden. Luke Graham and Tarzan Tyler initiated the lineage of the championship in 1971, four years after the retirement of the old U.S. straps and the brief recognition of a WWWF international tag team title. Others to hold the belts were Karl Gotch and Rene Goulet, and Haystacks Calhoun and Tony Garea. In the heavyweight division, the popular Bobo Brazil was often billed as the U.S. champion when he made appearances in the territory. Later, a North American/intercontinental title became the WWWF's secondary singles championship.

The Morales-Sammartino popularity debate continued, and many people soundly believed Pedro was the better draw. Widely respected publisher Nat Loubet editorialized in the February 1974 edition of *The Ring Wrestling* that "Madison Square Garden shows [were] drawing as never before." He wrote that Morales's reign was "outdoing" Sammartino, and that Garden gates were "hitting the 20,000 mark with consistency." Morales was well into his second year as WWWF king and had proven to be a distinguished and convincing champion. But there were still purists who wanted more technical aptitude from the top heavyweight, as shown by the NWA world titleholder.

In 1973, the Alliance belt passed from Dory Funk Jr. to Harley Race and finally to Jack Brisco, a scientific grappler from Oklahoma in the mold of Lou Thesz. Morales, though better skilled than given credit, was the antithesis of former NCAA champion Brisco in the ring. Nonetheless, the classic WWWF style wasn't going to change anytime soon. Northeasterners disgruntled with the punch, kick, and slam methods of the promotion were going to have to find their wrestling entertainment elsewhere.

Considering his options, McMahon decided to take the belt off Morales late in 1973. The idea was not based on a massive decline in the latter's popularity, although towns outside New York City didn't draw as well, but because of the planned reemergence of Sammartino. Since losing his WWWF championship, Bruno was one of the most coveted free agents in the world. He wrestled for promoters in St. Louis, Indianapolis, Detroit, Cleveland, San Francisco, and Los Angeles, and his reputation preceded him at every stop. He spent much of his time in the vicinity of his hometown of Pittsburgh, but when circumstances presented themselves, he ventured away, including several tours to Japan to work for Shohei "Giant" Baba's newly founded All Japan Pro Wrestling.

Sammartino made occasional showings in WWWF arenas. He wrestled in the semifinal at the Garden on January 15, 1973, and defeated Toru Tanaka. Around nine months later, McMahon offered Sammartino a stunning financial deal to return, and he accepted. He fulfilled an obligation to wrestle in Japan, where he spent Thanksgiving, and then made preparations for a December 10, 1973, appearance at the Garden in a hugely anticipated event. Meanwhile, Morales was in windup mode. His eventual conqueror, Stan Stasiak, challenged him for the belt twice at the Garden in August and October 1973 and was defeated. Morales had beaten Larry Hennig in November, and a rematch was set up for the following month. But before that bout could take place, the fateful Morales-Stasiak title switch occurred in Philadelphia, much to the surprise of enthusiasts.

The date was December 1, 1973, and the Philadelphia Arena audience, which slightly exceeded 5,000 people, was certain Morales was going to prevail in the contentious struggle. A backdrop sent both to the mat 17 minutes into the fracas, and a double pin resulted. Stasiak subtly raised his shoulder at the last second to vanquish Morales. Ring announcer Buddy Wagner purposefully curtailed his announcement and didn't flat out declare a new champion had been crowned. Apparently, officials feared a loud and possibly physical reprisal from youths in the crowd, and many of those in attendance left the venue believing Morales remained the WWWF titleholder. That changed in the days following, as news reports and McMahon's programming clarified the matter. Stasiak, a Quebec transplant to Oregon, was the promotion's new heavyweight champion.

Managed by the Grand Wizard, Stasiak filmed one week

of television as kingpin and fulfilled his booking at Madison Square Garden nine days later versus Sammartino. As expected, fans were keenly enthusiastic, chanting "Bruno" throughout the 12-minute, 14-second bout. The finish came when the challenger caught Stasiak coming off the ropes, slammed him, and scored the pin. Referee Dick Kroll raised Sammartino's arm, signaling his triumph, and announcer Bob Freed informed the 22,000 fans in attendance that the WWWF had a new champion. The crowd was elated, and McMahon had successfully pushed his organization's most heralded star back into the top spot.

The erstwhile system of booking Sammartino as an unstoppable force was antiquated but beloved in the Northeast. His charisma was unyielding. His courage and resilience never appeared to fade during his time away from the promotion, and he carried on in his lifelong fight against the "monsters" of the business. McMahon, once again, lined up a plethora of devious opponents beginning with 6'6" Don Leo Jonathan in early 1974. The powerful Russian heel Nikolai Volkoff, who was managed by Fred Blassie, came next, and then Sammartino's longtime rival Killer Kowalski. At the Garden, the champion beat John Tolos before 18,000 in July and twice teamed with Chief Jay Strongbow in battles against the crafty Valiant Brothers. Larry Zbyszko, Bruno's 20-year-old protégé and a graduate of North Allegheny High School in suburban Pittsburgh, routinely worked in preliminaries.

On September 13, 1974, wrestling lost one of its venerable pilots when Jack Pfefer died in a nursing home outside Boston. With four decades in the business, he was naturally skilled at creating and pushing new talent, including a wide assortment of freakish characters. Often paranoid and occasionally peculiar, Pfefer was exceptionally resourceful, and from his traveling road show emerged the likes of Buddy Rogers and the Fabulous Moolah. Few promoters have been as wily and successful on a national stage. In general, 1974 turned out to be a difficult year because of the added losses of former world champions "Scissors" Joe Stecher, "Jumpin'" Joe Savoldi, and Lee Wykoff. They each were indisputable legends and, like Pfefer, made their mark in more ways than one.

The rapport between Capitol Wrestling and the National Wrestling Alliance strengthened, and by 1973 McMahon was a member of the NWA board of directors alongside Jack Adkisson, Eddie Graham, Mike LeBell, Frank Tunney, and Don Owen. He supported Alliance initiatives, including donating $1,000 to the United States Wrestling Federation, an amateur organization, and featured NWA president Sam Muchnick in WWWF publications. As a further display of brotherhood, McMahon wanted to print photos of the board-sanctioned heavyweight, junior heavyweight, and light heavyweight titleholders in a 1974 Garden program. His allegiance to the NWA was obvious, and the revitalized camaraderie between promoters was a significant fact as box office numbers dipped.

Since the Alliance was in good shape and egos were in check, Capitol Wrestling had little to say in opposition to the broadcast of Graham's Tampa-based *Championship Wrestling from Florida* TV program on channel 47 in the New York City area. The syndicated show debuted in March 1973 and was presented on Tuesday nights. However, McMahon did have a problem with the arrival of another television broadcast, this one on his former flagship station, WOR-9. Pedro Martinez, a competitor going back to the 1950s, teamed with his son Ron, sports mogul Eddie Einhorn, and Robert F. Hatch to launch the International Wrestling Association (IWA), an outlaw organization with robust financial backing. Their local WOR broadcast debuted on Saturday, February 1, 1975, at midnight.

The corporation behind the promotion, Pro Wrestling International, Inc., maintained offices on Madison Avenue in Manhattan and initially named its local telecast *Wrestling from the Garden*. The IWA had designs on New York City, and McMahon had reason to be concerned. In April, Hatch put out a press release claiming IWA had five times the ratings McMahon had in New York and stated they possessed the "number one rated wrestling show in the country." They awaited licensing approval to run shows in the Tri-State Area and expanded their fast-moving television empire to include stations from Miami to Milwaukee and from Charlotte to Los Angeles. The IWA was a threat to be reckoned with.

Featuring recognizable performers such as former WWWF champion Ivan Koloff, Argentina Apollo, Bob Ellis, Ernie Ladd, and Mil Mascaras as the heavyweight titleholder, the IWA was striving to break the Alliance monopoly once and for all. Despite the impressive gains, the organization was doomed. The expanse of its territory was too much to cover, and heavy financial losses led the company to go out of business before the end of 1975. NWA pushback, of course, contributed to the collapse, and McMahon was no worse for wear at the end of the promotional war.

McMahon also took over the IWA's coveted Saturday midnight timeslot on WOR-9 and featured *Championship Wrestling* from Philadelphia. By September 1975, the promotion was crowing about a dominant 7.0 rating with a 32 percent share of the audience. Fans rejoiced at the return of the WWWF to the station, and live show attendance was unwaveringly good. Box office numbers were tumbling in wrestling as a whole, but McMahon was able to circumvent the trend. The popularity of the talent in the organization had a lot to do with it, particularly when it came to Sammartino, Morales, and Andre the Giant.

In 1974–75, Bruno stopped the challenges of George Steele and Ivan Koloff and had two remarkably vicious feuds with Bobby Duncum and former fan-favorite Spiros Arion of Greece. His May 19, 1975, bout against Waldo Von Erich sold out the Garden and packed the adjoining theater, the Felt Forum, for a total of 24,553 people—an incredible achievement. The following February 2, Sammartino and "Superstar" Billy Graham topped that figure after 25,600 spectators jammed the Garden complex to see their rematch from January. Bruno lost their initial contest by count out but returned to score a victory in 17 minutes and 55 seconds to wind up their feud.

During the summer of 1975, AWA world champion Verne

Gagne turned up as the tag partner of Andre the Giant in a Garden bout against the Valiants and won in two straight falls. Others to appear in the months following were Gagne's students Chris Taylor and Ric Flair and the co-trainer at his wrestling school, Billy Robinson. Antonio Inoki, the 32-year-old head of New Japan Pro-Wrestling, wrestled in the December 15, 1975, Garden show and cemented what would be an important working relationship with McMahon. Sammartino, conversely, still maintained loyalty to Inoki's promotional rival, Shohei "Giant" Baba and his All Japan Pro Wrestling, creating a level of friction. But the issue wasn't pushed and didn't derail what was important—making money.

Mike LeBell of the Hollywood Wrestling Office also had a good working relationship with Inoki, and the talent exchanges between New York, Los Angeles, and Tokyo were free flowing. Magazines noted that LeBell's office and New Japan held simultaneous membership in both the WWWF and the NWA, and Hisashi Shinma, an officer in Inoki's company, was acknowledged as the vice president of the WWWF. The friendly cooperation gave McMahon's organization an international flavor, and wrestlers such as Tatsumi Fujinami would demonstrate the vibrant Japanese grappling style, mixing technical wrestling with high-flying, for American fans in the Northeast.

Ring royalty in Los Angeles, LeBell was the son of Aileen Eaton, who, along with her husband, Cal, had dominated wrestling and boxing in Southern California since the 1940s. Mike attended the University of Southern California and immediately went to work in the family business upon graduating in the early 1950s. He served as the business manager of the Olympic Auditorium and continued operations following Cal's death and Aileen's retirement. As a wrestling promoter, he ran shows throughout the region under the World Wrestling Association (WWA) banner until joining the NWA in 1968. In August 1971, he broke the national gate record when $142,158 was taken in at the Memorial Coliseum in Los Angeles for a program headlined by Blassie and John Tolos.

With overflow crowds and political sway in the NWA as a

member of the board of directors (and later as first vice president), LeBell was one of the strongest promoters in North America. His television show was broadcast into New York and leveraged a sound partnership with McMahon that lasted into the 1980s. Tapes recorded at Madison Square Garden were sent back to LeBell for advertising purposes, and monies generated from the various TV deals were divided according to signed agreements. Unfortunately for LeBell, the bottom dropped out of his promotion only a few years after establishing the record gate at the Coliseum. He proved a survivor and managed to hang on despite the downward spiral of his business.

Boxing was a common interest between LeBell and McMahon. At different points in his career, McMahon delved into the fight game as a promoter, manager, and financial backer. In December 1966, he assumed the hat of a moneyman and offered up $100,000 to world light heavyweight champion Dick Tiger to defend his title against Bob Foster. The contest went off 15 months later at the Garden in New York City, and Foster won the championship in four rounds. McMahon offered $1 million to heavyweight champion Joe Frazier in 1971 for the rights to an East Coast fight, but he was more involved in the titleholder's 1974 rematch against Muhammad Ali. Teamed with promoter Bob Arum, he lined up a number of closed-circuit television outlets and was quickly brought up to speed on the valuable opportunity CCTV presented. McMahon and his son Vincent K. worked with Arum again that summer in the same capacity, exhibiting footage of Evel Knievel's Snake River Canyon jump.

Muhammad Ali was fully acquainted with pro wrestling. He was influenced by the legendary showman Gorgeous George, and since 1963 had been targeted by McMahon and his associates for a mixed match. Initially they wanted Ali, then known as Cassius Clay, to meet Buddy Rogers, but after the Nature Boy retired prematurely because of illness, the focus shifted to Sammartino. A $400,000 offer for the contest was made by Capitol to Ali's management, but they declined time after time. Ali was photographed at a range of wrestling events, posing with the likes of Andre the

Giant and Bobo Brazil, and appeared on *The Tonight Show* next to Fred Blassie. In 1976, he was presented with a new offer, one he'd have a hard time turning down. He wouldn't decline this time, and the stage was set for the most highly publicized mixed match in sports history.

The deal was offered by a Japanese contingent wanting Ali to face Antonio Inoki. Instead of $400,000, Ali was offered $6 million, and the proposition was too good to pass up. After some haggling over terms, the deal was signed, and McMahon and LeBell were named to a three-man rules committee also comprising boxing veteran Angelo Dundee. Arum was in on the deal as well, and in addition to the Tokyo match held on June 26, 1976 (June 25 in the United States), an extensive closed-circuit operation was organized. Over 100 different arenas and theaters would feature the unusual bout, some in conjunction with wrestling shows. McMahon went in full force, arranging the largest live spectacle in support of the CCTV broadcast at Shea Stadium. He even set up a mixed bout of his own between Andre the Giant and boxer Chuck Wepner.

But McMahon had an even greater attraction on his hands. Two months prior, on April 26, Sammartino had been matched with a Texas ruffian by the name of Stan Hansen. A football player in college, the 6'3", 300-pound Hansen was a star in the making, and his size and attitude made him a natural challenger for Bruno. During their Garden bout, the champion was legitimately slammed on his head and suffered fractured vertebrae in his neck. In spite of the horrific injury, Sammartino displayed exceptional courage in finishing the match, which was won by Hansen when the official halted action because of Bruno's bleeding forehead. In the days and weeks that followed, fans were told of Sammartino's broken neck and Hansen's lariat clothesline was blamed, instantly making him the most hated wrestler in the WWWF.

Sammartino was genuinely sidelined, and doctors warned him about ever wrestling again. As the Ali-Inoki contest approached, McMahon was forced to deal with the reality that sales were significantly poorer than he'd imagined. Critics relentlessly bashed the affair, and people were dismayed by the negative atmosphere. Between the guaranteed payouts and the rental of Shea, McMahon was far in the red, and Capitol was in danger of possible bankruptcy if things didn't quickly turnaround. His best chance at profit was the anticipated return of Sammartino in a revenge match against Hansen. McMahon convinced Bruno to appear much sooner than physicians recommended, and Sammartino saved the promotion by drawing an incredible 32,897 spectators. Ali and Inoki went 15 rounds to a pitiful draw, but the real story to WWWF fans was that Bruno beat Hansen by count out in 10 minutes, 19 seconds.

While chaos reigned in the East, Capitol Wrestling Corporation cofounder Joe Toots Mondt quietly passed away in St. Louis at the age of 82 on June 11, 1976. His visionary approach to pro wrestling helped trigger the dawn of a new era for the sport in the 1920s, and he was attached to the business for a total of 59 years, from 1910 to 1969. By the time Mondt had become a well-established promoter, most had forgotten that he had been a true catch-as-catch-can artist on the mat. He was a shooter on par with the greats of wrestling history, including "Tigerman" John Pesek and Ed "Strangler" Lewis. In his last years, he occasionally ventured over to the Kiel Auditorium with his wife to see matches presented by Sam Muchnick. His spirit endured, and Capitol Wrestling—and, in turn, the WWWF—would never have succeeded without him.

Muchnick had bowed out as National Wrestling Alliance president the year before and had been replaced by Jack Adkisson of Dallas, better known to the public as Fritz Von Erich. The loss of Muchnick as leader of the NWA was a severe blow to the organization. He'd been the face of the Alliance almost since it was founded, dealt with all the internal strife and politics, and warded off a damaging government investigation. Muchnick was an expert at maintaining friendly relations with promoters on all sides of the spectrum, and without his skilled efforts, it is unlikely that the WWWF and NWA would ever have reconciled. Like McMahon, he worked in the best interests of wrestling, and when he stepped down, he did so with the unanimous respect and appreciation of the NWA.

Back in the Northeast, the WWWF was overflowing with talent. Bruiser Brody, standing an intimidating 6'4" and weighing better than 250 pounds, was the Grand Wizard's newest title threat. A rabid warrior, he met Sammartino twice at the Garden in September and October 1976 and was defeated both times. Strongman Ken Patera, a versatile athlete out of Portland, was another notable heel challenger and beat Sammartino by count out at the Garden on January 17, 1977. On the other side of the ranks, Ivan Putski was a leading fan favorite and was also known for his enormous strength. In February, 31-year-old Dusty Rhodes, a Florida mainstay, debuted at the Garden and demonstrated his unique magnetism for the New York crowd. Audiences were receptive to his charm, and McMahon booked the star regularly.

The neck injury Sammartino had suffered was a constant anxiety, and Bruno told McMahon that his time as champion was nearing an end. McMahon needed time to strategize. He asked a few peers for recommendations, showing an inclination toward a straight-laced hero, and was steered toward Minnesota native Bob Backlund. An NCAA Division II tournament winner in 1971, Backlund was expected to be the next great amateur to make it big in pro wrestling, following in the footsteps of Jack Brisco and Danny Hodge. He toured Texas, Florida, and St. Louis and was an enthusiastic pupil, learning from many skilled mat men during his rise. A number of influential NWA promoters were impressed. McMahon was too. He was sold on Backlund but decided to shift the title to "Superstar" Billy Graham in the interim, ensuring the lineage followed the "good guy" to "bad guy" to "good guy" protocol.

Graham's earlier business with Sammartino in 1976 was outstanding, and the box office at the Garden exploded for their two-match series. Born Eldridge Wayne Coleman, he was a former bodybuilder and boxer from Arizona who had trained under Stu Hart in Calgary. Early in his career, he became a Graham "brother" and was purported to be related to Dr. Jerry and Eddie Graham, even though he wasn't. Nevertheless, it was a great story to sell to the public, and the Superstar's incredible strength made him a noteworthy heel on the circuit. He entered the Civic Center in Baltimore on April 30, 1977, as a dangerous challenger, but no one anticipated him actually winning the belt. The match was back and forth, but with Graham bleeding profusely, Sammartino took a commanding position and roused the crowd. Graham, ever cunning, surprised the champ, got him to the mat, and attempted a pin using the ropes for leverage. Referee Jack Davies counted to three and the championship changed hands.

People across the WWWF territory were bewildered and upset. The epic Sammartino reign had concluded in a disappointing fashion, and in his place was a crooked and cocky eccentric —but a man who seemed to have pro wrestling in the palm of his hand. Unfortunately, longtime enthusiasts in the Northeast were already depressed because of a tragic loss away from the scripted grappling scene. The month before, on March 15, icon Antonino "Argentina" Rocca passed away at the age of 49. Younger fans knew him from his TV commentary, but their parents had grown up watching him fly and tumble around the ring. He was a New York legend and, like Sammartino, meant a great deal to the audience he'd entertained for decades.

On the corporate side of things, Gorilla Monsoon and Phil Zacko each sold 50 shares of Capitol Wrestling stock to Arnold Skaaland in early October 1977. Skaaland, of Norwegian descent, became a wrestler following service in the Marine Corps during World War II. Since 1972, he had been a member of the company's board of directors, and for years, personally administered the New York office. Additionally, he managed Sammartino, and later Backlund, worked as a road agent for Andre the Giant, and promoted the Westchester County Civic Center in White Plains, near his childhood home. He was a trusted employee of McMahon, and it was only fitting that he became a partner. The ownership of Capitol, as of 1977, was the following: McMahon 50 percent, Monsoon and Zacko both 20 percent, and Skaaland 10 percent.

Andre the Giant, or the "Boss," as peers called him, remained a magnificent attraction. He traveled without the usual territorial restrictions and made lots of money. As an example, for the Calgary Stampede series in Western Canada in July 1976, he wrestled seven times and made $2,000, plus another $433 for transportation and $650 for Capitol in booking fees. The following year for the same event, he wrestled four times and made a total of $1,550. In contrast, NWA champion Harley Race appeared for eight matches during Stampede week and still made $550 less.

Andre was a favorite around the world, and McMahon witnessed his extreme popularity during an excursion to Japan in 1977. Prior to Andre's bout with Antonio Inoki, Vince delivered a specially prepared speech to the audience, which was well received. The next year, in need of a little rest and relaxation, McMahon took a little time for himself and ventured around the world.

As WWWF heavyweight champ, "Superstar" Billy Graham was gold. Exuding personality, he was the guy crowds loved to loathe, reminiscent of Buddy Rogers, and his reign of nine months and 21 days was the longest for a heel titleholder in the organization's history. Graham sold out the Garden nearly every time he appeared in the top spot, and the demand for him extended across the NWA. McMahon complied with outside requests, sending him often to Florida as well as stops in Los Angeles, St. Louis, and Atlanta. Backlund, throughout this period, developed as a performer and gained esteem in Northeastern rings. He worked his way up the card and was ushered into a February 20, 1978, match against Graham at the Garden. There, he defeated the WWWF king and won the belt.

For traditionalists, Backlund was lauded because he was a classically trained grappler with a preponderance of mat knowledge. He was considered the All-American boy and represented honorable behavior and sportsmanship. Often smiling, he was the epitome of the babyface wrestler. Others wanted more edge to their champions. Graham, Race, and AWA titleholder Nick Bockwinkel combined athleticism with a sharp attitude, and when they bent the rules to attain a victory, people howled in disapproval. Their dishonest actions were never a shock, and it was compelling to see just how far they'd go for a win. Backlund wrestled admirably. He never took the easy way out and prided himself on the square victory. The WWWF audience adjusted to the dramatic change from Graham to Backlund and accepted the latter's scrupulousness. He won over critics and carried the bulk of the fan base. Ticket sales were brisk, and things had turned out exactly as Capitol management had planned.

Willie Gilzenberg, the president of the WWWF since it was founded in 1963, passed away on November 15, 1978. The title of president came with real responsibilities, and Gilzenberg was not just a figurehead. He occasionally served a function on TV and handled the press, correspondence, and often traveled into the city from Newark to supervise the matches at the Garden. His 50 years of experience as a promoter, and general amicable nature, made him an invaluable associate to McMahon. One of his final on-camera appearances came in the summer of 1977, when Chief Jay Strongbow relinquished the tag title belts to him after his partner, Billy White Wolf, suffered an injury. New Japan's Hisashi Shinma succeeded Gilzenberg to the presidency, and veteran pro-moter Mickey Duff of England was named vice president.

In March–April 1979, McMahon shortened the name of his pro-motion from the World Wide Wrestling Federation to the World Wrestling Federation (WWF). The maneuver made sense in terms of advertising and the future implementation of promotional logos and trademarks. Relations among the "Big Three" promotions were stronger than ever, and Harley Race, still the Alliance champ, and Verne Gagne, owner of the AWA, wrestled at the Garden on April 30. McMahon used his Garden platform to feature the young talent of other promoters, offering them a substantial vehicle to get their stars over. It was incredible publicity for a grappler to have performed at the vaulted arena and meant a lot back in their home regions. There were dozens of up-and-comers in 1979–80 alone, including Roddy Piper, Dick Murdoch, Ted DiBiase, Tito Santana, Greg Gagne, and David and Kerry Von Erich.

The tremendous populace of the Northeast and opportunities for income intrigued wrestling promoters. The territory itself was almost too opulent for one promoter or one company to sustain. But McMahon managed to do it. He seized New York City, Boston, Philadelphia, and smaller cities in the East and never surrendered control. While Capitol Wrestling had its share of failures and was on shaky ground more than once, it persisted because of sound leadership and was rarely overextended. According to the financial records of Capitol established by accountants Leopold and Linowes of Washington, DC, the company took in $4.1 million in gross box office receipts in 1979–80 and another $115,197 in TV receipts.

Doing business was, however, costly. Between paying wrestlers and referees, advertising, rental agreements, travel fees, licensing, and television operations, over $3.6 million was spent. Additional expenses for salaries, insurance, telephone bills, and the fees tied to keeping the offices open accounted for another $380,000. The company had $639,083 in assets, and Capitol was solid. One of the contributing factors to the promotion's stability in the summer of 1980 was the great success of McMahon's spectacular at Shea Stadium on August 9, 1980. A huge 13-match program, headlined by Sammartino and his protégé, Larry Zbyszko, drew over 40,000 spectators and a gate of $537,421. The event was a resounding success.

As if there would be any question, Sammartino beat his opponent in a cage bout, much to the delight of the audience. In the semifinal, Andre the Giant defeated a 26-year-old blond heel from Tampa named Hulk Hogan. Standing 6'7" and weighing 300-plus pounds, Hogan was a sight to behold. He clearly needed further development, but Northeastern officials already knew he had immense potential. His future in wrestling was going to be bright. However, Sammartino, acknowledged as the "Living Legend," was facing a more difficult road. His importance in the promotion faded and he eventually departed under strained conditions. He'd later return as a part-time performer and commentator, only to experience an even greater estrangement with the WWF that continued until 2013.

Backlund was successful around the circuit, appearing on TV in Hamburg and Allentown, which became the location for

Championship Wrestling tapings in November 1978, and sold out the Garden versus Billy Graham, Ernie Ladd, Ivan Koloff, Swede Hanson, Sika, Stan Hansen, George Steele, Don Muraco, and Adrian Adonis. He also battled the likes of Sergeant Slaughter and highflier Jimmy Snuka in memorable contests. During a tour of Japan in November 1979, he was stripped of his WWF title by Antonio Inoki, but the title was declared vacant after a controversial rematch. Backlund beat Bobby Duncum at the Garden for the belt on December 17. The title was held up following a bout with Greg Valentine in October 1981, but Backlund managed to prevail the following month to capture his third WWF championship.

Through the years, innumerable old favorites returned to the promotion, from the popular Haystacks Calhoun to the cruel women's champion the Fabulous Moolah. The often-imitated, never duplicated "Nature Boy" Buddy Rogers reemerged after a long time in the shadows, and many older enthusiasts were reminded of his glory days as NWA and WWWF champion. Rogers was once angling for an ownership and secure promotional gig with Capitol, but the deal fell through, leaving him out in the cold.

Vincent Kennedy McMahon was an unyieldingly busy man during the latter stages of the 1970s, and by 1982, he was envisioning a full and complete buyout of the Capitol Wrestling Corporation. He maintained his duties as a commentator for WWF programming but began to display his entrepreneurial spirit in 1979, when he purchased the Cape Cod Coliseum in Massachusetts. Running concerts, wrestling, and other athletic events, he experienced a side of the industry that most promoters rarely encountered and gained a great deal of wisdom. On February 21, 1980, he incorporated Titan Sports, and while no one would have disagreed he was an enterprising soul, it wasn't yet apparent that he would soon be a significant force.

A few weeks shy of his 68th birthday, Vincent James McMahon was prepared to liquidate his shares and step down. The demands of full-time promotions and constant traveling were too much to endure. His health was also a concern. Understanding that his son Vincent Kennedy was a motivated buyer, McMahon engaged in preliminary talks and then received a formal proposal.

On June 5, 1982, McMahon and his three partners sold Capitol Wrestling and the contract specified that Capitol Wrestling was to remain a subsidiary of Titan Sports, Inc. Titan bought 385 combined company shares from Gorilla Monsoon, Phil Zacko, and Arnold Skaaland, paying $644,264, which was to be paid off within one year. Titan was to purchase the remaining 615 shares for $1 million. McMahon was to receive $822,132, Monsoon and Zacko $71,147, and Skaaland $35,574. Again, all money was to be paid off within a single year, providing for a grace period of 15 days. The sale was effective immediately, and if there was a default not "cured" within the 15 days, the shares would be returned to their original owners. In that case, all money paid to that point would be kept.

Vincent Kennedy and Titan Sports didn't default, and the sale was completed in June 1983. His designs on the wrestling business were uniquely aggressive, and expansion out of the restricted Northeastern territory was his goal. By signing deals with TV stations across the country and using superstation WOR and the USA cable network, McMahon planned to send his wrestlers into cities once protected by the National Wrestling Alliance. He was advancing on his father's former peers with a dedicated vision and the courage to force change. The unwritten rules that had been the foundation of the industry were erased, and McMahon tackled all promoters, big and small, with little fear. Nothing was going to be the same.

The NWA gathered for its annual convention in Las Vegas at the Dunes Hotel on August 22–23, 1983. Members were aware that change was imminent. The longtime secretary-treasurer of the organization, Jim Barnett, who would later work in various capacities for Titan, abruptly resigned the day before the first session convened. Vincent James maintained his membership in the NWA despite the sale of Capitol, but he didn't attend the Vegas conclave. Not shockingly, days later, on August 31, 1983, from his home in Fort Lauderdale, McMahon sent a letter to NWA president Bob Geigel, notifying him of his resignation. He wished "continued success" for his "many friends in the Alliance."

Regardless of the well wishes, NWA members weren't pleased and, in fact, didn't know the full scope of the younger McMahon's plans. His rapid advancement was eye-opening, and many of the old-school promoters hoped to stifle the movement by personally calling his father. But Vincent James McMahon's days at the helm were over. His responsibilities were limited to advising his son and traveling to the Garden for sporadic events. The budding wrestling war was going to happen without his generalship, and no one knew whether his son's attempt to establish the sport's first national company was going to succeed or not. Vince Jr., as he was called, was going to sink or swim.

Time was short, and few people knew that Vincent James was deteriorating due to progressive cancer. Married since the 1950s, Vincent and his second wife, Juanita Wynne McMahon, had moved to South Florida in 1971 and divided their time between residences in Rehoboth, Delaware (June to September) and Plantation (October to May), in the suburbs of Fort Lauderdale. In 1976, they relocated to a home just north of Fort Lauderdale Beach, near the Intercoastal Waterway. The warm climate and quiet atmosphere were a welcome change of pace, and Vincent enjoyed peaceful excursions on his boat. He got together socially with Willie Gilzenberg, who wintered in North Miami Beach, and other friends and met his business obligations by traveling to wherever he was needed.

In the spring of 1984, his condition suddenly worsened and he was hospitalized. Vincent James McMahon died on May 27. According to his last will and testament filed with the Broward County (Florida) Records Department, he left his entire estate to his wife. Had Juanita predeceased him, his will would have been divided his estate among several family members, including a portion to his sons, Vincent and Roderick. Juanita continued to live in South Florida and passed away in 1998. Both McMahons were buried at Our Lady Queen of Heaven Cemetery in North Lauderdale, Florida.

A man of honor and integrity, Vincent James McMahon was fondly remembered by his friends and employees. Much like his father, he was the kind of man who played by the rules and took few major risks. He rarely gambled on potentially unsafe deals and was thoughtful of promoters in other parts of the country. When it came to the grapplers themselves, he was excellent about payoffs, rewarded wrestlers at times with bonuses, and looked after their overall well-being. McMahon was adamant about the welfare of the workers in the inner circle of Capitol Wrestling, earning the lifelong loyalty of Gorilla Monsoon, Arnold Skaaland, James Dudley, and others. He went out of his way to financially take care of his ailing former ring announcer Jimmy Lake in the 1950s and kept people on the payroll even after their retirement, ensuring they were able to pay the bills.

The sale of Capitol Wrestling was kept secret. It wasn't until 1983 that publications announced Titan's ownership of the WWF and Vincent K. was acknowledged as the man in charge. Full of energy and ideas, McMahon was a definite risk taker, and differed from his father and grandfather in the way he approached wrestling. He was optimistic, and while many of his methods were distinctly opposite those of his ancestors, many were similar. He would earn the same kind of loyalty from his inner circle of employees and followed his father's custom of taking care of certain retired personnel. It was a McMahon family tradition and spoke well of their commitment to those who'd given so much to the company behind the scenes.

Champion for nearly five years, Bob Backlund remained the face of the organization until December 26, 1983, when he was defeated for the WWF title by the Iron Sheik of Iran. There was room to debate the next step, and there were two options on the table. One was to reestablish Backlund as their top star, and the other was to propel Hulk Hogan, the towering blond sensation fresh off an appearance in the mainstream film *Rocky III*, into the number one position. The younger McMahon didn't waste any time and made the biggest decision of his short career. On January 23, 1984, after a five-minute, 30-second match, Hogan pinned Sheik and won the WWF belt.

In an instant, Vincent Kennedy McMahon and his superstar Hulk Hogan slammed the door closed on one era and opened the door to another. The World Wrestling Federation not only survived but knocked out the competition, establishing a level of dominance never before seen in the history of wrestling.

PUBLISHED BY ECW PRESS
665 GERRARD STREET EAST
TORONTO, ONTARIO, CANADA M4M 1Y2
416-694-3348 / INFO@ECWPRESS.COM

EDITOR FOR THE PRESS: MICHAEL HOLMES
COVER DESIGN: TANIA CRAAN
COVER IMAGES: GEORGE NAPOLITANO
PHOTOS CREDITED "NOTRE DAME": REPRODUCED FROM
THE ORIGINAL HELD BY THE DEPARTMENT OF SPECIAL
COLLECTIONS OF THE HESBURGH LIBRARIES OF THE
UNIVERSITY OF NOTRE DAME.

LIBRARY AND ARCHIVES CANADA
CATALOGUING IN PUBLICATION

HORNBAKER, TIM, AUTHOR
CAPITOL REVOLUTION : THE RISE OF THE MCMAHON
WRESTLING EMPIRE / TIM HORNBAKER.

ISSUED IN PRINT AND ELECTRONIC FORMATS.
ISBN 978-1-77041-124-1 (PBK)
ISBN 978-1-77090-688-4 (PDF)
ISBN 978-1-77090-689-1 (EPUB)

1.MCMAHON FAMILY. 2.WRESTLING—UNITED STATES—
HISTORY. 3.WORLD WRESTLING FEDERATION—HISTORY.
I.TITLE.

GV1198.12.H67 2015   796.8120973
C2014-907625-8   C2014-907626-6

PRINTING: MARQUIS EXPRESS   5   4   3   2
PRINTED AND BOUND IN CANADA

GET THE EBOOK FREE

proof of purchase required

AT ECW PRESS, WE WANT YOU TO ENJOY THIS BOOK IN WHATEVER FORMAT YOU LIKE, WHENEVER YOU LIKE. LEAVE YOUR PRINT BOOK AT HOME AND TAKE THE EBOOK TO GO! PURCHASE THE PRINT EDITION AND RECEIVE THE EBOOK FREE. JUST SEND AN EMAIL TO EBOOK@ECWPRESS.COM AND INCLUDE:

· THE BOOK TITLE
· THE NAME OF THE STORE WHERE YOU PURCHASED IT
· YOUR RECEIPT NUMBER
· YOUR PREFERENCE OF FILE TYPE: PDF OR EPUB?

A REAL PERSON WILL RESPOND TO YOUR EMAIL WITH YOUR EBOOK ATTACHED. AND THANKS FOR SUPPORTING AN INDEPENDENTLY OWNED CANADIAN PUBLISHER WITH YOUR PURCHASE!